ECONOMIES OF DESIRE

ECONOMIES OF DESIRE

Sex and Tourism in Cuba and the Dominican Republic

Amalia L. Cabezas

TEMPLE UNIVERSITY PRESS
Philadelphia

Temple University Press
1601 North Broad Street
Philadelphia, PA 19122
www.temple.edu/tempress

♾ The paper used in this publication meets the requirements of the
American National Standard for Information Sciences—Permanence of
Paper for Printed Library Materials, ANSI Z39.48-1992

Library of Congress Cataloging-in-Publication Data

Cabezas, Amalia L.
  Economies of desire : sex and tourism in Cuba and the Dominican Republic /
Amalia L. Cabezas.
    p. cm.
  Includes bibliographical references and index.
  ISBN 978-1-59213-749-7 (cloth : alk. paper)—ISBN 978-1-59213-750-3
(pbk. : alk. paper) 1. Sex tourism—Cuba. 2. Sex tourism—Dominican
Republic. 3. Prostitution—Cuba. 4. Prostitution—Dominican Republic.
5. Women—Violence against. 6. Tourists—Sexual behavior. 7. Sex-oriented
businesses—Social aspects. I. Title.
  HQ161.A5C33 2009
  306.74097291—dc22   2008043758

  4   6   8   9   7   5   3

Dedicated to Antonia I. Castañeda and Arturo Madrid
and
Alfredo Cruz

Contents

Acknowledgments

When I was growing up in southeast Los Angeles, my mother Fefa, my sister Mila, and my aunt, Luz Divina, worked at a clothing manufacturer in downtown Los Angeles. When my mother worked on Saturdays, she took me with her to work. To the hum of sewing machines, I played, cut threads, and talked with the other garment workers. Wearing matching pink smocks, lipstick, and high heels, these women sewed at backbreaking speeds as they raced their sewing machines through the Frederick's of Hollywood lingerie line. Between piecework, musings, and jokes, they gave me advice: "Learn to speak English, so you will not end up in a factory like us." Teresita, Nenita, Romelia, Obdulia, Ofelia, Guillermina, Elena, Orquidia—*memorias de ellas* are woven into my life. I am grateful to the women of Susan of California who taught me valuable lessons about resilience, tenacity, diligence, and the dignity of labor. Without their example, I could not have completed this book.

Years later, when the garment factories became sweatshops, my mother would say to me, "Aquí estoy mi hija, trabajando como negra para poder vivir como blanca" (Here I am, my child, working like a black woman so that I may live like a white one). I am intellectually indebted to my parents, whose lives taught me about the racialized structures of labor and who inspired in me respect and gratitude. Without their example, I could not have completed this book.

I am thankful to the University of California's Humanities Research Institute for a postdoctoral seminar under the direction of Professor Marguerite Waller. This experience, made enriching by Margie Waller and the other participants, helped forge new directions in my research. I am grateful to all the participants for making this possible and to Margie Waller for her leadership, mentorship, and friendship. A one-year University of California President's Postdoctoral Fellowship allowed me to expand the Cuban research. I am privileged and deeply honored to have worked with Professor Ruth Milkman as my mentor under the President's Postdoctoral fellowship at UCLA. As a mentor, Professor Milkman generously shared her research, time, and resources. I am deeply grateful to her.

The University of California, Riverside, has been an inspiring and remarkable place to complete this work. I am thankful to my colleagues in the Department of Women's Studies for their encouragement and backing. A special thanks to Kris King and Reneé Deguire for their good humor and facilitation of my work. I am indebted to the Chair of the department, Alicia Arrizón for suggesting the title of this book. Financial support from the Academic Senate at UCR and from UC Faculty Regents Fellowships has provided considerable financial relief that has allowed me to undertake comparative fieldwork. This assistance was instrumental in the research and writing phases of this book. At UCR I have also been fortunate to work with outstanding librarians: Peter Bliss, Kenneth R. Furuta, Jim Glenn, Maria Mendoza, Janet Moores, Rhonda Neugebauer, I thank them for their diligent assistance and general helpfulness. Finally, I would like to thank Mike Chávez, Marlene Felix, Jenni Keys, Quyn Nguyen, Carolina Irma Rubio, and Martín Rodarte for outstanding research assistance and to the many brilliant students at UCR who have taught, motivated, and inspired me.

Many friends and colleagues have generously provided comments on various drafts of this book. Florence Babb, Marisela Chávez, Raúl Fernández, Anne Goldberg, Peter Johnson, Dorienne Kondo, Juliet Macmillan, Ruth Milkman, Nancy Paige Fernández, Ellen Reese, Mathee Rojas, Ana Sandoval, Ramona Sliva, Felicity Shafer-Gabriel, Chikako Takeshita, Carlos Vélez-Ibáñez and Margie Waller, have read and offered valuable comments on previous versions of the manuscript. I am also indebted to Steven Gregory and Todd Ramón Ochoa for sharing their wealth of knowledge about Santería practices and Yemayá. It was Anna Sandoval who initially helped me to further explore the figure of Yemayá in the narratives of Cuban women. I am thankful to her for her intellectual acumen and friendship. During the final revision phase, I joined a writing group that provided significant intellectual support and much-needed friendship. I am especially indebted to the stellar and wonderful Jodi Kim, Tammy Ho, Michelle Raheja, and Setsu Shigematsu for reading many of the chapters and providing insightful comments. A special thanks to *mi compay* Raúl Fernández, who has been a counselor, research assistant, advocate, and mentor all in one. Te aprecio mucho, mi hermano.

The women of MODEMU, the sex worker organization in the Dominican Republic, have been kindred spirits. They have opened their hearts and homes and given me much purpose in their struggles and fortitude. They never cease to amaze me in their steadfast *lucha* to craft lives of dignity for themselves and their *compañeras*. Gracias a todas. I am deeply grateful to Yamile Piñeiro Hernández for her resourcefulness, energy, warmth and talent. Tony de Moya, Francisca Ferreira, Gina Gallardo, and Santo Rosario have provided invaluable help. I am appreciative of my fellow travelers and friends, J.D. Andrews, Doris Arima, Peter Johnson, Wayne Middleton, Marilyn Smith, and Arnold X. Suzukamo for their solidarity and caring friendship. I also appreciate the hospitality, generosity, and child care provided by Josué Cruz, Jr., and Lollie Cruz which made it possible to complete this book.

Alfredo Cruz has been my number one champion, always ready to provide encouragement, support, and assistance. His sense of humor, patience, kind disposition, and gentle luminosity have nourished my life during the research and writing phases of this book. This book is dedicated to him in recognition of his dedication and support. I also want to thank our son, Alejandro, for bringing so much joy and happiness into my life.

Finally, I am blessed with a wonderful editor at Temple University Press, Janet Francendese, who has been both kind and rigorous. I am grateful for her expertise and knowledge and that of her staff. Special thanks to Gary Kramer for keeping me in laughs during this process and for being so helpful.

This book is also dedicated to Chicana/o scholar-activists Antonia I. Castañeda and Arturo Madrid. Antonia and Arturo are educators, cultural, and political workers who have dedicated their lives to creating and fighting for social justice. For over forty years, working in higher education, museums, public institutions, and community organizations, they have devoted their efforts to building better chances and deep transformations in the lives of many people. They have diligently constructed opportunities for many by mentoring thousands of students, teaching, editing, writing, giving speeches, joining picket lines, leading demonstrations, organizing and agitating, and aligning their fate with those who are marginalized and excluded. Separately and together, they have been sewing a new world order. I am grateful to have met them as an undergraduate student, for they have provided me with nourishment, guidance, a roof over my head, mentorship, and the chance to rewrite my history. Without the tireless efforts of Antonia Castañeda and Arturo Madrid, this book would not have been possible.

Introduction

Affective Economies of Sexualized Tourism

In 1991, my friend Sylviana Castillo, a Chicana feminist active in Cuban solidarity work, told me about an article that she had seen in *Playboy* magazine featuring Cuban women (Cohen 1991). Surprised to see the bodies of Cuban women displayed for mass consumption, we wondered where Cuba was heading after the fall of the Soviet Union. What happened to the ideal of liberating Cuban women from capitalist forms of sexual objectification? Why would the Cuban government, through its Ministry of Tourism, host a team of *Playboy* photographers and writers? Why, during the worst economic crisis of the Cuban Revolution, would it provide them with lavish accommodations and transport in helicopters, boats, and corporate jets? And where was the protective, vigilant, and image-conscious state patriarch in all of this? After all, was not this the only country in the Western Hemisphere that boasted the eradication of prostitution and beauty pageants, and that proudly supported women's professional accomplishments as doctors, scientists, and engineers?[1]

As it turned out, the *Playboy* team enjoyed the best of Cuban tourism, and its French photographer ended up marrying one of the Cuban models featured in the striking layout. Marriage soon became one of the paradigmatic outcomes of a new tourist economy in Cuba as increasing numbers of Cubans—mostly women—wedded foreign visitors and left the island. The *Playboy* article, appearing at a crucial period of economic and political uncertainty and transition, introduced an era of a mixed-market economy in Cuba and initiated a decade of growth in tourism, tourist-oriented liaisons, and marriage to foreigners.

Sylviana and I wondered if Cuba would end up like the rest of the Caribbean, viewed as little more than a destination for travelers from the affluent North. Would its scenic beaches be blocked from view by the cloned resorts so common in Cancún, Puerto Rico, and Jamaica? Would it capitalize on its infamous past as a pleasure playground to recapture the international tourism market? Were Cuban women destined to become the means of selling beaches and vacation packages, in much the same way as had happened to women in the Dominican Republic and in other tropical settings? Cuba, it seems, had discovered the benefit of exploiting one of its most precious resources. Was it any surprise that the *Playboy* display of the bodies of Cuban women on a global stage of sexual entertainment coincided with a massive infusion of tourists, more visitors than the island had seen in three prior decades combined?[2] The *Playboy* article ushered in a period of painful transitions for all Cubans, with women becoming the shock absorbers for the many changes that such cultural, social, and economic shifts entail.

At the beginning of the 1990s, a frenzy of international media attention to the resurgence of prostitution in Cuba did more to stimulate interest in the new sexual economy than any direct promotion campaign could have achieved.[3] Just as the international media buzzed with accounts of cheap, sexy, and brown Cuban bodies for sale, rumors circulated throughout Cuba about young women—*jineteras*—leaving for stints in Havana and Varadero and returning home with dollars, perfume, designer clothes, domestic appliances, foreign boyfriends, and invitations to marry and travel abroad.[4]

The contradictions were particularly heartfelt in the dusty, rural, central Cuban town where I was born and raised. During return visits, I listened as folks talked about young women who wore the latest fashions and spent time trekking through vacation resorts and the capital city. People equally envied, admired, and chastised them for their ability to navigate the social and economic changes taking place. In a period of instability and complex changes, *jineteras* embodied and symbolized the anxieties, dangers, and transitions that were beginning rapidly to transform Cuban society and culture away from a socialist ethos toward market reforms.

Before long, people inside and outside Cuba began saying that Cuba was becoming like the Dominican Republic—a major market and popular destination for Northern travelers seeking sex.[5] Uniformity in outcomes seemed a surprising assertion. After all, the Dominican Republic has long been a quasi-colony of the United States, while Cuba has remained a bastion of anticapitalist, anti-U.S. sentiment, having achieved some degree of independence from its powerful neighbor to the north. The Dominican Republic, on the other hand, was emblematic of the problems that could beset Cuba, troubles such as child prostitution, gambling casinos, widespread social inequities, and the pervasive lack of a social safety net for its citizens. Cuba had confronted and abolished all these problems shortly after the revolutionary government came to power in 1959. Therefore, unlike the Dominican Republic with its extensive marketplace of sex businesses, before the collapse of the socialist trading bloc and its entry into transnational tourism, Cuba had no widespread prostitution or sex establishments.

In contrast to Dominican women, Cuba's socialist policies guaranteed women a high level of investment in human capital formation, with large measures of juridical, occupational, sexual, and educational equity within the revolutionary process. *Cubanas* did not fit the formulaic representation of prostitutes, often portrayed as women lacking educational and vocational skills and agency.[6] It appeared to be an anomaly that foreign tourists were flocking to Cuba and buying sex as they did in other parts of the Caribbean. As a feminist, I was horrified to learn that women's socioeconomic independence appeared to dwindle to a small repertoire of options that included marriage and selling sex to foreigners. Certainly, the Cuban state and Communist Party apparatus owed more to women. By the mid-1990s, however, the erosion of women's status and material well-being made revolutionary Cuba resemble its Dominican neighbor more than in any other time in recent history.

Economies of Desire: Sex and Tourism in Cuba and the Dominican Republic explores the erotic underpinnings of transnational tourism by offering a comparative analysis of the complex affective economies of heterosexual sexualized tourism across Cuba and the Dominican

Republic. In so doing, it presents a reconceptualization and rearticulation of current understandings of sexualized tourism, the identity construction of the "sex worker," and the affective processes of globalized enterprises by focusing on the unifying tendencies of capitalist production in the area of tourism development.[7] In this book, I strive to challenge the notion of "sex worker" that is often applied to racialized working-class women who participate in relationships with foreign men by detailing the ways in which third-world women negotiate new economies and navigate the contact zones between the first and third worlds by using tactical sex. I explore the ways in which practices and identities are discursively inscribed to eroticize racialized, working-class subjects. My argument is that the exchange of goods and money for sexual services is not an unambiguous commercial endeavor but a discursive construction that is contested and in motion, changing across time and space.

Comparative Scope of This Book

The Dominican Republic and Cuba are ideal sites for a comparative investigation of sex and tourism. Indeed, César J. Ayala (1999) asserts that the nations of the Spanish Caribbean share a certain historical continuity that makes it appropriate to study them as a unified whole. For one thing, an intertwined history binds these neighboring countries. For example, migration between the islands has been a common occurrence throughout their histories, shaping many shared aspects of culture, economy, and society. Cuba and the Dominican Republic have also been constitutive in each other's anticolonial and other emancipation struggles.

The transatlantic slave trade that fueled the political economy of the sugar plantation, and the geopolitical incorporation of these two nations into a global order that is inherently unequal and uneven, mark their historical trajectory. During the colonial and neocolonial eras, both countries shared resonant histories of racial and capitalist formation, with a monoculture economy that underpins the structures of the transnational tourism industry in these islands today. As I point out in Chapter 1, the blueprint for tourism and leisure services was established with the plantation economies and the extraction of labor and natural resources in earlier eras. This historical and geopolitical grid thus constitutes the integration of these two countries into a global monopoly of leisure services. To a certain extent, Cuba was able to disengage from the empire of global capitalism from the 1960s to the end of the 1980s, but its insertion into capitalist markets—particularly through tourism—temporarily brought it back into line with the rest of the Caribbean. Thus this book is concerned with the "unifying tendencies" that are the basis for the formation of the tourism corporate structure of the Caribbean that creates similar outcomes to the plantation economies (Ayala 1999: 21).[8] The new kinds of sex-affective relations that I discuss in this book are present not just in Cuba and the Dominican Republic but in other parts of the Caribbean as well.[9]

My concern is with excavating the policies and politics that promote sexual-affective relations in tourism-development projects. I spend less time examining differences within and between the Dominican Republic and Cuba. These are nevertheless significant. For instance, in 2004 the Bush administration advanced the notion that the Cuban state was promoting sex tourism (Reynolds 2004a, 2004b). However, the sale of sex to tourists in the Dominican Republic, more widespread and with a longer history, has not engrossed the U.S. media and policy makers to the same extent. The ongoing hostility toward the Cuban government serves as a backdrop for wider coverage of this phenomenon by the U.S. media.

Another difference between the two countries is the high degree of state-driven human capital development in Cuba (Feinsilver 1993; Carnoy 2007). At many levels, the condition of Cubans is enhanced by state involvement in social welfare programs, not just in universal education and health care but in the use of social workers to alleviate social problems at the level of communities and households, as well as subsidies connected to housing and nutrition, entertainment and leisure. Cuba also has lower levels of interpersonal violence, drug use, and drug trafficking, problems that haunt the lives of Dominicans on a daily basis. Does social capital make for greater levels of agency in exchanges with tourists and more solidarity between Cubans and foreigners? Yes, even though during the early 1990s, at the height of the post-Soviet crisis, the desperation for survival was acute and fraught with dangers.

The Dominican Republic does have more class segmentation and stratification than Cuba, offering economic growth without social or cultural development and hence providing women a double-edged sword. In many ways, Dominican women take more risks and are more vulnerable in transnational encounters, but their longer history of engagement with transnational relations also offers more networks of support and protection. The greater development of civil society in the Dominican Republic also makes possible new avenues for women to seek redress and empowerment, albeit in limited ways. These are topics that deserve further research. Ultimately, however, as I argue in *Economies of Desire*, the global empire of capitalism flattened many differences between these two countries, conflating emergent opportunities with old forms of oppression.

Transnational speculations abound in island settings because people's orientation to what goes on *alla*, "over there," is part of daily parlance. In Cuba, comparisons were often made with the Dominican Republic: "No queremos ser otra República Dominicana" (We don't want to be another Dominican Republic), pronounced a conference participant in Cárdenas where I presented research findings on tourism and sex work in the Dominican Republic in 1997. "No queremos ser otra República Dominicana," a woman sociologist told me in Havana, referring to U.S. cultural and political imperialism in Dominican affairs. In daily conversations, as I discuss in Chapter 2, Dominicans were also eager to make comparisons between their situation and that of their neighboring island. Thus this book is an outcome of the ways in which Cubans and Dominicans pressed me to think and imagine comparatively.

Setting and Methodology

This book is the culmination of over ten years of engagement with the subject of tourism and sex in the Caribbean. It began with questions about Cuban women's participation in the new tourism economy, which led to preliminary research trips to the island in the mid-1990s. However, conducting research in Cuba proved difficult. Because I was a Cuban émigré living in the United States, my visits were regulated by the awkward, contentious, and erratic relations that characterize U.S.-Cuba affairs. Fraught with restrictions from both the Cuban and U.S. governments at every step of the process, I channeled my energies into investigating the situation in the Dominican Republic, where a sex-worker organization was forming, the Movimiento de Mujeres Unidas (MODEMU). In 1996 and 1997, I interviewed women who sold sex to foreign tourists in Puerto Plata and Sosúa, resort regions on the north coast of the Dominican Republic.[10] Subsequent visits took place in 2004, 2005, and 2007 to the capital city of Santo Domingo and the nearby resort setting of Boca Chica. This later period of research concentrated mainly on the organization of MODEMU and less on tourist-oriented sex work.

When the Clinton administration temporarily relaxed restrictions to allow U.S. citizens to travel to Cuba, with the ostensible goal of fomenting "regime change" and imposing democracy, I was able to partake of this opportunity as a researcher. Along with U.S. visitors of various cultural, racial, and age demographics traveling to Cuba, from 2000 to 2004, I averaged three yearly trips to the island, working as an assistant tour guide for educational conferences, business meetings, and music festivals in Havana, Santiago, and Varadero. Going back and forth provided both continuity and distance in the research process, and working within the industry gave me an insider's view of the culture at work within resorts, beaches, restaurants, discothèques, and other spaces that cater to tourists. I have taken precautions at every step of the research process to safeguard the identities and protect the anonymity of those I interviewed.[11]

Investigating a topic connected to stigmatized and criminal activities brought difficulties during early stints of fieldwork. As a Cuban living in the United States, I was entangled within the sociopolitical conflict between the United States and Cuba that continues to define those who travel to the island as dubious subjects with problematic political intentions.[12] We are admonished for traveling to Cuba by members of the Cuban American community who espouse total disengagement from the "Castro regime." No longer referring to Cuban Americans as *gusanos* (worms), the official national discourse in Cuba positions us as accepted members of *la comunidad* (the community) because of our remittances, which constitute one of the largest contributions to the national economy. With due cause, nevertheless, we are still distrusted as possible counterrevolutionaries, CIA informants, or potential enemies of the state.[13]

My nationality was not the only hindrance to my research. In both settings, the fact that I was asking detailed questions about sexual, stigmatized, and illegal activities raised suspicion and made it challenging to cultivate trust in research relationships. For example, a Dominican hotel clerk whom I befriended with the idea of obtaining an interview asked if I was really questioning him because of a study or because I was practicing prostitution in Santo Domingo. This situation and similar ones revealed how overidentified sex work is with women researchers and with women traveling alone. These types of experiences left me with the firm conviction that I was trespassing on cultural norms. Simply asking questions about sex work marked me as a moral transgressor and thus *una mala mujer*. As a bad woman, I crossed the boundaries of proper womanhood by traveling alone, openly asking and talking about sexual matters, and spending time in sexually demarcated spaces. Equally, I was configured as the good girl by sex workers who asked if I was a nun or an investigative reporter. Trapped in the binaries of social identities, I kept insisting that I was a researcher, much to everyone's chagrin.

Acting as both a tourist and field researcher produced a triangulation that continually located me in contradictory multiple subject positions.[14] Ultimately, my positionality illuminated particular social conditions and raised important questions about epistemological inquiries and theoretical frames. I turn to these issues next.

Theoretical Framework

My research on sex tourism in Cuba provoked a reevaluation of the categories of analysis that I employed when studying sex work in the Dominican Republic (Cabezas 1999, 1998).[15] Before long, I realized that the unified object of my research, the "sex worker," did not exist, was ambiguous, or at the very least was quite an unstable subject. Furthermore, most women in Cuba did not identify as a sex worker or a *jinetera*. Instead, I found many elusive travel romances and intimate encounters that did not fit the standard academic categories of "prostitute" or "sex worker." For example, in spite of living off remittances and gifts from their transnational boyfriends, many women did not identify themselves as sex workers or consider their romantic liaisons with tourists a form of prostitution. Rather, their situations presented the interstices of transnational linkages but did not confirm an easy fitting with the category of sex worker. I became fascinated by the indeterminacy and negotiation of decentered identities, the multivalent nature of encounters, and the affection and obligation of social ties that develop between locals and travelers. By way of clarification, I offer Yolanda's story, which follows, as a way to crystallize some of the challenges and ambiguities inherent in these encounters.

Yolanda's Story

Yolanda is a twenty-one-year-old mother of three from Puerto Plata, the oldest and largest tourist resort destination in the Dominican Republic. The day I met Yolanda, a tall, dark-skinned woman with long, shiny hair, she was on her way back from the capital city of Santo Domingo, where she had arranged a tourist visa to Austria to visit with her boyfriend in Vienna. This was quite a feat for a working-class woman who had never traveled outside the country.

At the age of twenty, Yolanda found herself with three children and no financial support. Her husband had left her, and had subsequently renounced all obligations toward his children. Her uncle, who had worked for many years at one of the many tourist enclaves in the area, helped her get a job as an "entertainer" at the beach resort. This work entailed facilitating recreational activities for the resort's guests, such as volleyball games, pool games, and conga dances. The wages were meager and did not fully support her family. She found constant sexual harassment from male tourists to be infuriating. They treated her as part of the entertainment. They touched her, grabbed her, and asked her to go back to their rooms or to go out dancing. This position, nevertheless, permitted her to meet some of her foreign boyfriends.

Her first long-term relationship was with a twenty-eight-year-old German tourist who invited her to go out after work. She agreed and thereafter saw him every night of his vacation stay. They dined in lavish restaurants and shopped at expensive boutiques. They spent a weekend at a tourist beach up the coast. When his vacation ended, he promised that she would visit him in Germany, and he left her *un regalito* (a small gift) of $300. She visited him in Germany a few months later but eventually ended the arrangement because she felt that he was unwilling to commit to a more permanent relationship.

Her latest boyfriend is a thirty-three-year-old Austrian engineer from Vienna whom she also met at the resort complex. They dated during his vacation stay and became romantically involved. Before leaving the country, he had a telephone installed at her house so that he could call her regularly. He also asked her to quit her job at the resort, promising to send her a monthly remittance to cover rent and help support her children.

Yolanda's experience and those of many other actors in the tourism landscape show that elements involved in what is called "sex tourism" can be ambiguous and go beyond the frameworks of victims and oppressors or the gender descriptors of "romance" versus "sex tourism" that characterize descriptions of transcultural liaisons.[16] Even in situations where money does change hands, ambiguity and inconsistency mark these relationships as something other than sex work.[17] We need to ask, therefore, who is considered a sex worker? Who identifies as one? When is it a productive category for instigating social change? When does it reify or challenge configurations of race and class? How does monetization and affective exchange in relationships lead to incomplete commodification in transnational encounters?

As I spent more time in Cuba and the Dominican Republic researching sex tourism, and as I learned from low-income women about the ways to navigate conditions of poverty, it became difficult to define all relations between foreigners and locals as "sex work." Reliant as they are on foreign sources of capital, both the state and individuals become enmeshed in a complex web of intimate interdependencies. Indeed, as I argue in the following chapters, it is often difficult to distinguish those who participate in the sex economy from those who do not. My work engages with and builds on three theoretical frameworks for thinking about tourist-related relations: affective and care work, sexual labor, and informalization theory. I elaborate on these here.

Third World Love: Affective Extraction

The circulation of affect in the sexual economy is one of the major themes of this book. I explore how intimate forms of labor are interwoven into the tourism product and how it is exploited by both transnational corporate capital and people on the ground. Although studies of the care economy have examined the privatization and commodification of domestic services, child care, and elder care, studies of sex work and sex tourism have omitted, questioned, or impugned the authenticity of the affective realm. Studies relating to the sex sector emphasize the exchange of sex for money. Even those who consider affective dimensions privilege the monetary aspect to the exclusion of ambiguous and contested meanings that are also present and traded for material gain. The artificial binary between sex work and care work obscures the constitutive properties present in both (Agustín 2007).

Feminist and postcolonial theories demonstrate the centrality of affective, intimate structures in the processes of racialization and sexualization in the colonial order (Stoler 2002; González 1999; McClintock 1995). For example, the centrality of sexual-affective processes informs Marta Savigliano's (1995) study of the tango with its attendant political economy of passion. Savigliano demonstrates how "a system of exotic representation that commoditized the colonials in order to suit imperial consumption" created homogenizing practices of exoticization and "exotic" objects (1995: 2). This scholarship insists on examining the ways in which the development of empires is entwined with intimately personal, sexual, or social relations (Ballantyne and Burton 2005). Thus, the affective formation of a culture is shaped by the political and economic structures of power (Hirsch and Wardlow 2006). The insights of feminist and postcolonial scholars are building blocks for an integrative framework that considers the extraction of affect and passion as crucial components in the enterprise of travel, hospitality, and the empire of global capitalism. Chapters 3, 4, and 5 detail the progressive development and deployment of identity and sexual practices connected to this practice.

Central to understanding the transference and circulation of affect between the global North and South is the scholarship on affect, money, power, and sex developed by feminist sociologists, philosophers, and economists (Folbre and Nelson 2000; Ehrenreich and Hochschild 2003; Zelizer 2005).[18] For example, Viviana Zelizer's scholarship proposes that we examine the widespread conviction that monetary exchange corrupts intimacy. Rather, her research into the varying practices of monetary and intimate exchange reveals the modes in which money and care are intertwined in various spheres where "participants are simultaneously negotiating delicate, consequential, interpersonal relations and marking difference between those relations and others with which they could easily and dangerously be confused" (Zelizer 2006: 304; 2005). Zelizer and other feminist scholars offer an analysis that begins with the proposition that money runs through all affective relationships. I suggest that we grant the same level of complexity to transcultural relations in third-world tourism settings where reciprocity is present and where sophisticated negotiations take place to delimit the possibility that participants are merely trading sex for economic advantages. This is an argument that I put forward in Chapter 4.

The different material and discursive conditions in which multiple kinds of sexual-affective practices are produced, distributed, and consumed call for an understanding of tourism as a process of extraction and transference of eroticized capital that is always already racialized and exoticized. However, unlike previous studies that equate these processes with monolithic forms of oppression, I am interested in the ways in which participants in transcultural liaisons negotiate power, local and global, through affect, sex, solidarity, and monetary exchanges. Intimate exchanges thus become a way to subvert systems of class and racial inequalities and allow for the creation of new identities.

Informalization

Unlike Yolanda, who had a paying job, most who labor in the service economy do so in connected spaces indirectly attached to the resorts and other tourism enterprises. They work in what is euphemistically referred to as the informal sector. Modernization theory of the 1950s and 1960s assumed that the informal sector—also referred to as the underground economy—would eventually disappear with the right combination of policies, economic progress, and modern industrial development.[19] Instead, throughout the 1970s and 1980s, the informal sector continued to expand, particularly in the low-income global South, where the International Monetary Fund (IMF) and the World Bank's austerity measures imposed the reduction of civil jobs and promoted entrepreneurship for the poor. Changes in the organization of production, including deindustrialization, deregulation of labor standards, and the expansion of the service sector, have multiplied insecurities and instabilities in people's lives. Large portions of the world's population must earn a living hustling in a broad spectrum of subsistence activities. Structural adjustment programs, leading to increases in income inequality, have further disenfranchised many people and forced them to eke out a living in unstable occupations (Thorin 2001). These are all practices that plague the Dominican Republic and are part of the dynamics in Cuba's new mixed-market economy, as I discuss further in Chapter 2.[20]

Debates have focused on how the informal sector subsidizes transnational capital and is interconnected with, and necessary to, the productivity of the so-called formal sector (T. D. Wilson 1998; Stephen 1997; Sassen 1994; Birkbeck 1978). This approach has been documented for the global circuits of commodity production in manufacturing (Freeman 2000; Itzigsohn 2000; Benería and Roldán 1987), but we know much less about how it operates in the service economy. How are sexual-affective services interwoven into the reproduction and accumulation of capital in the tourist product? Studies of the informal sector have traditionally treated it as spatially distinct and differentiated from the formal sector. In this book, I focus on the suppleness and presence of processes of informalization within hospitality services, challenging prevalent notions that tourist-related sex work is an unfortunate and marginal by-product of tourism development. I establish that whether they occur in the streets or in beachfront resorts, sexual-affective relations are structured by the transnational tourism industries as part of the product being sold. I situate sexual-affective relations operating within beachfront resorts and hotels in Chapter 3.

With the restructuring of the world economy in the 1970s, production reorganized into a more flexible system of production that made segmentation in tourism possible. Now niche markets cater to new consumption patterns, accommodating the mobile middle class and encouraging the expansion of markets in sexualized entertainment (Mullings 1999; Urry 1996; Poon 1990). These processes in organization and production have generated demanding changes for workers. In addition to subcontracting, the expansion of flexible patterns of work and part-time employment, lack of job security, the intensification of work, and the rise of casual labor have transformed wage work (ILO 2002). Consequently, "the informal sector" has become a euphemism for the lack of wage-based work, nonstandard employment, and the instability of income. Today, unemployed, self-employed, part-time, seasonal, and temporary workers dominate the global workforce (Gorz 1999; Rifkin 1995). In fact, the International Labour Organization (ILO) maintains that the share of the global workforce that remains outside full-time, stable, and protected forms of employment has been increasing over time (ILO 2002: 11).[21] As workers continue to suffer lack of control over earnings, a higher degree of discrimination, exploitative working conditions, and a lack of trade-union representation (Thomas 2002: 18), the central figure in global labor is no longer the worker identified with one particular trade or profession, but, as André Gorz (1999: 53) asserts, "It is becoming, rather, the figure of the insecure worker, who at times 'works' and at times does not 'work,' practices many different trades without any of them actually being a trade, has no identifiable profession or, rather, whose profession it is to have no profession, and cannot therefore identify with his/her work, but regards as his/her 'true' activity the one he/she devotes himself to in the gaps between his/her paid 'work.'" This description of the "insecure worker" has, of course, historically characterized the conditions of labor for many women or people of color, but with deindustrialization, contingent work has become more pervasive in other parts of the population. It is in these gaps of identity and labor—spaces of liminality—that we can situate the sexual-affective economies of transnational tourism. It is in the interstices of the global economy that Dominicans and Cubans can create malleable identities that provide distance from stigma and criminality, identities continually in flux. In this process of liminality, Cubans and Dominicans generate new opportunities to transcend local configurations of class, race, and sexuality. Later, I use the vignette of Camilo to illustrate these points.

The World Travel & Tourism Council estimates that 19 percent of total employment in the Dominican Republic (WTTC 2005) and 9 percent in Cuba (WTTC 2008) is in the tourism sector, but an even larger percentage carves out a living connected to tourists through informal, freelance activities. For instance, in the north coast of the Dominican Republic, outside and near the beach resort enclaves, young men stand across the street hoping to befriend a wandering tourist. Unemployed, informal tour guides are looking for opportunities that are few and far between—a tourist who ventures out of the all-inclusive beachfront compound on foot, a couple looking to try a local restaurant, or a small group wanting to get away from the resort enclave. Dressed in some of their finest threads, the young men will slowly and respectfully approach the foreigner with multiple offers: "Let me take you to eat at a typical Dominican restaurant," "How about if I show you around town?" and my favorite, "I can teach you to dance the *merengue*."

One day during one of my trips to the Dominican Republic, as I walked past the golf course and headed toward the main highway that goes from Puerto Plata to Sosúa, I could see a group of men congregating outside the resort. I had gone into the resort enclave to use a bank, which, along with the post office, shops, and a museum, produces a small town atmosphere. I found Camilo and Jorge waiting for tourists to break free from the rigidly structured recreation activities of the resort. Camilo, the younger of the two, approached me with an offer to be my guide. He thought that I could use an excursion to see the amber museum in Puerto Plata. I told him that I was there to work, and we stood around talking about Puerto Plata and tourism in the north coast. Camilo had recently heard from one of the resort's guests that the expatriate management team had been making disparaging comments about Dominicans during orientation meetings for the guests:

The hotels in Playa Dorada and Playa Naco have a 25 percent and 17 percent of occupied capacity. The little tourism that we have in the complex is being used and managed by foreigners [expatriates] who are the representatives of the tours and are responsible for telling them [tourists] barbarities, because they are the authorities. How is it that an Englishman comes here, for example, and when that guest is in the hotel they tell him, "You see that little Dominican that's right there? Don't mind him, he will lie and deceive you." At every step he will take the largest portion of the pie, and he will say the most barbarous things about this country. About a month ago I was reading a brochure that says that when you get to the airport, and if you have it, give only five pesos in tips. Those guys are hungry for tips. Now what duck laid that egg? What he [the airport worker] needs are gratuities. Do you think it's all right for representatives to speak ill of Dominicans and to give them wrong propaganda? Tourism last summer was more or less all right. It's the case that people working here for a few years are able to make a living. Those of us who have been working here for a few years we even speak Chinese, even sign language. I speak four languages. When a guest leaves the hotel, which is now rare, because now they don't go to Puerto Plata—the hotel has them tied, they have to do everything that the hotel representative tells them—they go to the lobby of the hotel to look for a taxi, and we explain to them that we will give them a tour of the city and that we charge a tip, whatever the guest wants to give. The guide says, "You give me whatever you want." And the guide does everything possible for them to feel good; to do a good job. When they use a hotel tour guide, they charge them $15 per person. I don't understand why all these foreign agencies have to use expatriates. I don't understand why they are replacing us in our country.

Camilo's statements emphasize the massive displacement of Dominican workers. Because the majority of resorts are managed by expatriates—many of whom do not appreciate the cultural, social, and economic realities of the countries where they work—locals are frustrated by the lack of respect accorded by their bosses and the severe competition for resources and employment. This displacement has led many citizens to feel like strangers in their own land. Treated like outsiders in their home country, they are a marginalized workforce, performing roles and functions similar to those they would perform as undocumented workers in Europe or North America. Informality, however, is not just about exclusion from formal jobs. It is also a counter-economy to wage labor. As Camilo's narrative reveals, and as Steven Gregory (2007) points out, it is also a structure that allows for oppositional resistance to the hierarchy of race and class that constitutes labor markets.

Deported for selling drugs in New York, Camilo was fluent in English and felt comfortable escorting Canadian and German tourists. After waiting for public transportation that never arrived, we started walking back to the main square of town, and Camilo shared how he often became romantically involved with the foreign women whom he met. Sometimes they were one-night stands, but often he cultivated an ongoing friendship.

"¿Eres sanky?" (Are you a *sanky panky*?), I asked in a teasing manner because he wore his hair in dreadlocks; an unusual hairstyle for Dominican men, but used by *sankys* as a way to signal their desire to attract foreign women.[22]

"No," he said. "Los sankys se acuestan con cualquiera" (*Sankys* sleep with anyone), alluding to the male-to-male sexual relations that were increasingly stigmatized. "Yo estoy interesado en la amistad" (I am interested in friendship), he added with a smile.

The affective dimensions of his work as a tour guide allowed Camilo to reposition himself as not simply an unemployed worker hustling a living, but rather as someone who nurtures relationships with foreigners for mutual benefit. He could cultivate malleable social and labor roles, thereby repositioning himself as a friend and a cosmopolitan subject. Lasting bonds with foreigners may ultimately position Camilo as a lover and a friend and assist him in asserting and maintaining a subjectivity of resistance to the exclusionary practices of transnational tourism capital. Informal arrangements thus generate the possibility for the emergence of new subjectivities. They also enable local people, who are otherwise shut out, to align themselves with transnational class relations. The sexual-affective exchanges that Camilo and others negotiate at the margins contest the dominant relations of the political economy of tourism. Thus these affective arrangements both complement the accumulation of capital and siphon profits from the state and transnational enterprises. Intimacy functions as a countereconomy.

Sanky pankys and the multitude of new social-sexual actors emerging across the global South who craft affective and sexual encounters are the touchstone of new power relations between transnational capital and labor that are at the core of "flexible accumulation" practices and are consequences of changes in the structure of global production (Robinson 2004). Scholars point out that the restructuring of the labor process has diminished the differences between formal and informal labor arrangements. This is particularly evident in the enclave model of tourism, as I discuss in further detail in Chapter 3. The casualization of labor in transnational tourism calls upon shifts in gender and sexual subjectivities while articulating class and racial hierarchies that require policing (Gregory 2007). This is a theme that I explore further in Chapter 5.

The late feminist philosopher Linda Singer suggests in "Sex and the Logic of Late Capitalism" that sexuality emerges in late capitalism as "both that which is to be disciplined, and that which remains as excess or resistance to discipline and therefore must also be pacified, accommodated, indulged. It is also, consequently, that which must also be socially managed and coordinated to maximize its social utility, i.e. its profitability" (Singer 1993: 35). *Economies of Desire* is concerned with the accommodation and the resistance that sexual-affective relations present for people involved in marginal and elusive relations connected to travelers.

Selling Sex

Studies that have appeared in the last thirty years have unearthed an extensive historical and cultural variability in prostitution (Gilfoyle 1999). No longer regarded as the world's oldest profession, prostitution is now seen as existing within specific cultural contexts and fields of power (O'Connell Davidson 1998). One of the most important influences is the feminist reformulation of prostitution as a form of labor. The reconceptualization of prostitution as a form of labor—"an income-generating activity"—is instrumental in distancing women from moralizing discourses that stigmatize those who sell sexual services (Kempadoo and Doezema 1998:4). It provides women in the sex industry a discourse to demand better working conditions and new forms of redress and protection (Kempadoo and Doezema 1998). Sex workers have organized to gain legitimacy through labor rights and decriminalization of the sex trade (Nagle 1997; S. Bell 1994). The sex-worker identity is closely aligned to labor rights and facilitates the formation of collective action to raise awareness about abuses in the sex trade. This topic is further explored in Chapter 5. New forms of sex work, such as acting in pornographic films, erotic dancing, escort services, erotic massage, and telephone and cyber sex, can be subsumed under the category of sex work.

Controversies between feminists on the issue of prostitution and sex work focus on what exactly is sold in prostitution.[23] Some argue that the prostitute's body is bought and sold, rendering the transaction alienating and dehumanizing, particularly for the person selling the sexual service (O'Connell Davidson 1998). For other feminists, commercial sex is a service rendered similar to other forms of body work (Nussbaum 2005; Kempadoo and Doezema 1998; Chapkis 1997). Wendy Chapkis (1997), for example, locates sex work as the performance of emotional labor where only certain parts of the body and practices are provided for sexual access. In other words, the entire body is not being sold. This position draws on the sociology of emotions to argue that sex-work providers distinguish between intimate love and paid sexual services (Chapkis 1997). It maintains that sex workers separate and demarcate their intimate selves from their working lives in much the same way as other professionals, such as flight attendants, actors, psychotherapists, masseuses, and child-care workers. It stresses a commonality with all those in occupations that use emotional labor as part of their work but can divorce themselves from the more pernicious aspects of entanglement.[24]

Some feminists bitterly contest that sex work can be just another form of labor because women are forced or coerced by poverty to sell sex in conditions of poverty, and this contributes to women's overall social subordination (Lacsamana 2004; Barry 1995; Satz 1995). In conditions of poverty and within structures of male domination, they maintain, the lack of choice renders sex workers survivors or victims who lack agency and self-determination because of economic constraints. But privileging liberal humanist notions of "choice" obscures the complexities that frame labor under capitalism. Since labor lacks ownership of the means of production, it is unable to survive except through the commodification of its labor power for wages (Joseph 2005: 389). Furthermore, race, gender, sexuality, and cultural capital structure labor markets, relegating most women laborers to very few occupations.[25] Although women who participate in the sex economy often have few options, their agency is not obliterated.

For feminists who contest the meaning and significance of sex work, Marx can provide some important insights. In Marx's early writings, prostitution served as a metaphor for capitalism.[26] Marx argued that labor itself was a commodity. The idea that, in prostitution, the commodity being sold is the self is partly articulated through the notion that the whole body is commodified and that the prostitute is completely powerless and subordinated.[27] In his later writings, Marx no longer conceptualized prostitution as the selling of a body (van der Veen 2001; Tucker 1987). Instead, he developed concepts such as labor power, use value, exchange value, and class as processes by which surplus labor is appropriated and distributed. He moved away from the notion of prostitution as the sale of the body and toward that of prostitution as the sale of a service. Thus Marx emphasized that prostitution could be conceived as selling "the service of *labor-power* in the production of a *service* sold to clients" (van der Veen 2001: 43).

The idea that the sale of the commodity is shaped by class processes is useful in allowing us to analyze situations in which class processes shape the commodity diversely. Instead of trying to subsume all sex work under the rubric of sexual slavery, as some prostitute groups, advocates, and feminist scholars have done, we can examine the context—not just class, but the cultural, gender, racial, political, legal, and economic processes—in which the commodity is produced. In situations where sex is provided within informal, freelance arrangements, the provider may be able to exercise control over his or her sexuality and minimize the possibilities for degradation. In other words, the provider has some control over producing and appropriating the surplus value, being able to determine "what is provided, when, where, with whom, how, and at what price" (van der Veen 2001: 47). The affective economies of transnational tourism effectively fuse exchange value with use value.

The category of sex work, however, does not apply to all erotic cross-cultural encounters. What of situations that are not clearly marked commercial endeavors? Or where sex is not present at all, but gifts and other forms of financial reward play a prominent role? What of relationships that combine pleasure, intimacy, and monetary support? The inability to read the subtle and liminal aspects of these encounters and an overemphasis on the sexual component risk privileging the sexual component as the most important aspect of interpersonal relations. Nicole Constable (2003), for example, argues that the overemphasis on analyzing the sexual component of transcultural relationships obscures other elements present that are equally important. She contends that this is a form of Orientalism and the exoticization of the "other." Here I put forth a number of assertions to raise concerns with the category of sex work.

First, there is an overarching perspective that implies that "sex" and "sexuality" are understood as a universal category as projected by the European Enlightenment, a notion that anthropologists argue does not apply to many Asian, African, and African-based cultures (Waller and Marcos 2005; Wekker 1999; Kendall 1999; Herdt 1980). Expanding the cultural context of the meaning of sex, in Chapter 4 I analyze how the term *sex work* is not applicable within the religious cosmology of Santería, since superimposing a Western notion of sex denies the particular local meaning that connects sexuality to spirituality.

Second, the imposition of the term *sex worker* reveals an indiscriminately racist and classist perspective. I argue that the label *sex work* is difficult to apply to the new forms of flexible, contingent practices that may contain elements of partial commodification but that do not conform to rigid categories of commercial sex work. *Sex worker* is also a problematic descriptor for sex-for-money exchanges that take place in all-inclusive resorts (as discussed in Chapter 3). Furthermore, it is difficult to apply this term within the context of some same-sex desires and practices (Allen 2003).

In an ethnography of the Boca Chica tourist resort in the Dominican Republic, Gregory (2007) ascertains that the notion of sex work fails to capture the challenges that *dominicanas* face and the fortitude with which they struggle. Tourist-local relations in Boca Chica, Gregory argues, could be "reducible neither to 'sex' nor to 'work' but instead embraced disparate practices through which women renegotiated and contested hierarchies that were secured *simultaneously* in terms of gender, sex, race, and class" (2007: 134). Consequently, I make a case against portraying all practices and social relations within tourist economies as sex work and against subsuming significantly different forms of sexuality under the category of *sex worker*.[28]

Sex worker presupposes a fixed identity and thereby creates and freezes differences and subjects. This identity may be fixed where institutions like brothels or pimps control the conditions of women's sexual activity, but not necessarily in less constrained situations. *Sex worker* is an empowering term in situations where the woman or man does not have substantial control over the disposition of sexual activities because it marks those activities as labor and therefore as entailing worker rights. In situations where sexual commerce is unclear or where full commodification does not take place, the sex-worker discourse proves futile in shaping identities that clamor and organize for rights. We need a more nuanced theoretical lens to understand these relationships and practices, one that can provide more ample recourse for social justice.

Transnational travel and leisure produce geographies that generate and reproduce the racialization of sexualized, eroticized bodies that are necessary for the ways in which tourism is imagined and shaped. The landscape of transnational corporate tourism makes it possible for erotic encounters between people of different racial-ethnic backgrounds to involve subject formations and practices that are more productive than "sex work." The general tendency in the scholarship to assume that participants in these relationships misrecognize their roles or are deluded about their actions misreads intentionality and the ways in which people negotiate and express desire with economic exigencies. It is more useful, I suggest, to interrogate our opposition between love and money. Instead of reading all relationships where there are monetary exchanges, gifts, and travel as immoral, oppressive, and exploitative, I reveal how money cultivates relationships, and gifts create identities in relationships that can be more fruitful to both participants than the alignment with "sex work."

Overview of Chapters

In Chapter 1, "Tourism in Cuba and the Dominican Republic," I elucidate how and why tourism development in the Caribbean, contrary to the conjecture of politicians and policy makers, increased internal inequality, external dependency, and expanded informal-sector activities and unstable, low-paying jobs. By closely examining the framework for incorporating Cuba and the Dominican Republic into the global economy, I trace the foundation of the macrostructural patterns prevalent in tourism development. This chapter explains how the establishment of mass tourism development has produced similar effects and created new kinds of sex-affective relations and identities in both places. This chapter underscores the homogenizing practices of global capital.

Chapter 2, "Neoliberal Times in Cuba and the Dominican Republic," is an analysis of economic restructuring after the fall of the socialist trading market that places Cuba within the larger global, neoliberal framework. Using features of structural adjustment programs, Cuba increased joint ventures and foreign investment, privatization, and retrenchment of state services as it quickly moved to a mixed-market system during the 1990s. These changes reintroduced vestiges of the prerevolution capitalist social order, such as prostitution, drugs, beggars, and maids. As a consequence, by the end of the 1990s, Cuba appeared more like the Dominican Republic than at any other time in the previous forty years. This chapter throws light on the multidimensionality of the crisis and Cuba's move to the market. It specifically analyzes the cumulative effects of economic restructuring with attention to their impact on race and gender. Although the reforms exacerbated vulnerabilities for Black Cubans and women, connections to the global economy also provided unprecedented economic and social resources.

Having established an understanding of the political economy of international tourism in the Caribbean and the implications of restructuring with features of structural adjustment, I turn to the erotics of transnational tourism in Chapters 3 and 4. Chapter 3, "Eroticizing Labor in All-Inclusive Beach Resorts" is the first ethnographic study of all-inclusive resorts in the Caribbean; it draws on participant observation and interviews with Cuban workers to interrogate the use of race and sexuality in the organization of labor in transnational firms. This chapter examines Cuba's new, all-inclusive beach resorts in Varadero, where workers are asked to enact scripts of affective labor, sexual enticement, and servility in the delivery of their occupational roles. Most studies of sexualized labor argue that resistance occurs when workers do not comply with management's demands. Instead, in this chapter I argue that workers' resistance can be found in the appropriation of their sexualized labor. This chapter illustrates the working of a hidden site for sexual-affective encounters that is invisible in studies of sex tourism.

In Chapter 4, "Daughters of Yemayá and Other *Luchadoras,*" I use the narratives of women involved in relationships with tourists to explore the complexity of sexual-affective encounters. Drawing on the spiritual guidance of the Afro-Cuban deity Yemayá, women embrace tourists as divine intervention to help them support their children and to find love and spiritual affirmation. This chapter exposes a wide range of experiences in the Dominican Republic and Cuba that cannot be easily subsumed under the category of "sex work." Instead, these narratives reveal heterogeneity in experiences that move us away from a monolithic view of relationships, sexual practices, and sentimental entanglements. I employ the notion of *tactical sex* to capture the diverse, amorphous ways in which sex is deployed in tourist economies. The aim of this chapter is to problematize dichotomous categories employed in sex tourism and to show how essentialist notions obscure ambiguities and reinscribe racialist paradigms.

In both the Dominican Republic and Cuba, I found ample evidence of the ways in which women use sex work to escape domestic violence, only to end up exposed to further violence at the hands of the state. In Chapter 5, "Tourism, Sex Work, and the Discourse of Human Rights,"

I present evidence of human rights abuses connected to gender and sexuality by exploring them as outcomes of the tourist-based economic ordering of the state. I establish that the intensification in state-sponsored violence against women is an outcome of the tourism development project. I explore how and when the term *sex worker* is fruitful for political organizing and for women's empowerment. I discuss state enforcement of the category "prostitute" in tourism settings, particularly with regard to working-class women, and the response of organizations such as MODEMU in the Dominican Republic that clamor for human rights for sex workers.

Without question, trade in travel and tourism services at the turn of the century poses great challenges for the people of the Caribbean. A comparative study such as this book, therefore, provides an important departure in understanding how sex and love are intertwined within the structure and organization of transnational tourism and processes of the global political economy. I hope that this book will move us away from the focus on and stigmatization of erotic relationships and toward discussion of the human costs and disparities imposed by the expansion of a corporate empire of capital.

1 / Tourism in Cuba and the Dominican Republic

In October 2005, I stepped off an airplane into the humid Caribbean air in the late evening. Tired and dazed from a short plane ride that entailed waiting five hours at the Miami airport, I caught a taxi and settled into the backseat for a twenty-minute ride. The taxi driver sped along toward the colonial area of the capital city. After about five minutes of sitting in the backseat alone, I got restless and decided to strike up a conversation with the driver. I asked him how things were going in the country. "¿Como esta la situación en el país?" He was somewhere between thirty and forty years old, with café-au-lait–colored skin, dark hair, and a mustache. He drove through the dark, traffic-congested streets, smoking a cigarette with the same hand that he used to steer the compact Japanese car. With the other hand, he punctuated his sentences with wide hand gestures, sometimes switching the cigarette from hand to hand, while looking into my eyes through the rearview mirror. I was impressed by his agility and noticed that he had long fingers and rough-looking hands. I wondered if he had another job— one that involved manual labor—on the side. However, dressed in nicely pressed khaki pants and a white shirt, he looked more like a store manager than a construction worker. He avoided my direct question, and after some short exchanges, we talked about Hurricane Katrina. He was both articulate and well informed about U.S. racial

politics, with answers that stemmed from an analysis of social inequality in New Orleans. Finally, I inquired again how the political and
economic situation was unfolding in the country. It had been a couple
of years since my last visit, and I was eager to learn about the current
debates, dramas, and tragedies that plagued this little piece of the
world.

"¿Pa' que le cuento?" (Let me tell you). He started in with a litany of
complaints as I settled into my seat in the role of a studious listener.
This is a familiar role for me. I often find a taxi driver's take on the
political-economic situation keen and a good precursor of how my trip
will unfold. Taxi drivers, I conclude, are astute readers of the cultural
pulse, and they often forewarn of what awaits during my stay. The
bombardment of criticism against the government is customary, however, and resonates with those of previous trips. He told me that the
new tax system was killing his business, the cost of food had gone up,
and everyone was sick and tired of the many power outages. In fact,
the electricity only came on during the early morning hours, when
everyone was sleeping. Workers were losing ground all the time, he
told me. Tourism was down for this time of the year. He rhetorically
asked, "How can I pay for my children's school costs this year?" All
of sudden I began to feel disoriented, as if the long airport wait was
catching up with me. I looked ahead to see the tall buildings that lined
the Malecón (the sea wall of the capital city) in the horizon. Where
was I? Cuba or the Dominican Republic?

Free-trade zones attracting foreign investment with low-wage labor,
dependence on remittances from its migrant citizens laboring in the
North, the blazing development of uniform tourist resorts along the
coastal beaches that daily dismantled coral reefs and marine ecology.
Where was I? Cuba or the Dominican Republic? Since Cuba reentered
the world capitalist economy in 1990, it appears to resemble the Dominican Republic more every day. Tourist-oriented prostitution, transnational labor migrations, and other forms of orientation toward the
global economy emphasize the focus on *aya,* over there. Just as in other
parts of the Américas, the whims of the "Washington consensus" or the
neoliberal order of the capitalist economy increasingly disadvantage
local populations. Where was I? Cuba or the Dominican Republic?

The taxi driver's many complaints momentarily transported me
to Cuba, where people incessantly analyze and reflect on the dizzying

Fig 1.1   Colonial area of Santo Domingo, Dominican Republic

pace of social and economic changes that have taken place since the fall of the Soviet Union. However, the taxi driver's anxiety about paying for his daughter's education reminded me that I was in the Dominican Republic, where a broken and fragile social infrastructure cannot provide treatment and medicine for the sick, and where collective resources are not used to create and sustain an educated citizenry. In this late stage of global capitalism, Dominicans suffer acute forms of social vulnerabilities and dispossession. This marks an acute divergence from the situation of Cuba.

Had I been in Cuba and not in the Dominican Republic, my taxi driver could have been a former electrical engineer, a mathematician, or an economist educated by the state. Unable to work or make a living in state industries, many elite professional workers migrated to tourism services in the 1990s, at that time the only viable venue for decent jobs. But as in the Dominican Republic, taxi drivers, bartenders, and chambermaids were all forced to lead double lives. Laboring in formal tourism-related jobs and trying to find other ways to augment income and attain some stability amid the constant disruption created by market forces, people call upon all their emotional and social resources to transcend the limited possibilities of their lives. A gratuity or an enduring friendship with a foreigner relieves the daily struggle for survival, *la lucha,* and makes prominent the role of affect in navigating and assessing contact with the outside world. I gave my taxi driver a large tip and walked into the air-conditioned hotel feeling inconsolably like an exploitative foreigner.

Cuba and the Dominican Republic? In this chapter, I examine the geopolitical framework for Caribbean tourism and argue that the threads of a common history, combined with the transnational control of travel and hospitality services, create common unifying tendencies in regional industry. I explore why tourism has little chance to substantially alter the relations of these countries to the global economy. The concern here is with the framework under which multinational hospitality and tourism monopolies establish themselves in the Dominican Republic and Cuba. The processes of tourism economic development that I investigate in this chapter include an examination and analysis of the so-called informal economy that makes possible the emergence of new social-sexual actors in Caribbean tourist destinations.

I begin by briefly tracing the foundation of macrostructural patterns and dynamics created through historical processes of colonialism. This history of economic, political, and social subjugation is the basis for the current global market in Caribbean tourism. I conclude by examining tourism in Cuba from the 1960s to the 1980s, a period in which Cuba focused on providing leisure and recreation for the working class, peasants, and other marginal populations. This proved to be an unusual and refreshing alternative for the Caribbean as a whole.

Developing International Mass Tourism

Capitalism in the Caribbean has its roots in conquest, consolidated through the enslavement and demise of local populations and the subsequent importation of African slaves. From the sixteenth century, when Europe established itself in the Americas, capitalism continually expanded through access to cheap labor, land, resources, and markets. The violent decimation of the indigenous peoples of the Caribbean, which began in 1492, preceded the equally brutal transatlantic slave trade. The outcome of conquest and colonialism created the structures for the subjugation of labor, and firmly planted racial inequality.

From the discursive construction of the exotic "tropics" to the neocolonial arrangements, tourism's roots lie in a colonial order of conquest, violence, pillage, and exploitation that scraped clean natural resources for foreign profit. Gold, fine woods, ore, nickel, and copper became the fuel for the massive accumulation of European wealth. "Without deliveries from the Caribbean womb," as Benítez-Rojo (1992: 5) states, "Western capital accumulation would not have been sufficient to effect a move, within a little more than two centuries, from the so-called Mercantilist Revolution to the Industrial Revolution." Thus the massive transfer of wealth to European colonizers places the Caribbean center stage in the history of capitalism.

The Caribbean was shaped economically, socially, and politically by the European plantation system. This ordered the region into a parallel configuration that shared similar structures, producing a morphology that was "repeated, becoming more or less ascendant from colonial times until the present" (Benítez-Rojo 1992: 38). The "great plantation machine," which required enormous sums of resources in labor, transport, agriculture, technology, administration, and commerce, ravaged local economies in ways later supplanted by tourism. Today, the replication of the plantation takes place in the insular tourist resort enclaves of Jamaica, Barbados, Puerto Rico, Antigua, and other locations.

Under the all-inclusive-resort model of enclave tourism, Caribbean beaches are privatized, and the surrounding communities are excluded from entering hotels and beaches. Little is done to incorporate local communities or to gain their participation in conceptualizing the transformation of their environment. In Havana, for instance, a city-level survey on the impact of tourism development revealed that residents were not included in any of the stages of planning and implementation of new tourism facilities (Colantonio 2004). The consumption of tourism-oriented infrastructures is restricted exclusively to foreigners, and local residents do not benefit from them (Colantonio 2004: 36).[1] Similarly, the United Nations Development Program's Human Development Report (2005) for the Dominican Republic characterizes the resort enclave as a tourist facility that literally and figuratively turns its back on the local community and culture, a homogeneous product subject to little state regulation (69).

As the sugar plantation economy evolves into the tourist resort, coastlines, native plants, open spaces, and wildlife in general are demolished to create large hotel complexes that house, nourish, and nurture primarily North American and European travelers. Transnational capital is not compelled to pay the environmental costs it exerts on fragile ecosystems through large-scale resort development. The devastation of coral reefs and the degradation of the surrounding environment are regarded as a national, not an international, catastrophe. Once the seven-to ten-year tax exemption has ended, multinationals move to a new location and begin the cycle of exploitation elsewhere. As with maquiladoras and other forms of export-processing zones, there is no obligation to compensate for the environmental costs of exhausting the physical environment. Given the lack of commitment to developing human capital in host societies, local Caribbean populations have developed ways to negotiate these fleeting and temporary global interactions.

The experiences scripted for the rest and recreation of "guest" populations relegate locals to rigid roles as entertainers and subservient workers (Crick 1996). Many hospitality workers, who actively resist their subjugated status by crafting affective relations with guests and adopting cosmopolitan desires, emphasized this point. For instance, Elías a Cuban waiter in his late twenties, told me that he would like to travel anywhere: "I don't want to leave Cuba, no. What I want is to see the world. Just like you come to visit here, I want to visit there. I want to visit you, and I also want to go to Paris." Elías echoed a sentiment that Caribbean writers and artists have expressed in various forms. For instance, Antiguan writer Jamaica Kincaid, in her critique of tourism in the Caribbean, writes about the putative exclusion of residents in her poetic essay *A Small Place* (1988).

Leisure travel and the values of hedonism that tourists seem to pursue do not escape the notice of those trapped in labor regimes of servility and exclusion upon which transnational tourism builds its foundation. In fact, leisure travel, as we know it in the world economy, is structured by the geopolitical inequalities of global capitalism whereby "a peculiar pattern of rich, temperate, countries of origin connects tourists to a much larger number of less affluent and warmer destinations comprising a 'pleasure periphery' on a world scale" (Lea 1988: 1). This pleasure periphery is composed of former colonies with few choices to develop financial viability within the global capitalist system. As Britton (1982: 355) declares, "The more a Third World country has been dominated by foreign capital in the past, the greater like-

Fig 1.2 Hotel Nacional at 2 A.M., Havana, Cuba

lihood there is of the prerequisites for establishing a local tourist industry being present." As former colonies, gendered and raced spaces
eroticized along a colonial axis of power, the tourist plantations reinforce all the former divisions of labor, capital, and power.

Organizational Structure of Tourism

International tourism is set up to meet the needs and demands of in-
dustrialized countries and reflects the asymmetrical distribution of
power and economic resources between former colonies and their colonizers (Nash 1977; Fanon 1963). This structure of dominance is such
that wealthy countries use their technology, management resources,
marketing, and commercial power to control third-world tourist destinations. Tourism's tendency to perpetuate patterns of economic dependence and vulnerability for developing countries is most evident in the
island nations of the Caribbean, where small local suppliers have limited access to tourist-generating markets. Because of monopolization
practices by powerful foreign wholesalers and retailers, particularly

networks that restrict and control accommodation and ticket reservations, the institutional organization of the tourist industry impedes small economies from generating sufficient foreign exchange and viable employment or promoting the participation of the most marginal segments of the population (Cabezas 2008; PSTT 2004).

By contrast, travel and tourism in Europe and North America emerged because of subsidized state-led development. Growth in the infrastructure and technology needed for expansion was realized with state-sponsored research and development funds. For example, in the 1950s, the U.S. Senate authorized more than $12 million to support the development of improved transport aircraft. According to Truong (1990), the United States designed an "air policy which encouraged and fostered the development of civil aeronautics and air commerce inside and outside the US" (103). Use of U.S. aviation equipment, U.S. aeronautical procedures, and the English language as the world standard in aviation guaranteed the United States global dominance in the nascent aeronautics business. In Western Europe, the concept of "participatory enterprise," by which airlines are owned in part or in full by governments, helped cover the losses incurred by the operation of initially unprofitable but strategically important routes. In essence, both the United States and Western Europe established, subsidized, and cultivated the global travel infrastructure and set up the regulations and norms of the industry for air transport. Consequently, U.S. and European carriers control the Caribbean skies today. Major airline corporations such as American Airlines, the biggest regional airline in the Caribbean, Virgin Atlantic Airways, British Airways, United Airlines, and KLM lead the industry.

During the late 1950s and 1960s, travel and tourism enterprises grew rapidly as they sought to capture the disposable earnings of wageworkers in the booming postwar economies of Western Europe and the United States. Leisure time was quickly transformed into a multibillion-dollar market for mass consumption (Shaw and Williams 2002). The growth was enhanced by a burgeoning consumer society, the hard-won creation of social legislation for holiday time off, and changes in production. The United States furthered its political and commercial interests by promoting travel and tourism as a method for economic development in the Caribbean. As Truong (1990: 104) explains in her study of the rest and recreation industry in Southeast Asia:

The promotion of tourism itself mirrored the awareness of the relation between air transport and economic development. This intervention has two main advantages for the US. From a commercial perspective, such intervention contributes to the strengthening of the U.S. position as a manufacturer and exporter of aircraft and navigation equipment. From a political perspective, it helps to consolidate the direction of social and economic development in the Third World, which benefits U.S. interests under a screen of peaceful understanding.

Thus tourism allowed the United States to maintain and extend its economic dominance of the region. In due course, the growth of travel and hospitality services became a "peaceful" method of attaining long-lasting political power and financial control in the markets and politics of developing nations, particularly through flows of direct and indirect foreign investment in transnational tourism corporations (Lanfant, Allcock, and Bruner 1995).

In tourism, as with subcontracting in the manufacturing industries, transnational corporations have increasingly disarticulated the production of services through a flexible management and ownership control system, leasing arrangements, franchises, technical service agreements, and management contracts. For example, the emergence of international trade and production networks in tourism means that subcontracting and fragmenting practices extend to the design, construction, and management of hotels. Globally dispersed production and distribution chains are now so prevalent in the industry that an analyst with the Dominican association of hotels told me that he could not decipher who owns what in the majority of hotels in the country. Nevertheless, only a handful of the largest chains dominate the industry (ILO 2001). Regardless of the vicissitudes of globalization, the organizational framework remains firmly rooted in multinational firms that are responsible for creating and generating standardization, also referred to as "McDonaldization" practices in the leisure industry (Ritzker and Liska 1997). Multinational corporations aim to standardize every aspect of the tourist experience, from the style of the facilities to the roles of the workers (Greenwood 1989). In Chapter 3, I elaborate on the practices that combine standardization of the labor process with the exoticization of workers in commercial hospitality.

As I detail in Chapter 3, tourism is a racialized process that depends on transnational linkages that move leisure migrants from the global North to the South in search of pleasure and recreation. This process stimulates the mobility of Caribbean migrants who travel to the North in search of labor and economic stability. Leisure migrants' citizenship rights, privileges, status, and comforts are often enhanced in ways unknown to them in their own countries. The concurrent flow of black and brown bodies receives a different kind of reception in the powerful nations of the North, where they encounter criminalization of their labor, xenophobic attacks, and racism. Affective relations between tourists and locals are a means to mitigate this hostile terrain of global uneven exchange.

Paradise for Consuming Masses? The Enclave Model of Tourism Development

Tourism is characterized by the monopolization of capital—a historic system that has developed for more than five hundred years and is in a new stage of accumulation governed by transnational global production and consumption (Robinson 2004). Monopolization in tourism is evident in the commercial system and organization of the industry, which is dominated by a handful of transnational corporations (ILO 2001). The great plantation machine is present all over the Caribbean, where a homogeneous market of enclave, beachfront resorts dot the coasts. Controlled by international chain hotels and tour operators and managed by expatriates,[2] the mass-marketed, mass-consumed, all-inclusive tourist package, in which tour operators and travel agencies combine the components of a destination's attractions—food, lodging, and transportation—into a single product, is the most widely used monopolizing practice in Caribbean tourism. The all-inclusive tourist package accounts for 95 percent of all visitor stays in the Dominican Republic and ensures that most of the money is spent before the trip even begins, in the place of origination (Tuduri 2001b; ASOHARES 2005). The mass tourist resort of the sun-sea-sand type is associated with economies of scale and is therefore dependent on bargain prices offered to middle-class consumers (Torres 2002). Since most countries in the region compete with one another to offer the same experience, the sameness of the resorts means that there is little to differentiate one location from another.

Transnational corporations dominate global markets that control the beachfront resorts. In beachfront resorts, a Fordist mode of production and consumption with a rigid standardization of the product and mass replication has generated similarities in architecture, facilities, corporate culture, and forms of entertainment and marketing images that have created a standardized product (Torres 2002). As I discuss in Chapter 3, management increasingly implements "personalized" forms of services to circumvent the homogeneous and sterile environment of resorts. Although many vacation destinations do offer some alternatives and variations to the beachfront resort model, these monopolize smaller niche markets that provide "products" such as ecotours, community tourism, and health tourism. These alternatives are offered as an extension of the same model and are circumscribed by the same practices. Described in tourism theory as post- and neo-Fordist models of consumption and production, they provide differentiation and flexibility in the product design but are still relatively small markets that do not alter the framework of control for the industry (Torres 2002; Ioannides and Debbage 1998; Poon 1990).

The resort-hotel model is mediated by transnational accommodation providers and tour operators, where foreign corporations control advertising and international transport. Where the monopolistic practices of tour operators can effectively dominate the flow of visitors to a destination, "no one tourist destination is able to gain satisfactory control over viability of its own tourist facilities" (Britton 1996: 160). With few alternatives, in large part because of their lack of technological development and capital, small nation-states cannot eliminate the intermediaries and deal directly with tourist consumers.

Tour Operators

In addition to travel agents, trade, and the consumer press, tour operators—a transnational industry based in Western Europe and the United States—market and control tourist destinations. In mass international tourism, tour operators are the link between consumers and providers of tourism services. They bring together various components of travel services into one single product that they can market and regulate by managing a large volume of travelers with low-cost vacation packages. These economies of scale allow tour operators to pressure hotels to operate in accordance with their wishes. Besides the monopolizing practices of tour operators, expensive air transport fares to developing countries and aviation protectionism in the wealthy countries allow tour operators to exert control over consumers themselves.[3]

Travel and tourism are integrated vertically and horizontally by the information technology revolution that has further created a circuited system combining air transport, accommodations, sea cruises, tours, and car rentals into a worldwide monopoly. Computerized reservation systems with high access charges have rapidly become the industry norm, leaving out the small tour operators and hotels. The Internet has additionally facilitated the vertical integration of airlines, car rental companies, and tour operators.[4] Air travel is controlled by Western nations through worldwide marketing campaigns that create demand and ensure a steady flow of visitors. This allows for not only the promotion of destinations but also the domination and control of the flow of visitors (Britton 1996). Fierce price wars keep the competition stiff among countries that constitute the pleasure periphery. Neither the Dominican Republic nor Cuba is a luxury market; rather, they cater to middle-income earners looking for an inexpensive vacation package. Increasing per visitor spending in these countries thus becomes the holy grail of the industry.

Given the extent of the globalization of leisure and travel services and foreign control of the organizational structure, experts argue that tourism development brings dubious economic benefits for local participants. As Urry (1996: 215) explains, "Much tourist investment in the developing world has in fact been undertaken by large-scale companies based in North American or Western Europe, and the bulk of such tourist expenditure is retained by the transnational companies involved; only 22–25 percent of the retail price remains in the host country." In the Dominican Republic, tourism has been weak in creating linkages to agriculture, manufacturing, and other sectors of the economy (Freitag 1994). This is compounded by lack of a diversified product outside the enclave resorts, neglect of other sectors, and the repatriation of profits to metropolitan locations through tax incentives and vertically integrated institutional structures. Some evidence, however, suggests that Cuba has been able to provide horizontal linkages to other sectors of the economy in foreign venture relationships, although these linkages have been difficult to implement (Jensen 2003). Further, it is difficult to quantify what linkages have been made: "it is not possible to estimate the direct or total impact of foreign direct investment related to the tourism sector on the Cuban trade balance, even though anecdotal evidence suggests that it is positive and conforms with domestic upgrading efforts" (Jensen 2003: 450).

Excessive reliance on one industry renders destinations extremely vulnerable to external markets and to natural catastrophes (Cabezas 2008). Anything that debilitates demand for a destination tends to undermine the national economy.

International Management

Dependence on foreign technology and foreign-influenced managerial styles is also a prominent feature of the tourism and travel sector in the Caribbean, a trend that keeps local populations laboring primarily in low-paid service positions. In the many joint ventures that are developed with management firms or with foreign investors, it is a common occurrence for the executives, managers, chefs, and comptrollers of most resort enclaves to be foreign males imported to perform these functions. Alexis, a disaffected Cuban hospitality worker, discussed the way the Cuban manager employed by a Spanish hotel chain is treated:

> A Cuban will never make the kind of money that the Spaniard is making. We cannot make serious decisions because no one will back us up, you understand? That is all I am complaining about. We are here to fill a space without real power to implement changes. They are the ones that govern this place and it is not even their country!

Complaints about uneven labor arrangements are also common in the Dominican Republic. Dominican hotel workers complained that they made less than half of what Spaniards made doing the same job (Tuduri 2001b). Furthermore, in the Dominican Republic, even small businesses that rent equipment for water sports or that provide ecological tours are foreign owned and operated. This leaves very few opportunities for locals, the majority of whom lack access to capital, training, English-language skills, and the network of connections to the industry that are necessary to develop even small enterprises linked to the tourism sector. The ability to provide the "product" that the westerner desires relies on managers who are socialized to procure these services, in essence, tourists themselves.

International Tourism in the Dominican Republic

The particularities of developing tourism in the Dominican Republic for mass international consumption have their roots in external relations created in its colonial past. Central to this history is the role of the hegemonic political and military power that the United States exercised in the Western Hemisphere. Since the nineteenth century, Dominican-U.S. relations have been distinguished by dominance and dependence. Receivership, intervention, annexation, and occupation are all part of this history. Dominican *caudillos* tried unsuccessfully to sell, lease, and annex the Dominican Republic to the United States during the nineteenth century, and by the early twentieth century, the United States began to profit more from its dealings and to play a more aggressive role in Dominican affairs (Wiarda and Kryzanek 1992; Ferguson 1992). This marked the beginning of intimate relations between the two nations.

In 1907, the Dominican Republic entered into a receivership agreement with the United States to pay off a loan of $295 million. This was followed by the invasion and subsequent occupation of 1916, which lasted eight years, and generated considerable opposition. The rise to power of Rafael L. Trujillo, a U.S. trained lieutenant of the National Guard, facilitated the continuing domination of the U. S. in Dominican affairs. In seizing the opportunity to exert its influence on the unstable nation, the United States paved the way for U.S. enterprise to begin to dominate the social and political context of the republic. The use of force to impose its rule and transform the Dominican nation ensured United States profit interests. The United States occupation of 1916–24 consolidated U.S. domination and developed the Dominican Republic from a subsistence economy into a vast sugar plantation (Ayala 1999; Ferguson 1992). Trujillo turned out to be one of the most brutal and corrupt dictators in Latin American history and remained in power with United States support for thirty-one years (Roorda 1998).

Sugar became the single crop that fueled relations between the Dominican Republic and the United States (M. R. Hall 2000). The sugar plantation economy privatized large landholdings into the hands of U.S. firms, creating low-wage labor and dependence on external markets and foreign credit (Ayala 1999; Betances 1995). By 1925, U.S. monopolies controlled sugar production and vast tracts of land. Sugar became the most dynamic sector of the Dominican economy and its primary means of integration into the global economy.

These patterns continue today. The presence of multinational corporations, authoritarian and disorganized political structures, a brutal and corrupt governmental apparatus, a large foreign debt, a fragile sovereignty, and the strong and dominating presence of the United States have prompted observers to remark (Wiarda and Kryzanek 1992: 75), "It may safely be said that, along with the military and the economic elites, the United States is a major domestic political force—and not necessarily ranked behind them."[5]

When sugar declined in the 1980s, foreign companies continued to wield extraordinary power and influence. Tourism supplanted sugar as the most important national industry without changing the orientation of the political economy of the nation. The analogous trade modes of sugar and tourism can best be appreciated in the case of U.S. conglomerate Gulf and Western, which became the largest landowner in the Dominican Republic in 1967. This conglomerate was able to maximize profits when sugar prices were low by trading in the sugar futures market (Ferguson 1992). Gulf and Western also invested in state-sector sugar on the futures market and realized immense profits that it failed to pass on to the Dominican state. Under threat of a lawsuit, the company agreed to share the profits, but Gulf and Western never actually paid the Dominican state its fair and due allotment. Instead, it created "projects of social value," such as the Miss Universe contest, the Altos de Chavón complex, and a luxury tourist enclave that it operated (Ferguson 1992: 10).[6]

Although Barbados, Cuba, and Jamaica developed their tourism infrastructure in the early twentieth century to accommodate North

American travelers, the Dominican Republic did not become a tourist destination until the late 1960s. The nation's negative image during the Trujillo era reflected a violent political system.[7] The United States grew increasingly uncomfortable with the Trujillo regime and sponsored his assassination in 1961. The subsequent invasion and occupation by 23,000 North American troops led to political instability and did not project an enticing image of tropical paradise. The physical security of guests, an essential component in the packaging of vacation destinations, could not be ensured.

In 1966, Joaquín Balaguer, an old crony of Trujillo and an anti-Communist ally of the United States, came to power through corruption and force, effectively displacing the democratically elected reformist president Juan Bosch (Chester 2001). The United States, the United Nations, the World Bank, and the Organization of American States guided Balaguer's regime in their effort to create a favorable climate for the development of international tourism (Lladó 1996; Miolán 1994; Barry, Wood, and Preusch 1984). Through World Bank loans and development packages, the productive structure of the country was transformed, and its economic strategy was redirected to absorb foreign investments in tourism. The old U.S. interventionist role in Dominican affairs is now played by the multilateral agencies that dictate and control many aspects of national sovereignty.

United States Cold War, anti-Communist policies in the region became more pronounced after the Cuban Revolution, and tourism appeared a safe approach to foment a free-market economy and discourage brewing socialist tendencies in the region. The Dominican Republic was poised to capture the displaced North American traveler. International tourism in the Dominican Republic grew slowly at the end of the 1960s as a way to generate development without making large investments in manufacturing and technology. By 1968, the Plan Nacional de Desarollo had established the outline of a strategy for the tourism sector (Castellanos de Selig 1981). Through loans and incentives, and with the technical expertise of the World Bank and the Inter-American Development Bank, tourism offered the possibility of solving the chronic balance-of-payments deficit.

Multilateral agencies created specialized units for the evaluation, approval, and granting of financing for projects of their member countries. For example, in the 1960s, the Inter-American Development Bank, the U.S. Agency for International Development, and the World Bank directed their lending in Latin America toward tourism development (Monge 1973). The Organization of American States also promoted financial resources for tourism development. In the Dominican Republic these efforts were enhanced by legislation to promote tourism development. Law 153-71 (Ley 153 de Promoción e Incentivo del Desarollo Turístico) granted generous tax concessions to tourism investors and corporations. By 1980, corporations such as the Dallas, Texas–based Jack Tar Village opened in Puerto Plata. Its subsidiary, Adventure Tours, began marketing all-inclusive packages that included chartered airplanes. Shortly thereafter Club Méditerranée (Club Med) opened a resort with an ample financial package of financing and tax abatements (UNDP 2005). By the late 1990s, Spanish mega hotel chains, such as Sol Meliá, Iberostar, and Riu, were among the many firms to prosper under the generous tax concessions and legislative incentives offered by the state.

The transition to a tourist monoculture restructured the economy away from sugar and state-led industrialization and toward tourism and free-trade zones (Atkins and Wilson 1998). As the price of sugar fell in international markets, the government began to push the development of nontraditional industries, such as export-manufacturing plants in free-trade zones. The sugar revolution that started in 1875 was quickly fading by the end of the twentieth century. Currency devaluation, along with tax abatements, further made the Dominican Republic an attractive place for foreign capital. The plantation machine quickly shifted from producing sugar to producing experiences of leisure, sensuality, and psychic recuperation.

Beginning in 1984, tourism displaced sugar as the country's major industry. As of 1997, tourism was generating more than half of the country's total foreign exchange (Jiménez 1999). By the beginning of the twenty-first century, commercial services—the economic category that includes tourism—accounted for well over 50 percent of gross domestic product (World Bank 2004b; Mullings 2004). Travel and tourism are by far the fastest-growing sector of the Dominican economy, with export-processing manufacturing, agro-industrial production, nickel, and ferronickel following far behind (WTTC 2005; Raynolds 1998; Safa 1995).

The Dominican Republic has become one of the principal tourist destinations in the Caribbean region, with 4 million international

Fig 1.3   Tourists in colonial Santo Domingo

tourists arriving in 2007—surpassing all other Caribbean countries, including Puerto Rico, the leader in the Caribbean for forty years (UNWTO 2007). However, according to the United Nations Human Development Report (UNDP 2005), the Dominican tourism workforce in hotels, bars, and restaurants earns less than the national average. Workers who are mostly female, young (60 percent below thirty-nine years of age), and with low levels of formal education (over 60 percent have only an elementary-school education or less) characterize these sectors. In fact, the median salary in tourism is 16 percent below the national average. In addition, this group of workers is distinguished by other disparities, such as unequal compensation by gender—women earn 68 percent of men's salaries and are less likely to hold positions in administration and management (UNDP 2005: 78).

The government has facilitated the promotion of hospitality services and has funneled many of its resources into building the infrastructure of resort enclaves. This approach to development creates economic distortions because the country has continued to reduce investments in health and education and in other areas of human capital formation. Thus the state is forced to borrow more money to implement remedial education, health programs, and social infrastructure projects (World Bank 2005; 2004a; 2004b), reproducing a cycle of indebtedness for generations to come.

By the beginning of the twenty-first century, the Dominican Republic was registering some of the highest rates of growth in Latin America and the Caribbean (UNDP 2005). However, this economic growth has not benefited the majority of the population, which suffers from deficiencies in the areas of health, education, housing, employment, and sanitation.[8] Equally important, hospitality workers do not make enough money to enjoy leisure and recreation themselves. The waiter for a French-owned boutique hotel in the capital city of Santo Domingo told me:

> Amalia, when I took my last vacation, I could not afford to take my family anywhere. We went out for dinner once and that was the vacation. I could not afford anything else. We cannot buy a house. I am even thinking of leaving for Puerto Rico where a friend owns a car wash. Maybe there the situation will improve for me. But here all there is is work with little pay.

National elites and foreign capital have been reluctant to implement policies that democratize the benefits of tourism and redistribute the gains to the most vulnerable segments of the population.

International Tourism in Cuba

Historically, Cuba was the quintessential pleasure destination for U.S. travelers, who came to escape cold winters, Prohibition-era policies, and moral reforms. Attracted by Havana's vibrant nightlife, which featured entertainers such as Nat King Cole and Frank Sinatra and internationally acclaimed dance reviews, in addition to drinking and gambling, Cuba was the destination for throngs of East Coast secretaries, honeymooners, and military "boys." During the period from 1915 to 1930, Havana was the city with the largest number of foreign visitors in the Caribbean. Mass-marketing campaigns stimulated pleasure-seeking visitors to come to a place that was "so near, yet so foreign," as one travel poster proclaimed—in essence, a place that was exotic but not too exotic. During a period in which the United States restricted "pleasure" activities, Cuba provided an outlet to satisfy the demand.

Visitor arrivals steadily grew in the twentieth century. In the heyday of North American tourism visitor arrivals increased from 180,000 in 1940 to a high of 350,000 in 1957 (Villalba Garrido 1993: 54).

Known mainly for its decadence—drugs, gambling, and sexualized entertainment—Cuban tourism before 1959 was principally foreign owned and operated. The extensive sex industry, partly foreign owned, included everything from live sex shows to pornography (Villalba Garrido 1993). Louis A. Pérez (1995) declares that during this period "pornographic theaters and clubs were expanding everywhere in the capital. Brothels multiplied through the early 1950s; by the end of the decade, 270 brothels were in full operation. By 1958, an estimated 11,500 women earned their living as prostitutes in Havana" (305). Cuba embodied the essential characteristics of a playground atmosphere where "anything goes." In his autobiography, Frank Ragano, an attorney for the Mafia during the 1950s, recalled a conversation with Mafia boss Santo Trafficante about Havana (Ragano and Raab 2002: 164):

> Frank, you've got to remember, over here there's something for everybody. You want opera, they have opera. You want baseball, they have baseball. You want ballroom dancing, they have ballroom dancing. And if you want sex shows, they have live sex shows. That's what makes this place so great.

Although foreign travelers accounted for a significant portion of the demand for sexual services, Cubans represented the major clientele (R. Schwartz 1997). However, U.S.-based transnational corporations were the main beneficiaries of the profits generated by the airlines, hotels, car rental companies, cruise ships, and entertainment establishments. Cuban tourism reeked of imperialism.

Revolutionary Tourism

The rise of the revolutionary government in 1959 and the political tensions with the United States quickly dissolved the carnivalesque atmosphere that characterized Cuba's pleasure-oriented tourism. Inspired by the egalitarian zeal of the revolutionary project of the 1960s, Cuba rejected the model of hedonistic tourism that emphasized hospitality coupled with subservience. The government outlawed drugs and gambling by disbanding the structures that supported these enterprises. It shut down casinos, and hence Mafia bosses returned home. Prostitutes and pimps either left Cuba or participated in training and work programs in other occupations (del Olmo 1979). The government reoriented production primarily toward sugar. Although Fidel Castro initially welcomed and encouraged U.S. tourism, this changed in 1962 when the United States ended diplomatic and trade relations with Cuba and imposed an embargo on the movement of goods and people between the two countries (R. Schwartz 1997: 203). Cut off from its principal market, the government began to legislate fundamental changes in the country's tourism structure. Tourism as it had existed came to an abrupt end.

The revolutionary government divested and nationalized major hotels, such as the Sevilla Biltmore, the Nacional, and the Hilton, that previously had been U.S. owned. Exclusionary practices that kept Black Cubans and working-class people from beaches, hotels, clubs, and other hospitality and entertainment businesses were dismantled. Afro-Cuban poet Nicolás Guillén captured the common glee in the revolutionary social changes in his epic poem "Tengo" (Guillén 1973: 191–93):

I have, let's see:
The pleasure of going,
Me, a peasant, a worker, a simple man,
I have the pleasure of going
(just an example)
to a bank and speaking to the manager,
not in English,
not in "Sir,"
but in compañero *as we say in Spanish.*

I have, let's see:
that being Black
I can be stopped by no one at
the door of a dance hall or bar.
Or even on the desk of a hotel
Have someone yell at me that there are no rooms,
a small room and not one that is immense,
a tiny room where I might rest.

> *I have that having the land I have the sea,*
> *no country clubs,*
> *no high life,*
> *no tennis and no yachts,*
> *but, from beach to beach and wave on wave,*
> *gigantic blue open democratic:*
> *in short, the sea.*

For the first time in Cuban history, democratic practices prevailed in tourism and other forms of leisure and recreation. The revolutionary government created the National Tourist Commission (INIT) to stimulate national tourism by implementing a number of decrees, such as the one creating the Departamento de Playas para el Pueblo, the Department of Beaches for the People (Miller and Henthorne 1997). Edward Boorstein, who spent three years working in Cuba during the early 1960s, recalls:

> For the people, it was like a fiesta. They could go everywhere as equals. Ordinary people all over Cuba began to use the sandy white beaches. Instead of having to dive into the rocky waters around the Malecón (the Sea Wall), Havana youngsters could now use the beach of the Havana Biltmore Yacht and Country Club where even Batista had not been welcome because he was partly colored. (1968: 42)

Cuba formulated an alternative approach to tourism, reorienting the sector from foreign tourists to Cuban vacationers. In promoting tourism for the masses, room rates in luxury hotels throughout the island, including the prime tourist destinations, were discounted up to 70 percent (Villalba Garido 1993: 151). Restaurants offered reduced prices for Cubans while keeping the same prices for foreigners. Further efforts created affordable recreational destinations throughout the island by charging low prices in the most exclusive establishments, creating easy payment plans that allowed local workers up to twelve months to pay for their vacations, and promoting special sightseeing packages and excursions for every budget (Villalba Garrido 1993).

These policies created access for those excluded in the neocolonial economic and social order. During a research trip to Havana, while walking near the hotel Habana Libre, formerly known as the Havana Hilton, I spoke to Moyito, a *guajiro,* a peasant from central Cuba, whose family had been poor and illiterate before the revolution. He pointed to the top of the building and said,

> M: You see up there? I had one of the best meals of my life. I ate a steak the size of a blanket.
>
> ALC: What were you doing there?
>
> M: This was during my honeymoon. In my workplace they gave you two weeks of vacation when you got married, and you could choose a city or beach to visit. I decided to come to Havana and stay at the Libre. ¡Y yo que ni siquiera había estado en La Habana antes! [And I, who had never even been to Havana before!].

Moyito enthusiastically recalled his all-expenses-paid stay in one of Cuba's finest hotels. He and other peasants from the central and eastern provinces were encouraged by special marketing campaigns with slogans such as "The city is for all Cubans!" "The hotels are now for the working man!" and "This weekend, come visit your Havana." Moyito felt comfortable in his first visit to Havana; he was a welcomed guest.

The Cuban Revolution enabled those previously excluded by race and class to partake of travel, leisure, and entertainment. Targeting workers and peasants, the revolutionary government created promotional campaigns designed to make them feel comfortable visiting the capital and venues of recreation. Workers were given incentive vacations at their workplace through El Plan de Turismo Obrero-Campesino (the Plan for Worker-Peasant Tourism), which sought to promote tourism in work centers, cooperatives, and farms and to reverse the neocolonial pattern of saving the best beaches, accommodations, and entertainment for foreigners and elite classes.

By 1968, international tourism to Cuba had dwindled to about 3,000 tourists annually (Miller and Henthorne 1997). Cuba's economy geared toward sugar production for the socialist markets. In the early 1970s, Canadians began to travel to Cuba for winter excursions. By 1974, 8,400 tourists, mainly from capitalist countries, visited Cuba (Espino 1991). Also arriving in Cuba during the 1970s were Soviets and Eastern Europeans who traveled to Cuba to experience the sunny beaches, palm trees, and Communist rum.

During the 1980s, Cuba's tourism inflows grew rapidly from 132,900 visitors in 1981 to 340,300 in 1990 (Espino 1991). Although the tourist inflows doubled from 1980 to 1987, Cuba still accounted for only 2.9 percent of all tourist arrivals to the Caribbean region. In comparison, the Dominican Republic's share in 1987 was 9.5 percent (Espino 1991). Accommodations expanded across Cuba as new hotels were built and others were rehabilitated. In 1988, 321 hotels and motels were operating in the island, 54 more than at the beginning of the decade (Espino 1991). Although there was growth in the number of visitors and the infrastructure, the neocolonial character of the Cuban industry did not reemerge. Tourism continued to be available for a broad sector of Cuban nationals. Beatriz, a forty-year-old office worker, recalled tourism for the masses during the 1980s:

> When you got married, you could stay in the best hotels, the Nacional, the Habana Libre, the best hotels. You could choose the hotel you wanted. I stayed at a hotel in Santiago, and we even went for a few days to Guardalavaca, a beach that is now only for foreigners. It used to be that anyone could vacation in Varadero. You did not have to have a lot of money to spend two weeks in Varadero. Everybody went there for their vacation, and you could stay in a beautiful villa. This was before the nineties when everything changed.

Instead of forming part of the "pleasure periphery," from the 1960s to the late 1980s Cuba advocated national and "solidarity" tourism. Many came to witness the socialist experiment in the Western Hemisphere. Solidarity groups such as the Venceremos Brigade—composed of Chicano and Black nationalists, along with others in the U.S. Left— and the Antonio Maceo Brigades, made up of young, radical Cuban émigrés, came to harvest coffee and tobacco, cut sugar cane, and build schools. Instead of training a nation of "bellhops and chambermaids," Cuba, assisted by the Soviet trade partnerships, expended resources in human capital formation in areas of science, such as biogenetics and pharmaceuticals, and in the arts and sports. The state prioritized the arts, generously supporting Cuban ballet, music, and film and earning the island international recognition. Black Cubans made exceptional gains in law, education, and medicine. While the national advertising campaigns of other Caribbean islands, such as Barbados, Dominica, and the Dominican Republic, instructed citizens to smile and promote friendliness toward foreigners, Cuba proudly proclaimed an educated and healthy citizenry with sovereignty from transnational tourism capital.

New International Tourism in Cuba

This legacy of democratic forms of leisure and recreation, affordable and available to the masses, came to an abrupt end at the beginning of the 1990s. The disintegration of the Soviet Union and the socialist-bloc Council for Mutual Economic Assistance ended the favorable trading terms that Cuba had enjoyed for more than twenty years. Tourism development became once again the engine for economic growth, an economic sector for foreign investment, albeit in more controlled, limited fashion than in the prerevolution era. Although Cuba has continued to make hotel accommodations accessible to outstanding workers and students, its capacity to provide democratized tourism to all citizens ended. Few Cuban workers can partake of leisure and recreation activities in the new tourist economy. Beatriz explained the changes:

> All tourist hotels are now inaccessible to the population with any kind of currency. You cannot go into a hotel no matter how much money you have. But there are options for the managers and high functionaries of the principal enterprises. It's mainly for the directors and such. The state gives them an incentive, it's like a prize, a week of vacation. For example, the director of the provincial vanguard [an organ of the Communist Party] has every year one week of vacation with her family in an all-inclusive hotel in Varadero. The state pays for everything. For workers of another category there are cheap hotels, but they are not in five-star hotels. They are in lower quality with roaches in the rooms. But that's just a minority. Ninety percent of the population does not take a vacation.

Cubans resent the new policies because they articulate their exclusion and relegation to subservient roles within the international order. Even the new policies instituted in 2008 by Raúl Castro, Fidel's successor, that allow Cubans to stay in hotels are an empty gesture. Cubans cannot afford the steep prices. This is another commonality with Dominicans, who cannot afford to vacation in the hotels that they build and service.

Given the current situation in Cuba, the project of tourism for the masses is no longer a viable option. Instead, the objective of Cuban tourism is to provide foreign travelers with the provision of enclave tourism as the primary product in the new market. In 1994, the government created a new Ministry of Tourism that combines market socialism with high levels of commercialization and market orientation (Jensen 2003: 440). Tourism grew from 340,300 in 1990 to 1.8 million in 2004, with approximately 80 percent of foreign travelers visiting in Havana and Varadero.

The Cuban government has successfully attracted foreign investment to finance construction in the hospitality sector.[9] Joint ventures with Dutch, French, German, Italian, and Jamaican capital and particularly Spanish investors have renovated hotels and old mansions in Havana and expanded tourism throughout the island. Free from U.S. competition, foreign joint ventures in Cuba enjoy some of the same tax breaks and profit repatriation that multinational hotels enjoy in the Dominican Republic. In addition to these benefits, Cuba can deliver a

Fig 1.4   Vista del Cristo, U.S. travelers overlooking Old Havana and Havana Bay

healthy and well-educated workforce at a relatively low cost. Joint ventures pay the Cuban government for the use of their labor force, and the government in return pays the workers 5 percent of that fee. Although tourism workers live better than most Cubans, with access to gratuities and other benefits, they must pay taxes and contribute a percentage of earnings as a "donation" for the national health-care system. Additionally, their wages are stretched to support multigenerational and extended-family units.

The state runs major hotel corporations, Cubanacán Corporation, Habaguanex, Gran Caribe, Gaviota, among others, but most of the large resorts (with over one hundred rooms) are foreign joint ventures (Cerviño and Bonache 2005). A case in point is the Sol Meliá hotel chain, which operates hotels under the names Meliá, Tryp, Sol Hotels, Paradisus, and Hard Rock Hotel and is one of the ten largest hotel and resort companies in the world operating in Cuba. In 1991, the Sol Meliá began to invest in Cuban joint ventures and became the major investor in tourism by 2005, with more than twenty hotels throughout the island. Foreign joint ventures contribute hard currency, management, technological services, and operational expertise; Cuba supplies the land, labor power, and construction materials in these deals.

From Colonialism/Empire to Globalization/Tourism

Although the world has changed significantly since the sixteenth century, the basic political and economic relationships between colonies and empires remain largely structured along a colonial axis of domination. The enormous transfer of raw materials and labor power from the Caribbean to Europe and North America continues to follow the fundamental patterns established during the colonial era. The underlying relationships between features of the industrial countries in the North and poor countries in the South have remained constant. Patterns in the circulation and distribution of commerce, money, and migration were established during the colonial period and have continued to the present. For instance, air jet travel revolutionized transportation after World War II, following previously established navigational travel routes from the global North to the South. Today tourists circulate primarily within metropolitan areas where the top three travel destinations are France, Spain, and the United States (UNWTO 2008; Keller 2002).[10] As in the colonial period, most travelers continue to be Western European and North American men. Travel from the global South is generally connected to labor migrations, wretchedly circumscribed by immigration laws, and to dislocation due to political-economic turmoil.

This framework replicates the ways in which the formative political, economic, and social processes established during periods of imperial expansion resonate with the current structures of transnational corporations. Tourism production and consumption articulate the interests of metropolitan centers and displace and further marginalize local populations. But through traffic in emotions and sentiment, local populations can access some of the wealth that tourism can potentially impart. By examining these practices, we can appreciate how the new international division of labor relies on the transmission of care and love. I turn to this topic in Chapter 3.

In order for the Caribbean region to become more than a low-wage production location, Mullings (2004) argues for an exploration of a pan-Caribbean regional integration strategy for the development of the service sector. Further possibilities include trade negotiations calling for a "liberalization" of tourism services by dismantling trade barriers and increasing access to markets for poor nations. For example, the Dominican Republic led a lobby at the World Trade Organization to adopt a mechanism to address anticompetitive practices in the tourism sector of the Caribbean (PSTT 2004). Although this measure was defeated, it points the way to possibilities for future advocacy and solidarity. The emergence of regional integration and cooperation in tourism services and through the Caribbean Community and Common Market (CARICOM) could begin to address the monopolistic practices of transnational corporations in Caribbean tourism. These small measures will not entirely remedy the lack of access to markets and the gargantuan monopolistic mechanisms that maintain competition of Caribbean states against one another. However, some of these practices could potentially open the way to diminish foreign domination of the hospitality and travel markets of the Caribbean.

Caribbean citizens dream of being leisure travelers, of holding decent jobs, and of securing a better future for their children, but the transnational tourism industry is not arranged to provide decent wages and equitable standards of living for local populations. Various scholars have documented the ingenuity and resourcefulness of the Caribbean people in seeking out opportunities to benefit from tourism, but the spaces and potential for significant democratizing practices and social change are modest and too often absent (Gregory 2007; Padilla 2007; Brennan 2004; Cabezas 2004; Fosado 2004). The new configuration of capital in the Caribbean shuts out the local population from meaningful participation in many aspects of the tourism industry. Consequently, local populations look toward foreigners as a way to resist their exclusion.

Conclusion

At the beginning of the twenty-first century, Cuba and the Dominican Republic remain unevenly integrated through transnational corporations into the new global circuits of capital accumulation. This integration depends on the intensive accumulation of capital through the exploitation of services and labor that have been traditionally associated with women—unremunerated labor connected to social reproduction, the servicing of bodies, and the care of emotions—and are now part of the new global circuit of accumulation. As I argue in this chapter, transnational tourism reactivates historical patterns of production—the changes from a sugar plantation to a tourist one—and integrates Cuba and the Dominican Republic into a transnationalization of production that generates the unification and homogenization of both countries.

In transnational tourism, former colonizers and new transnational classes travel to the Caribbean to consume the scenery, beaches, and, ultimately, brown bodies. A new kind of brown sugar is consumed, one that calls upon locals to strategically use affect to maximize their survival and promote their well-being. A new regime structures not only the exploitation of labor but also of emotions. In doing so, however, it also sets up a reverse dynamic: while tourism has been long studied as the consumption of place, culture, and people, only recently have we begun to explore the ways in which those who are the object of the "tourist gaze" also consume tourists.

2 / Neoliberal Times in Cuba and the Dominican Republic

Sosúa is a town that is a little different even if it is in the same region, and it is very close to Puerto Plata. Its dynamic of social reproduction is different. Its economic dynamic marks the type of relationships that are developed there. Prostitution is not like it used to be. Previously in Puerto Plata prostitution was a street; you went there and everyone knew what you were looking for. It was a controlled situation. Now it is different in Puerto Plata but even more so in Sosúa. The whole town is like one big cabaret. It's a big center of recreation. Sosúa is a little town that is very cosmopolitan, in every sense of the word; here it is not! Not in Puerto Plata. And I think that marks everything. In its totality it is about recreation. It is disposed for that; it is the business of the city. The business of sex there is different. The women there establish a different relationship with the tourists than they do here. The relationships are less questioned. The city there is oriented towards that. Tourism is here but it does not have the same weight.

—RUBÉN, TWENTY-EIGHT, PUERTO PLATA

S itting at an outdoor restaurant, Rubén and I were sharing a plate of *mofongo,* a tasty dish of African origin that is made from plantains and is familiar to me in its Cuban version, *fufú.* We were in Puerto Plata, a large historic city—founded in 1496 by Bartolomé Colón, Columbus's brother—with a population of approximately three hundred thousand, in the north coast region of the Dominican Republic, about two hours away from Haiti, and near the tourist resort of

Sosúa.[1] On the eve of a national strike, Rubén, a young Dominican sociologist, and I had been talking about sex work in Cuba and in the Puerto Plata and Sosúa area. This area of the Dominican Republic is full of Cuban history (Moya Pons 1995). It was here in Puerto Plata that the foremost Black general of the Cuban War of Independence, Antonio Maceo, led the Cuban anticolonial struggle in 1880, assisted by Cuban émigrés and General Gregorio Luperón, president of the Dominican Republic. We were near the plaza of Puerto Plata, where there is often a lot of frenetic activity going on.

> R: It is not the same thing if they call you a *cuero,* that's what
> we call sex workers here as a pejorative term, a term of so-
> cial condemnation, than if they call you *sanky panky.* A
> *sanky panky* commercializes sex the same as the other, but
> they have a different tact.
> ALC: But a *sanky panky* can be a woman too?

"Chica!" (Girl!) Ruben exclaimed with some exasperation and looked at me with a smile that softened his reprimand. He went on to explain that a *sanky panky* could also be a woman. *Sanky panky* was more about practice, a new modality and social identity that appeared in the area with the arrival of foreign visitors looking for romantic attachments, friendship, and sex. At the center of these interpersonal connections are economic transactions linked to affective relations (Zelizer 2005). Mark Padilla, in his ethnographic study of gay sex tourism in Boca Chica, the Dominican Republic, reveals the malleable character of the *sanky panky* and the unstable boundaries of identities:

> Indeed, the ad hoc and shifting nature of the economic activities
> in which sex workers—and indeed most individuals employed
> in the pleasure industry—engage can make it difficult to deter-
> mine in a specific case whether sex work or a "supplemental job"
> is the primary income-generating activity (Padilla 2007:59).

It is difficult to find stable referents for *sankys* and others who operate in tourism geographies because as Rubén and Padilla motion, most people are called upon to face the crushing volatility and insecurity of their lives with all available resources.

Ruben was employed as a program director for a local nongovernmental organization (NGO) delivering sexual health messages that target women working in sextablishments that cater primarily to Dominican men. However, he seemed uneasy about the stability of his job
because it depended on the funding priorities of philanthropic organizations in the global North. The conversation revealed the uncertainty
and social insecurity that even middle-class professionals felt as all
structures of the country were increasingly oriented toward the global
North and away from local exigencies. Rubén also seemed worried by
what he termed the "loss of social values." This became a theme that
he kept stressing:

> If you are a *sanky panky*, you are at another level in social sta-
> tus. You are appraised differently because you are connected
> to the business in a different modality. It is not socially con-
> demned because it offers you an opportunity that the other
> does not. It offers you the opportunity to accumulate money, to
> really get out of your problems. If there is an opportunity to be
> with a tourist that will take care of your [economic] problems,
> and those of your family, then that is not condemned. You are
> resolving your problem and that of your family. It is justified.
> When the girl from the *barrio* goes to work at a bar, then she is
> a prostitute, but if a North American visits her, a Canadian for
> example, that's fine. Even if everyone suspects what's going
> on. People will say so-and-so has luck. She is trying to get out
> of her situation. When there is love, it's something else.

Rubén came back to this idea of restoring social values because the
new economy of the tourist trade had strained and radically challenged
the boundaries of gender and sexuality. The dichotomy that existed
between sex and work and between "good" girls and "bad" girls or
mujeres libres and *mujeres de la calle* (free women, women of the
street) was beginning to unravel.

In Puerto Plata and Sosúa, it was perturbing to many folks that the
old gender demarcations could not sustain the new social order. Without
a specific geographical site of stigma, like a brothel or street corner, the
mujeres de la calle (women of the street as prostitutes are called) and *mujeres de su hogar* (so-called decent women of their home) were now dif-

ficult to distinguish. Many of my informants kept saying, *"Ya no se sabe quien es cuero aqui"* (We no longer know who is a prostitute here).

In this chapter, I examine how neoliberal policies have created material conditions for the transformation in social practices and the emergence of new sexual identities connected to the global capitalist order (D'Emilio 1989). I detail the policies that were generated in post-Soviet Cuba for a number of reasons. For one, the adoption of neoliberal market-oriented policies presented a glaring ideological contradiction for the socialist regime. That Cuba, a country that celebrated its independence from international financial institutions such as the IMF and the World Bank, would adopt neoliberal policies similar to those that subjugated Caribbean, Latin American, Asian, and African nations under the tutelage of these institutions is striking and deserves scrutiny. Second, it is these policies, coupled with the end of Soviet preferential trade agreements and the rapid insertion into capitalist markets, that aligned Cuba with its Dominican neighbor.

I trace the implementation of neoliberal policies in Cuba, the attendant withdrawal from market-based solutions to the economic crisis, and the ways in which this course structured deep racial and gender inequities, thereby producing new sexual formations. The new modalities of sexual-affective exchanges are produced by neoliberal paradigms within the political economy of late capitalism. These new modalities break with prerevolutionary prostitution in Cuba and with the institutional forms of sex work that operate in the Dominican Republic. My aim is to indicate the ways in which the implementation of neoliberal policies results in a gendered, sexual, and racial process that impels the emergence of new sexual formations.[2]

The Neoliberal Paradigm

That Rubén and I were leisurely sitting and talking over an early morning lunch, with full awareness that a national labor strike had been called for the next day, seemed odd to me. Somehow this felt like the calm before the storm. Labor unions and civic supporting organizations had called for a national strike to demand wage increases, and we did not know what degree of violence might erupt. Unaware of what would unfold, we were scared about the level of government repression. Through the mass media, the government insisted that it had the police, the national guard, the army, and the navy, which, along with helicopters, were "ready to keep the peace in the northeast" (Navarrete and Calderón 1997). I had already been warned to stay indoors for the next few days by the management of the hotel where I was staying in Puerto Plata. "If you stay in here," the receptionist told me, "you don't have to worry. There will be no problem. You are a tourist."

I knew that I should be cautious. The food riots in 1984, caused by the IMF-prescribed austerity policies, unleashed a wave of violence in the Dominican Republic that was characterized by police and military killings, hundreds of wounded citizens, mass arrests of demonstrators and union members, generalized repression, and millions in losses and damages (A. Díaz 1997; Espinal 1995; Mañon 1986). Violent opposition to the structural adjustment programs and generalized resistance through riots and international migration continued to take place through the 1980s and into the 1990s.[3]

Like many other countries in Latin America, the Dominican Republic during the 1980s reoriented its economy in accordance with the desires and prescriptions of the IMF and the World Bank. The reign of free-market fundamentalism failed to take into account local culture and society, and in particular, the effect of such policies on vulnerable segments of the population, such as female heads of household, agrarian communities, and the large numbers of people living in urban poverty.

Structural adjustment policies helped place the needs of transnational capital above all others. Under the guidance of the IMF, the country decreased the role of the state in education, health, water, and social services, creating a chaotic quotidian experience. Institutional and policy reforms set into practice features of structural adjustment programs— privatization, trade liberalization, and currency devaluation—that brought a decline in the social well-being of the population. Structural adjustment meant that currency devaluation forced wages to one of the lowest levels in the Caribbean (Safa 1995: 32).[4]

The transformation of the economy in the Dominican Republic along the neoliberal paradigm also increased women's participation in paid labor and contingent forms of work without increasing the quality of their lives. Women entered into wage labor arrangements characterized by low remuneration, which compelled many to pull together various informal activities to meet their income needs. A case in point is a young woman whom I met on a bus ride back from Boca Chica to the capital. This twenty-year-old woman worked in the nearby free-trade zone and was traveling to Santo Domingo to purchase a blender to raffle off at work. This represented extra income to supplement the low wages at the export-processing factory where she worked.

Coincidentally, some of the sex workers whom I interviewed in the Puerto Plata region had previously been employed in export-processing plants, but the low wages, long hours, and oppressive labor practices induced many into the sex trade. Others, unable to find work altogether, pieced together an income through casual forms of labor. For example, Juana, a single mother in her late thirties from Puerto Plata, remarked that her income consisted of selling lottery tickets, vending fried foods at the beach, and offering sexual services to local and foreign men.

Recent research indicates that *dominicanas* are hampered by sexual inequalities in the workforce. Indeed, in 2005 a UN Human Development Report indicated that *dominicanas* are mainly employed in positions with little mobility, whose functions are governed by gender stereotypes, and where they receive compensation inferior to that of their male counterparts. The report points out that even though *dominicanas* have higher levels of education than men, they nevertheless earn less income than male workers (UNDP 2005).

Since the 1980s, the hegemonic position of the United States in Dominican affairs has been expressed through IMF policies. However, these have been met with wide-scale resistance (Gregory 2007). IMF agreements have had deleterious effects for low-income and middle-class households (Silié and Colón 1994; Deere et al. 1990). By the end of the millennium, the Dominican rate of poverty was higher than the average of other Latin American and Caribbean countries (UNDP 2005). The lack of social services, safe and accessible drinking water, education, housing, and health care poses grave challenges for the population (La Forgia et al. 2004). A small oligarchy, in alliance with transnational capital, continues to enjoy affluence and comfort.

The Transformation of Tropical Socialism

Cubans did not experience the chaos and tragedies of the neoliberal paradigm that plagued the Dominican Republic and Latin America during the "lost decade" of development, the 1980s, when neoliberal practices led to declines in the standard of living, large-scale emigration, reliance on remittances, and increases in inequality, casual labor, and sex work. In contrast, Cuba's economy expanded in the 1980s with its citizens enjoying a relative measure of economic growth and well-being (Pastor and Zimbalist 1995b). Nevertheless, during the 1990s structural reform quickly led to similar IMF-style impacts and changes, shaking the foundation of tropical socialism to its core.

Cuba's alliance with the Eastern bloc initially sheltered it from experiencing the tumultuous effects of the globalized capitalist economy, but in due course, the dissolution of the Soviet Union brought Cuba in line with the rest of the third world. Cuba responded to the downfall of the Soviet Union by quickly integrating into global capitalist markets, using neoliberal measures like those implemented in the Dominican Republic. Consequently, Cuba's misery grew overnight and developed more drastically than anywhere else.

Looking back, we can say that without question that when the Soviet Union disintegrated in 1989, Cuba, a tropical island 5,968 miles away, experienced extraordinary hardship and large-scale misery. Social observers consider Cuba's downward spiral to be worse than the Great Depression of the 1930s in the United States (Anderson 2001). Indeed, during the Fourth Congress of the Cuban Communist Party, held in October 1991, a resolution regarding economic development emphasized that without a doubt, the current international economic period was the most unfavorable that Cubans had experienced during the entire history of the revolution. In 1991 alone, the economy contracted by more than 10 percent, and the effects were quickly felt throughout Cuban society (Roque Cabello and Sánchez Herrero 1998). The Cuban government termed this *Período Especial en Tiempos de Paz,* or the special period of crisis in times of peace, also known as the Special Period.

To halt further deterioration in the standard of living, the state-party apparatus implemented wide-reaching reform measures such as decentralization, the opening of all sectors of the economy (except education and health) to external influences through foreign investments and joint ventures, and other market-oriented policies, which contradicted or reversed some of the government's most egalitarian socialist-based principles. The Cuban reforms appeared to be based on principles very close to those of neoliberal economic strategies and had all the features of structural adjustment programs, except that they were internally generated and not prescribed by the IMF. Báez (2004) and Anderson (2001) argue that the Cuban and IMF models of reform share similar characteristics, with the major difference being that the Cuban model prioritized social welfare. Nevertheless, in terms of social outcomes, both Cuba and the Dominican Republic experienced similar effects.

1990–96: *El Período Especial* (the Special Period)

Cuba's dependence on Soviet preferential trade arrangements through the auspices of the Council for Mutual Economic Assistance (COMECON)—the socialist economic trading camp created in the 1970s—guaranteed development but also placed Cuba in a marginal position vis-à-vis global capitalist markets.[5] Trade with socialist economies represented 85 percent of Cuba's trade (Báez 2004). Through COMECON, Cuba was guaranteed the sale of its sugar at above global market prices and the purchase of oil at below global market prices. Between 1989 and 1992, imports declined from $8.1 billion to $2.4 billion, and exports declined from $5.4 billion to an estimated $1.7 billion (Spadoni 2008; López 1998). Gross domestic product fell by 35–45 percent between 1989 and 1993 (Pastor and Zimbalist 1997a: 4).

Cuba's reinsertion into the capitalist economy could not have come at a less propitious moment. The drop in oil imports and machinery parts generated large-scale reductions in productivity, the closure of plants and factories, extended electrical power outages, and massive transportation scarcity. The contraction of the economy brought about not only the tumbling of production, investment, and consumption but also the decline of basic consumer goods, with diminished variety and quantity of foodstuffs. In response, the underground economy proliferated as people sought to alleviate their suffering. Disease and malnutrition were rampant. A previously unknown epidemic, peripheral neuropathy, which damages parts of the nervous system that transmit information from the brain and spinal cord to every other part of the body, impaired some 40,000 people between 1991 and 1994 (Centers for Disease Control 1994). Medical researchers attributed this epidemic to a highly deficient diet, lacking in protein, vitamins, and minerals (Centers for Disease Control 1994). Per capita daily caloric intake declined steeply. General health standards deteriorated, and the rates of contagious diseases such as tuberculosis, hepatitis, and syphilis increased. Unemployment and underemployment climbed, and deficiencies of housing, child-care centers, basic household goods, and social services became acute. Cuban scholars maintain that the situation diminished the incentives for state-based jobs and expanded illegal activities (I. Díaz 2000). The consequences of economic decline and privation were extreme. Odalis, a thirty-year-old mother of two from Santa Clara in central Cuba, made this clear in 2000:

> We had days of not having bread, although it would have cost less than twenty cents to feed the three of us. We went without food, clothes, and shoes. Because there was no soap, I used a rag with alcohol to bathe. My boy, who was the youngest, cried when taking a bath instead of liking it like normal children his age. He would scream, and he would tell me that his skin burned. And at that, the baths did not even happen every day. It's just that in Cuba there was nothing. But at least I made a broth, put in plantain or sweet potatoes, and that was lunch and dinner. The milk that they gave the kids the majority of time went bad because we did not have a refrigerator. The truth is that we suffered a lot. If I had to tell you everything I went through until 1994, it would fill a book.

Free market-oriented reforms were put into place primarily during the first four years of the Special Period, creating a noticeable recovery by 1996. However, the reforms were followed by a period of contraction, which I detail in a later part of this chapter, as the government sought to rein in capitalist tendencies and maintain firm control of the political system.

Restructuring the Cuban Economy

What appeared initially like a move toward a market economy was in actuality a temporary way to adjust state supremacy—a method for the state to ease the crisis. The state implemented a number of measures to attract capital investment without attracting wide-scale capitalism. To recuperate from the crisis, Cuba sought to stimulate a mixed-market socialism that could quickly integrate it into capitalist markets.

These policies, including the proliferation of joint ventures and foreign investments (from 1990 on), the authorization of a dual currency (1993), the legalization of self-employment (1993), the reopening of farmers' markets (1994), and the authorization of gastronomic services (1995), were all initiated to earn income quickly and to alleviate immediate conditions of hardship.[6] Experts commented that these modest reforms were weak and could be derailed (Pastor and Zimbalist 1995a), but they were nevertheless an ideological threat to the egalitarian structures of the state. As Pastor and Zimbalist (1997: 4) conclude, "All of these measures implicitly recognized the importance of both markets and private (or cooperative) incentives and initiatives and thus marked a sea change in Cuban economic policy."

Joint Ventures

Joint ventures in tourism quickly attracted foreign investment. The law on joint ventures, passed in 1982, eased restrictions on foreign investors (Glazer and Hollander 1992). The law on foreign investments, which had been on the books since the 1980s, allowed the repatriation of profits and the importation of management teams. Although privatization and joint ventures enticed capitalists from all over the world to invest in Cuba, the law did not allow Cuban citizens to invest, profit, or benefit directly from capitalism.

Joint ventures accelerated expansion of the tourism infrastructure and also made significant impacts in other key areas such as petroleum exploration, nickel extraction, transport, and the textile and chemical industries. The state began commercializing its products, particularly new medical and pharmaceutical ones. The number of joint ventures grew from 80 in 1992 to 260 in 1996. Reported direct foreign investment expanded from $54 million in 1993 to $442 million in 1997. The policy managed not only to attract European and Canadian capital but also to support South-South solidarity by giving preferential treatment to Latin American investors (Glazer and Hollander 1992).

The Dual Monetary System

The devaluation of the peso that since the 1980s had created havoc in the lives of Dominicans (Duany 2005) was also introduced in Cuba as part of the restructuring process. The dual-currency system, which exonerated the use of the dollar, or *fula,* the slang term that Cubans use, was one of the most effective policies introduced in the process of restructuring the Cuban economy. This reform helped relieve financial stress, but it also created social fissures and class disparities.[7] The dollarization of the economy profoundly demarcated social classes, leading to class segmentation, most notably along racial lines. It also produced a striking contradiction for a state-planned economy, because most Cubans needed U.S. dollars to provide for a household's survival on a daily basis. The Cuban system of distribution that supplies subsidies in housing, food, education, health, utilities, transportation, and recreation came under attack with the austerity measures. For example, the *libreta,* or ration book, a system of distribution that provided monthly subsidies for basic necessities, became practically obsolete due to shortages that ravaged the delivery structure. Beatriz, an office secretary for a state bureaucracy in Havana, recalled:

> It was catastrophic. In 1989 we were still getting products from Czechoslovakia, but by 1990 everything was gone from the store shelves. Before, in the stores we didn't have products from France, like we do now. But we used to get products from Czechoslovakia that were accessible to our salaries. We used to protest because the clothing lacked style. But it's like the saying goes: "You don't know what you have until you lose it." I saw doctors make *picadillo* [a ground beef dish] using only plantains. I saw professors at the university, and people with a good education that were washing their clothes with *maguey* [a plant species used to make alcohol]. They were making their own soap. Students were going to school with holes in the bottom of their shoes. It was very hard. We had not seen that before. These were very hard times.

Rationed goods were in scarce supply in the state stores,[8] with the *libreta* providing at most ten days of food supplies. Essential provisions could be purchased only in dollars or through the underground economy at very high prices, thereby establishing universal dependence on dollars to obtain necessary items, such as soap, cooking oil, and foodstuffs.[9]

To recuperate hard currency—mainly remittances from Cuban Americans and tourist shoppers—the state introduced dollar stores, *tiendas de recuperación de divisas*, that Cubans termed *chopin*, a Spanglish rendering of "shopping." The dollar stores, like many other measures in the parallel economy, were justified as a method of maintaining equality in Cuban society. For example, the hard currency subsidized the daily liter of milk guaranteed to all children younger than seven years of age at 25 cents.[10] But the *chopins* also made consumerism desirable as new products from Canada, Italy, France, and Spain began to line store shelves in a country where consumption had been a minimal aspect of social life for four decades. In stark contrast to the bleakness and deprivation that were seen in the state-managed stores, with their drab, dark, and empty shelves, the fully stocked, air-conditioned, and well-lit *chopins* proliferated throughout the island.

The mixed-currency economy promoted market relations in aspects of social life where none had existed before. As more people were forced to sell goods and services, the informal sector burgeoned. Moreover, the deficiencies that shocked the economy, such as scarcities of fuel, electricity, and manufacturing parts, and that shut down manufacturing plants and factories further pushed workers into entrepreneurial and illegal activities.

The dual economies, with an exchange rate of 150 pesos to the dollar during the period from 1990 to 1996, turned a state salary into pocket change. The average monthly income for 1994 was 180 pesos (Ritter 1998). For those still employed in the state sector, the paltry salary did not justify the time spent working because these salaries—at less than $10 a month—did not provide subsistence provisions. The demoralizing effect was felt in ideological and economic terms because "the wage—the economic and social reason to work—ceased to be the fundamental route for obtaining individual and family well-being" (Carranza Valdés, Gutiérrez Urdantea, and Monreal González 1996: 15). It was far more gainful to sell goods and services informally and to look for other avenues to provide support.

There was a mass exodus of professionals—doctors, lawyers, economists, engineers—from the state sector, where they were paid just less than a dollar a day, to myriad activities connected with the tourist trade and hustling in the informal sector. As taxi drivers, hotel housekeeping staff, waiters, and bartenders, they could earn better salaries and dollar incentives, effectively inverting the social pyramid and relegating professionals to the bottom of the hierarchy.

Remittances

The Cuban state fell in line with the rest of the Caribbean, Mexico, and Central America in authorizing remittances from abroad, mainly the United States. Although U.S. dollars had been circulating in Cuba for some time before the Special Period, anyone found exchanging dollars was criminalized before 1993. As a way to salvage socialism, the decriminalization of the dollar in 1993 made it possible to receive remittances, or *remesas,* legally from family and friends residing overseas, thus stimulating an influx of remittances to ameliorate the daily *lucha,* the struggle for survival.[11]

In both Cuba and the Dominican Republic, remittances ensure dependence on outside relationships to generate an extra cash flow for families or for household survival. It is no wonder that Cubans refer to their foreign-residing family members as *fé,* the acronym for *familias en el exterior* (families in the exterior). This is often said with irony since *fé* means "faith" in Spanish. In the Dominican Republic *remesas* are a vital source of revenue for over 10 percent of households and a major resource of foreign exchange (Oficina Nacional de Estadísticas 2002). The majority of overseas Dominicans and Cubans reside in the United States, followed by Puerto Rico (Duany 2005).[12]

By 1999, overseas remittances to Cuba were an estimated $890 million (Orozco 2002). These remittances were used to start businesses in Cuba or to exit the state sector altogether. A transfer of $100 a month, for example, provides comfortably for a family of four in most parts of Cuba. Those without foreign support, however, suffer the most.[13]

Cuentapropismo *(Self-Employment)*

Besides legalization of the dollar, another important form of economic liberalization during the early 1990s in Cuba was the introduction of new forms of self-employment, previously illegal, which helped stimulate the economy and ease the burden on the state.[14] Self-employment, known as *trabajo por cuenta propia* was legalized in more than 150 occupations

(Ritter 1998; Núñez Moreno 1997; Lutjens 1996). *Cuentapropistas* could use "family labor" but were prohibited from employing or selling the services and goods of others. By 1994, fewer than 50,000 Cubans applied for a self-employment business license (Millman 1994), but by 1996 the number had risen to an estimated 160,000 to 205,000 (Molyneux 1996). Many tried their luck at selling sandwiches and *frituras* (fried foods) on the boulevards of Havana or at train stops. Although heavily regulated and controlled, enterprises such as *paladares* (small restaurants in private homes) and *casas particulares* (rooms for rent) grew in popularity and proliferated quickly in urban areas throughout the island. *Cuentapropismo* also included work connected to the global economy, such as that of musicians, artists, entertainers, taxi drivers, and sellers of artisan products for the tourist market. The self-employed sector "ceased to be the counter-revolutionary" and became essential in absorbing superfluous labor power (Pearson 1996: 1). The market-based remedies, ironically, facilitated the survival of the Cuban regime.

Cuban Democracy Act and Helms-Burton

Amid the crisis, the United States seized the opportunity to further tighten the trade embargo that had been in existence since February 1962, when the United States broke off all economic, financial, and commercial ties with Cuba (Murray 1992).[15] The Torricelli bill, known as the Cuban Democracy Act (CDA) of 1992, sponsored by Representative Robert G. Torricelli, a New Jersey Democrat, tightened the noose around Cuba's neck by imposing an extraterritorial law prohibiting foreign subsidiaries of U.S. companies from doing business in Cuba (Landau 1992). The CDA seeks to sanction countries that provide assistance to Cuba and to confiscate any boat that docks in U.S. harbors after being in Cuba within the previous six months (Torricelli Bill/Cuban Democracy Act, September 18, 1992, *Congressional Record, Senate,* S14135–S14136; Reeve 1992–93; De Córdoba 1992).[16] In violation of international law, this law applied to such ships even if they only entered U.S. territorial waters; this alone permits the government to capture and seize the boat and sell its merchandise.

Even U.S. allies within the Organization of American States, the United Nations, and the European community argue that the Cuban Democracy Act violates the most basic international free-trade practices, treaties, and respect for national sovereignty and nonintervention (López 1998; Landau 1992: 819). Since 1990 a UN resolution has called for the end of the embargo, with the United States consistently opposing the resolution. Nevertheless, the overwhelming majority of UN General Assembly members have backed the resolution criticizing and calling for the end of the embargo. The conservative sector of the Cuban American exile community, however, has advocated for tighter penalties and measures to remove socialism from Cuba.[17] These new policies for regime change need to be examined within a longer historical context of U.S. imperialist politics going back to the nineteenth-century Monroe Doctrine.[18]

In 1996 the Torricelli bill was followed by even tougher measures in the Cuban Liberty and Democratic Solidarity Act (known as the Helms-Burton Act), which sought nothing short of the strangulation of the Cuban nation.[19] Introduced in the Senate by Jesse Helms, a Republican from North Carolina, and in the House of Representatives by Daniel Burton, a Republican from Indiana, the Helms-Burton Act sought extraterritorially to penalize countries and individuals investing in Cuba (Brenner and Kornbluh 1995). It expanded the jurisdiction of the U.S. federal courts by allowing U.S. citizens to sue U.S. subsidiaries trading in the island.[20] It also denied visas to executives or investors who had business dealings with nationalized companies formerly owned by U.S. citizens (including Cuban Americans) and imposed new sanctions on U.S. citizens traveling to Cuba.[21] Further trade and travel sanctions were imposed by the Bush administration, culminating in May 2004 with restrictions on remittances and travel that went so far as to limit travel of U.S.-based Cubans to one visit every three years and only to immediate family members.

The cultural, economic, social, and political impact of the embargo on Cuba and the United States cannot be underestimated. Helms-Burton had a chilling effect on foreign investments. Many investors canceled their contracts out of fear of liability and concern that their executives would be denied entry into the United States. The largest investor in Cuba at the time of passage, Grupo Domos from Mexico, divested its share in the Cuban telephone company. The intensification of the *bloqueo* (blockade) limited the country's ability to secure foreign investments, trade in global markets, and obtain financial credit and raised the costs of interest payments and transportation

(Morales Domínguez 1998). Economists claim that just a partial lifting of the embargo could double "import capacity and [bring] a 25 percent hike in Cuban national income" (Pastor and Zimbalist 1995a: 9). Others attest to the ready-made legitimacy that these punitive policies against Cuba provide the current regime. Thus far, the Cuban state-military apparatus has been able to integrate into the hypercompetition of the global capitalist economy even while facing the continued aggression and hostility of the U.S. empire.[22]

Civil Disturbance

Unlike the riots, demonstrations, and national strikes that have continually been part of Dominicans' repertoire of resistance against globalization, Cubans faced the worst crisis of their existence without massive collective protest. The most debilitating period of the crisis occurred between 1991 and 1994. At the time of what were the first and only riots in Havana, there seemed to be no end in sight to the challenges of daily living. Electricity and running water were sporadic, and food was scarce. On August 5, 1994, in Centro Havana, a working-class, predominantly Black, overcrowded neighborhood sandwiched between Old Havana and the Vedado, where many new tourist hotels, shops, and restaurants are situated, a group of rioters took to the streets, throwing bottles, yelling obscenities, and looting stores (Landau 2002). The united anger and frustration of the crowd turned into the first antigovernment fracas in the history of the revolution (Brenner and Kornbluh 1995). An irritated, tense, and hungry population resorted to a mass demonstration of dissent. More than seven hundred people broke store windows, threw rocks, and shouted anti-Fidel sentiments as they marched along the Malecón, the seawall that lines Havana. Besides this manifestation of frustration and dissent, the most public demonstration of dissatisfaction with the crisis was the large impetus toward migration.

Balseros, Yoleros, and Makeshift Migration

In the Caribbean, the movement of people between and across borders is a prime characteristic of its history. In times of economic and political upheaval, people emigrate to find better life chances, as they did in the Dominican Republic with the U.S. occupation of 1965, and in the 1980s and beyond with the continuing economic and political crisis (Duany 2005). Since the first recorded illegal migration from the Dominican Republic to Puerto Rico in 1972, a steady stream of undocumented migrants have attempted to cross the Mona Passage in "unseaworthy" *yolas*, as these ramshackle boats are known, into Puerto Rico (Duany 2005). "No one knows how many *yolas* capsize every year," claims Duany (2005: 249), but the Dominican print media regularly report that *yoleros* are intercepted and seized by the U.S. Coast Guard, while others capsize and perish at sea (Hilario 2004).

Similarly, the trickle of people leaving Cuba in the early 1990s in ramshackle, precarious, homemade sea vessels, known as *balsas*, became a flood by 1994, creating a dilemma for U.S. immigration policy and an embarrassment for the Cuban government.[23] Most of the *balsas* left for U.S. territory, but in addition to Florida, destinations included the Guantánamo military base, the Cayman Islands, Jamaica, the Bahamas, and the Dominican Republic (Aja Díaz 2001). While I was in the Dominican Republic, I met a *balsero*, a Cuban engineer who had left Cuba for the Dominican Republic in a makeshift raft with his wife and child during the mass exodus in 1994. In 1997, when I spoke with him, he was unable to find work in the Dominican Republic. His temporary, part-time job as a lifeguard at a hotel swimming pool in Puerto Plata left him dependent on remittances sent by his aunt in Miami.

It is not unique to Cubans that when there seems to be no end to their desperation, people take to the sea. The desperation fueled violent, reckless, and dangerous acts, including the hijacking of Cuban vessels for transportation to Florida and the murder of a boat captain.[24] Perhaps as a response to the civil disturbance and the increase in illegal migration and to ease the rising internal political dissatisfaction among the population, Castro announced on August 5, 1994, that all those who wanted to leave could do so in small rafts. The Cuban Coast Guard stopped patrolling the coast and allowed emigrants to leave.[25] People left not only from Havana but also from other cities and coastal areas, including Santiago and the eastern provinces, in makeshift boats, inner tubes, and crude rafts made out of plywood, with or without motors. As many as twenty people piled into a single makeshift vessel. Many lost their lives trying to escape the Cuban catastrophe, while some 30,000 other *balseros* (rafters) were picked up by the U.S. Coast

Guard and interned at the Guantánamo military base (Brenner and Kornbluh 1995).

A Cuban study conducted in August 1993 by the Centro de Estudios de Alternativas Políticas (CEAP) of the Universidad de La Habana found that 85 percent of the *balseros* were white males, with 50 percent under the age of thirty (Martínez 1998: 77). The CEAP investigation concluded that young men left Cuba for economic rather than political reasons. A study conducted in Miami also confirmed that most *balseros* were young males under thirty (Ackerman 1996). For many Cubans of African descent, U.S. racism posed a new set of challenges that many were unwilling to accept. Furthermore, chain migrations, which characterize Latin American migrant processes, are weaker for Cuban Blacks who lack family in the United States.

On August 18, 1994, the United States announced that it would intercept and detain the *balseros,* reversing a twenty-eight-year-old policy of granting all Cubans automatic political asylum (Brenner and Kornbluh 1995). Cuba argued that U.S. policies, such as the denial of U.S. visas to Cubans, the economic embargo, the welcoming reception of hijackers by the U.S. Coast Guard, and the prompting to leave by U.S.-sponsored Radio Martí broadcasts, were fueling the exodus of émigrés. The avalanche of new immigrants during an election year, at a time when the United States was less willing to take on new migration, prompted the Clinton administration to agree to talks.

Caridad, a twenty-something-year-old single mother whom I met in Cárdenás, experienced the *balsero* phenomenon firsthand. Standing on the balcony of her apartment in a late afternoon in August 2002, she related the tragic events that transformed her life at the age of seventeen. She recalled this moment vividly, so much so that I felt transported in the telling of the story to that fateful moment that changed her life. She recounted how on a dark and early Sunday morning in 1993, her childhood sweetheart stridently knocked on her wooden bedroom window, waking her up in an unsettling way. She tried not to awaken her little sister, with whom she shared a bed in a small and stuffy room near the bay of Cárdenas—a part of the city that often seems to languish in a peculiar smell that combines the perfume of the nearby rum distillery with the putrid pollution of the bay. She stepped outside the porch of her house to speak to him on the sidewalk, making sure that her parents did not wake up. Her boyfriend looked scared, resolute, and too wide-eyed for the early morning hour. Without saying a word, he took a gold chain from his neck and put it in the palm of her hands. "Esto es todo lo que tengo. Me voy," (This is all I have. I'm leaving) he told her. "I didn't know if I would see him again," she recalled. "But I knew that I would be very much alone after he left."

Years later, as we were standing on the balcony of her apartment on the outskirts of Cárdenas, in a huge modern housing complex of dilapidated apartments in need of paint and repairs, her son walked in to ask her a question. Without answering him, she instead turned and told him to leave her alone, yelling, "Déjame tranquila." Her tone of voice was strikingly hostile and unwarranted. The young boy walked away sheepishly, looking down as if ill at ease. Attempting to justify her violent reaction, Caridad turned to me in a confessional manner that let me know that I was privy to a story of origins which her son did not know. I leaned forward, and in a hushed and soft voice she continued:

> I was three months pregnant, still living at home with my mother, sister, and stepfather. My boyfriend was in the same position. We didn't have work, money, and a place to live. We didn't see a future. Everything seemed like more of the same suffering. Like a *martirio*, martyrdom, those endless days without power in blistering heat, the hunger . . .

Without finishing the sentence, she looked off into the distance and smiled sadly. Her boyfriend had joined a raft of *balseros* that same morning. His body had never been found, and she had not heard from him since. "*Agua, agua,*" she told me. "*Hay mucha agua en ese mar y muchos corazones*" (Water, water, there's lots of water in that sea and many hearts). As her eyes swelled with tears, I looked inside her living room, where her son was playing on the floor. On his neck was a gold chain, a repository of hope and faith.

The *balseros* phenomenon that ravaged so many lives opened the way for U.S.-Cuba diplomatic discussions regarding the visa situation, but the United States refused to discuss the embargo. The immigration accords reached in September 1994 granted 20,000 visas a year to Cuba, including about 6,000 chosen by lottery (Bradley 1994). From then on, *balseros* intercepted by the U.S. Coast Guard would be returned to Cuba under a policy that came to be known as "dry feet, wet feet." Those who managed to step on U.S. territory would gain an entry permit and eventual permanent residency (Brenner and Kornbluh 1995: 33).[26] No such concessions have ever been made to Dominicans, who continue to battle the treacherous Mona Channel to reach Puerto Rico.

1996–2000: Cutbacks, Regulation, and Repression

The stormy international political climate, the riot, and the exodus of *balseros* did not deter a modest economic recovery and the continuing overall stability of the socialist regime. In 1996, there were signs that the economy was turning around. It grew 7.8 percent in 1996, and GDP grew 2.5 percent (López 1998: 54; Susman 1998; Hamilton 2002: 24).[27] Nevertheless, Cuban scholars commented that even though there was recovery at the macro level of indicators, in daily life most families did not perceive a favorable economic change. Cuban scholar Mareelen Díaz Tenorio (2000: 14) observed that the economic recovery was very slight, and Cubans did not know if it had truly recovered or if they just got used to the crisis and adapted to a new way of life.

By 1996, the government had begun to roll back reforms and further control, tax, and clamp down on the free-market tendencies that had been unleashed in the early 1990s. The period after 1996 marked the stabilization of the crisis and the tendency for the state to rein in and reverse the reforms that had made the expansion of the private sector possible during the initial Special Period. What seemed like an *apertura,* an opening, or at least forbearance, in the early 1990s became a hostile environment of "punitive, restrictive, and discriminatory" measures (Ritter 1998: 64). For example, a burdensome tax accompanied by a regulatory and inspection system was implemented, leading to the contraction of microenterprises, particularly *paladares* (private, home-based restaurants), areas of food production, and rooms for rent (Ritter 1998).[28] The private *paladares* and restaurants created competition for state-controlled restaurants and foreign joint ventures. Furthermore, an August 1996 statement issued by the Cuban Communist Party noted various negative impacts from the continuing crisis, including weakened political support, widening inequalities, rising crime, and the appearance of "entities not committed to state or government action," that is, the private sector. As Pastor and Zimbalist

(1997: 11) point out, Cuba viewed the "winners" from the reform "as potential enemies of the state."[29]

The time was propitious to reverse the *apertura*. Instead of viewing the reforms as part of a gradual opening toward market forces, the government saw them as transitory, unfortunate adjustments that were necessary for the short term, not the long. Ritter (1998) speculates that many private entrepreneurs were driven once again into informality. For the Communist leadership, fears over the erosion of socialist principles and the growth of corruption, crime, drugs, and prostitution became paramount preoccupations. Beginning in 1996, a period of social contraction, reversals, and severe repression was instituted that would set the tone for the rest of the decade.

Repressive Taxation

The period after 1996 was marked by the implementation of policies to keep the capitalist tendencies firmly in check. Three years after legalizing self-employment, the government instituted policies that discouraged the growth of petty capitalists (M. Beck 2001). It introduced a system of fees, inspections, and regulations in the private sector that created a process of contraction and disincentive for the self-employed small business owner. This process culminated with the introduction of a repressive system of taxation.[30] Marshall Beck's study of artisans working in the Havana craft fairs, for example, indicates that fees, licenses, and taxes were increased between 1,700 and 6,000 percent over earlier fees (M. Beck 2001). The system of taxing gross earnings, coupled with the *impuesto adelantado* (tax-in-advance), forced all *cuenta propia* businesses to pay taxes, regardless of earnings, driving many out of business.[31] The new system was prohibitive for many, and ultimately only a few, well-capitalized businesses survived.

Palestinos: *Crackdown on Internal Migration*

The irony would not be lost on the late Palestinian scholar Edward Said (1979), who might have been amused to know of Cuba's organic Palestinians who come from the Orient, or *Oriente*, as the eastern part of the island is known. Popularly called *palestinos*, a term used to encapsulate all those leaving areas deemed similar to the war-torn conditions of

Palestine, they moved through chain migrations to become one of the most vulnerable sectors of the poor in Havana in the 1990s and beyond. Cuban *palestinos* are internal migrants, people of African descent. Discursively, *palestinos* represent that Oriental "other" in need of management, regulation, and ultimately exclusion from the new economy of tourism and the social and cultural fabric of the rapidly transforming socialist nation.

Palestinos in Havana or in the western part of the island share a fate similar to that of Haitians in the Dominican Republic, a racialized and criminalized people with "weakened or non-existent claims to the nation and its resources" (Gregory 2007: 39). Haitians in the Dominican Republic are an internal colony that provides low-cost labor in sugar cane plantations—in slavery-like working conditions—and in urban areas where they are mainly employed in construction and informal activities. Haitians are routinely deported, particularly during scapegoating and "negrophobic, anti-Haitian campaigns" (Gregory 2007: 181) that seek to blame them for the lack of social infrastructure, decent jobs, public health, and affordable housing.

The eastern provinces of Cuba have traditionally been a periphery to Havana. Historically, the area of Oriente has been plagued by higher poverty and unemployment, structural deficiencies in sanitation and water, and lower standards of living than the urban areas of Havana and in the western part of the island (Mesa-Lago 2002). The eastern provinces have some of the most marginal segments of the Cuban population, including a predominantly rural and Black population. As new waves of internal migrants made their way to Havana, particularly from rural areas and the eastern provinces, most had to settle into casual labor and hustling connected to the tourism market. Few of these internal migrants were able to improve their lives in Havana, given the precarious living conditions in this overcrowded city of 2 million, where sanitation, housing, water, and electricity are in short supply (Fosado 2004). Attracted by opportunities in the tourist sector, *palestinos* lack documents showing legal residence, which pushes them into a state of noncitizenship. *Palestinos'* undocumented status in Havana means that they forgo any of the social safety provisions available, such as shelter and food (Hodge 2005).

The government sought to respond to the increasing numbers of *palestinos* by making internal migration to Havana illegal (LaFranchi

Fig 2.1 Police and pedestrians in Obispo and Cuba streets, Old Havana.

1997). The controversial new law, Decreto Ley 217, sought to completely restrict migration to the most densely populated neighborhoods
of Old and Central Havana—El Cerro and Diez de Octubre—areas
near the new tourist zones.[32] The government cracked down on *palestinos* by sending them back home, fining them, and increasing surveillance through racial profiling in the tourist areas of Havana. Police in
Havana began a process to routinely stop racially marked pedestrians
and unaccompanied women by requesting proof of residency in the
city. The increased surveillance of the undocumented status of *palestinos* and other racially marked subjects led to the further spatial exclusion of racialized subjects from hotels and the vicinity of tourism centers of recreation.

Gender and Race in Cuban Neoliberal Times

The austerities of the Special Period forced all Cubans to be inventive,
diligent, and creative with few resources. Terms such as *resolver, inven-
tar,* and *luchar* (to resolve, to invent, and to struggle) embody the communal resistance to poverty and characterize the daily struggle for

working people not only in Cuba but also in the nearby Dominican Republic. The responses differed according to social characteristics, systems of stratification, and the specificity of the country. Gender, race, and class dynamics play important roles in determining household subsistence strategies. For example, leaving Cuba in makeshift rafts was a gendered and racial response on the part of *balseros,* primarily young white males, while many Blacks, resisting the discrimination and racism that kept them out of formal employment, crafted income-earning ventures in the Cuban underground economy rather than face an exodus to a country where they would lack family networks of support and encounter increased racism.

The Special Period had a heightened impact on the lives of Cuban women. At the forefront of family reproduction, and as heads of households, they were forced to *luchar* (struggle) more than ever before. Molyneux (1996: 30) asserts that Cuban women bear the brunt of macroeconomic policy because "they constitute a greater proportion of the vulnerable groups—the elderly and infirm, single-parent households, and low-paid workers." The underrepresentation of women in leadership positions and in spaces of decision making, the scarcity of services that diminish domestic tasks, and the lack of child care and leisure time placed women in a weaker position to meet the crisis than men (Núñez Sarmiento 2004; Lutjens 1995).[33]

Placed under acute hardship as they sought to meet domestic obligations with scarce resources, Cuban women used the resourcefulness and ingenuity of their communities, families, and networks while performing multiple roles inside and outside the home. In contrast to North American feminists who use the term the "second shift" to describe women's double duties of work and family responsibilities, Cuban women are said to perform a minimum of four shifts. They are active in volunteer work through mass Communist Party organizations, in addition to their roles in child rearing and elder care, the labor force, and domestic duties (Molyneux 1996). Moreover, most women take on additional income-earning activities in the informal sector to supplement low pay in the state sector. Juanita, a nurse in Santa Clara, recalled the extra work she did to survive:

> I made and sold yogurt and cheese. I was a manicurist. I sold used clothing. I know many women who were with foreign

men. Many did it because they liked it, but I also know that many did it because of the economic situation. I knew doctors who raised pigs in their bathtubs. The moment was propitious for everything; we were so pounded and bitter by the Special Period that people did whatever they could.

"¡No es facil!" (It's not easy) became an incessant refrain as Cubans recounted the trials and tribulations of the Special Period.[34] The phrase acknowledged the gravity and challenge of daily survival. Going from poverty to misery, women all over the island met the daily struggle for survival head on. In the countryside, women went back to cooking with firewood and tilling the land with oxen, just as their grandmothers had done generations before. In comparison with Havana, it was not as difficult for rural inhabitants to procure food, but other goods, such as soap, toothpaste, shoes, and toilet paper, disappeared from rural areas. In the urban cities, where more than 70 percent of the Cuban population lives, the dearth of food was acute, but manufactured items, such as shoes and soap, were comparatively easier to obtain. Women in urban areas created community gardens, growing produce for household consumption. Others brought pigs and chickens from the countryside into city apartments and backyards to raise for consumption or sell for cash. As schools and workplaces stopped providing meals, both rural and urban women improvised in order to feed their families.

The restrictions placed on self-employment during the second half of the 1990s hurt women the most. The gendered nature of economic reforms was felt in food stands and *paladares*. Cuban-Nicaraguan theologian María López Vigil (1999: 163) argues:

Cuba has made economic changes without accompanying them with specific, gender-based policies. Neither the inevitable structural unemployment nor the authorization of self-employed work took sufficient account of women. At the end of 1996, when the government hiked the taxes on *cuentapropistas,* food preparation was one of the most heavily taxed sectors. Did anybody link the hike with the high percentage of women in that category and high percentage of women who are heads of households?

Women's energies were taxed to the limit in these small enterprises. The regulations for self-employment did not permit hiring employees or purchasing inputs from any source other than the state. Reliance on family labor quickly translated into women's uncompensated work. Consequently, the crisis hurt women because of specific gender vulnerabilities, such as social reproduction, that were not addressed in the changes to market-based initiatives and in the counterreforms. Both socialist and capitalist tendencies failed to grasp and address the ways in which women's social reproductive labor is invisible, taken for granted, and at the service of capital and the state.

Women emigrants from the eastern and central regions of the island were placed under increased scrutiny and surveillance in the migration crackdowns that began in 1996. The new law allowed the police to detain pedestrians and request to see their *carné de identidad*—the national identification card. Those stopped and questioned were often Black male Cubans or young, darker-skinned women without male companions.[35] Ironically, this was happening at a time when the tourism economy was marketing and otherwise promoting sexualized images of *mulatas* and Blacks for tourist consumption.

Racial Inequality

The restructuring of Cuban society in the 1990s reinforced historical racial inequalities as well. From literacy campaigns and universal education programs to health-care coverage and housing for all citizens, Cubans of African descent have benefited from socialist reforms that privileged the poor, most of whom were Black. Yet inequalities remain in all areas of social life, attesting to the deep legacy of white supremacy and the failure of race-blind policies (Hernández 2000). As Tanya Hernández reminds us, Afro-Cubans were disproportionately situated to experience the worst effects of the crisis (Hernández 2000: 1146).[36] Even though the Cuban state-military apparatus has done the most in the Western Hemisphere to address the class-based inequalities that besieged Black Cubans, making discrimination based on race and color unconstitutional and providing opportunities for education and employment, the structural and cultural life of racism has not been sufficiently and adequately addressed in Cuban society. The opportunities provided by class equality have not materialized into equality of results, and white supremacy continues to persist in everyday life.

Structural factors and the distribution of dollars and jobs in the dollarized economy play a role in the continuing marginality and increased vulnerability of Black Cubans (Pérez Sarduy and Stubbs 2000). As de la Fuente (2001: 89) makes clear, "Not only has racial inequality increased along with other forms of social inequality, but racist ideologies and prejudices seem to be operating with greater freedom than before the crisis started."[37] For instance, two of the most dynamic areas of the contemporary Cuban economy are remittances and tourism. In both of these economic sectors, Black Cubans are disadvantaged in relation to whites. Cuban émigrés to the United States tend to be primarily of lighter skin and of Spanish descent. Anthropologist Jafari Allen argues (2003: 178): "The majority of those who left the country and are now able to remit funds to their families on the island are (structurally) white. U.S. dollars coming to Cuba this way are therefore *raced* at entry" (italics in original). Black Cubans, who did not migrate at the same rates as whites, receive approximately less than half the dollar remittances that whites receive.[38]

Another site of exclusion and discrimination for Black Cubans is joint ventures and foreign investments in tourism development (Espina 2008; de la Fuente 2001). Alejandro de la Fuete notes that Black Cubans should have been in a good position to reap the benefits of tourism investments, since they were well represented in the services sector during the 1980s (de la Fuente 2001). In the contemporary tourist economy, they "face significant obstacles to both finding jobs and getting promotions" (de la Fuente 2001: 77). The notion that racialized subjects in Cuba lack *buena presencia* (good presence, understood as being white), for example, is often used as an expression of racial discrimination in jobs (M. Beck 2001; Hernández 2000; McGarrity and Cárdenas 1995).

Buena presencia is a euphemism also used in the Dominican Republic and Venezuela, a thinly veiled judgment on the aesthetics of race (Valdéz 2005).[39] In the Dominican Republic, where Spanish ancestry, combined with Catholicism, reifies racial hierarchies that privilege lighter tones of skin pigmentation and straight hair, *buena presencia* denotes that which approximates whiteness and is often considered distinct from Haitians or people with dark skin. *Buena presencia* and other expressions of racism are common in daily parlance in Cuba and the Dominican Republic. However, as I discuss in Chapter 3, my research reveals that the exclusion of Blacks from tourism jobs is not undifferentiated and fixed. Rather, when employed in the hospitality sector, dark-skinned Cubans are relegated to positions that have less contact with international travelers or are featured in racially segregated and sexualized entertainment occupations.

Internal migrants from the eastern provinces, where the largest concentration of Black Cubans live, were especially disadvantaged by the dollarization of the economy. For example, the uneven development of the dollar economy that privileged the western part of the island disadvantaged those from the provinces in the east. In 1996, 40 percent of the *chopins* were located in Havana, and only 10 percent were located in Oriente (de la Fuente 2001). Likewise, on the basis of national figures, Anthropologist Gisela Fosado (2004: 54) estimates that between 1994 and 2000, the "salary in Oriente averaged 3 to 5 percent lower than the median salary for Cuba," and this is grossly underestimated because workers in joint ventures (mostly located in Havana) receive unreported dollar incentives as part of their salaries.

In Cuba, the acute economic crisis created differences between those who receive remittances, employees in mixed enterprises or foreign firms, hospitality workers, and small business owners, all with regular access to dollars, and those not receiving remittances and without tourism or foreign joint-venture jobs.[40] The new laws drove *palestinos* underground and further harassed, disenfranchised, and criminalized those who were working in informal activities The new changes exacerbated racial discrimination and marginalization, adding to a society increasingly polarized along racial and class divides.

Emerging Sexualities

As Rubén's comments at the beginning of this chapter indicate, traditional commercial forms of sexual exchange have changed and are challenged by new modalities and subjectivities that have materialized with the continuing integration of the Dominican economy into global markets. The formation of new agentic subjects connected to tourism markets has altered how sex work is generally perceived and practiced. Before the introduction of mass tourism, social lines were clearly demarcated with regard to the stigmatization of women involved in prostitution. The identity of a *cuero,* or *puta,* was fixed. But economic restructuring has opened up the possibility of creating new spaces for the enactment of multiple subjectivities, as evinced by Rubén's earlier exegesis of *sanky panky.* Here I am not gesturing toward an emancipatory realm free of contradictions, given that neoliberal free-market practices, whether in Cuba or in the Dominican context, have legitimated structural violence against women and racialized bodies, as I discuss in Chapter 5. It is under neoliberal politics that the most marginal are called upon to shore up the failed policies of development and the hegemonic geopolitical interests that operate, for instance, in the Dominican Republic. My intention, therefore, is to situate the new sexual formations within policies that are made in the name of progress, modernity, and development or to shore up faltering socialist projects.

In the wider Caribbean, the socioeconomic conditions and the demand for sexual services have given rise to new sexual identities that alleviate economic, racial, and class dislocations and respond to emerging cultural shifts. Since the late 1970s, scholars and social observers have been documenting heterosexual relations between Caribbean men and visiting women and same-sex relations between local and foreign men.[41] Investigations from other third-world tourism geographies, such as the Gambia, Mexico, Belize, Sri Lanka, Hawaii, and the Sinai, report similar patterns of tourist-local interaction in tourist settings (Cantú 2002; Dahles and Bras 1999; Dahles 1998; Ebron 1997; Bowman 1996; Kelsky 1994; Crick 1992). These new sexual subjects are often referred to as rent-a-dreads in Jamaica; they are known as beach-boys in Barbados, *pingueros* and *jineteros* in Cuba, and *sanky pankys* in the Dominican Republic. They have emerged with the introduction of international mass tourism and the demand to enact racialized scripts. These new masculinities interrupt the crushing tendencies of the neoliberalism and also serve to reinscribe racist paradigms (Hernández 2005).

Increases in male forms of sex work and affective relations with tourists are common in the Dominican Republic and Cuba. At the level of state regulation, these are subject to oppressive and repressive policies that target people for not having proper work documents and residency permits. As racialized bodies, they are exposed to racial profiling and increased scrutiny by the state-military apparatus (Gregory 2007; Padilla 2007; Hodge 2005; Fosado 2004). However, as I argue further in Chapter 5, it is mainly women who have been the targets of criminalization and gender rehabilitation campaigns. In other words, in the judicial system and at the level of culture and society, it is primarily women, and especially women of color, who bear the burden of stigma in the sexual exchange.

One of the discourses of globalized capital penetration is that racialized peoples are hypersexualized subjects. The effect is a savage racial and class configuration that equates *jineterismo* and *sankys* primarily with racially marked bodies. This has reinforced the view that sex work is associated with people of color and promiscuity, illegality, immorality, and pathological tendencies, leading to the perception that the bulk of the population is not involved in rent-seeking and multifarious forms of hustling behaviors. Yet what the next chapter makes abundantly clear is that demarcations between the lives of people who sell sex, those who do not, and what exactly they are selling are not easy to categorize. Contemporary forms of oppression based on race, class, and sexuality in the Cuban and Dominican tourism landscape suggest that socioeconomic deprivation, labor-market exclusion, and global and local forms of injustice have a marked effect on promoting and maintaining systems of sexual-affective exchange and transference.

Conclusion

Within the context of the political economy of the third world, little was special about the so-called Cuban Special Period. The countries of Africa, Asia, and Latin America had experienced similar effects because of IMF and World Bank policies that aggravate insecurity, erode the social safety net, and create dislocation for the most vulnerable segments of the population. During the structural adjustment of the Special Period, Cuba was able to resist U.S. hostilities while trying to preserve some of the social gains of the Cuban Revolution. By the end of the 1990s, the economy had recovered somewhat, and Cuba was able once again to register significant improvement in education and infant mortality rates. Scholars sympathetic to Cuba are not the only ones to point out that "health, education, and social security were held up, at the expense of defense and business subsidies" (Anderson 2001: 76).

Then president of the World Bank James Wolfensohn, surely no friend of Cuba, acknowledged that Cuba's social welfare indicators were better than those of the World Bank's own client states. The World Health Organization also honored Fidel Castro for Cuba's model of health care. After declines in the Special Period, social indicators of life expectancy and infant mortality rates actually improved during the 1990s. What is remarkable is that doctor-to-patient ratios, literacy rates, and life expectancy at birth are better in Cuba than in the United States, attesting to the power of prioritizing the health and educational needs of the population and the continuing importance of the redistributive effects of the nation-state in the welfare of its citizens.

The intimate connections between the United States and the Dominican Republic have not guaranteed a better livelihood for the majority of Dominicans. U.S.-Dominican preferential trade policies have not wiped out the armies of shoe-shining children that patrol the streets of the country. As in previous generations, school-aged girls still end up as live-in domestics for wealthy households because their own families cannot afford to support or send them to school.

The social impact of the Special Period, in creating and exacerbating inequalities, was unprecedented in the history of the Cuban Revolution. It eroded previous gains that women and Blacks had made and increased inequality throughout the island. The cumulative effect of the Special Period was to marginalize the most vulnerable segments of the population, excluding them through gender-neutral and race-blind policies that burdened them with uncertainty and inequitable access to resources. In the gaps and margins of these processes, the formation of new agentic subjects surfaces, challenging these conditions even while reinscribing old modes of oppression.

3 / Eroticizing Labor in
All-Inclusive Resorts

Jorge is a privileged worker in Cuba's revived tourism economy. He is a waiter at a hotel resort in Varadero and lives in the nearby town of Cárdenas.[1] In a country where a surgeon earns $25 a month, Jorge can earn that, and more, in a day. As a *trabajador del sector mixto,* he works in one of Cuba's new mixed-sector enterprises, a joint-venture resort hotel involving foreign capital and management. Jorge earns gratuities and an incentive payment that is part of his salary in the new convertible currency. He travels eighteen kilometers to Varadero in a tourism-industry air-conditioned bus that picks up hotel workers and delivers them to the "gilded ghettos" where foreign tourists, mainly Europeans and Canadians, come to vacation, sunbathe, relax, snorkel, and play golf. Jorge is single, tall, slender, light skinned, amiable, and bright. He relied on networks in the tourism industry to procure entrance into the local tourism-training school, where he received instruction in hospitality services. Other contacts helped Jorge gain employment in the restaurant of a Spanish joint-venture resort development where he currently works.

Jorge and his family represent some of the paradigmatic challenges facing Cuba's youth today. The schism between generations, those who had experienced and benefited from the redistributive practices of the revolutionary government, such as agrarian reform laws, and those who came of age during the Special Period, is well articulated in Jorge's family. Jorge's parents, for instance, maintained a commitment to the revolutionary government. Jorge, on the other hand, felt disinherited and alienated from the Cuban Revolution.

Originally from the countryside near Cárdenas, his parents found their lives changing for the better during the 1960s. His father, Raúl, learned how to read and write during the literacy brigades of the 1960s and later went on to attend school. He was twelve years old when he set foot in a school for the first time. Later he joined the military and worked in a factory. Jorge's mother, Marta, who also came from a humble background, trained to be a nurse. Both realized that without the social changes that sought to lessen the gap between those stricken by poverty and Cuban elites, their lives would have turned out remarkably different. When I first met them in the late 1990s, Raúl was working as a truck driver, Marta had retired, and they lived in a comfortable, well-maintained cinder-block home with a wide porch.

Even though his parents went through hard times during the Special Period, their linkages to the countryside helped them survive. Later in the decade, they took in Marta's parents, both in their late seventies. In addition to Jorge, there is also his younger sister, who is completing medical school training and continues to live at home. On most weeknights, they sit on the rocking chairs on their front porch, with an open widow and door to their living room, while the color television set blasts in the background. Scenes likes this made me marvel at the social security that they enjoyed and the strong sense of belonging that their life experience had produced.

Without reservation, Raúl and Marta are ardent and militant nationalists who continue to support Fidel Castro and the Cuban government. They regarded themselves as Communists, they told me, and although they wanted the economic situation in Cuba to improve, they did not want the system of government to change. Both often talked about the economic crisis, about how desperate the situation had gotten and how painful it was for them. On many occasions they told me that the blame was to be placed on the U.S. embargo of Cuba. All the same, they often related whatever antirevolutionary jokes were in vogue at that time, such as "Cuba tiene tres problemas: el desayuno, almuerzo, y comida" (Cuba has three problems: breakfast, lunch, and dinner), even while maintaining steadfast support for the

Cuban Revolution. Where else in the world, Raúl asked me, would their daughter be able to go to medical school for free? "She's gone all the way through medical school and I've never had to pay a cent," he pointed out in one of his particularly passionate revolutionary diatribes. Thinking of my own student loan debt, I looked down silently, raising my eyebrows and shaking my head in assent.

In contrast to his parents' devotion to Cuban socialism, and in common with the generation that did not experience neocolonialism, Jorge's sense of citizenship diverged from that of his parents. He sought solace from the hopelessness and misery of the Special Period in the evangelical church. His conversion from atheism came early in the 1990s when, as an adolescent, he experienced disillusionment coupled with economic need. In search of meaning and hope, he became a Christian.[2] Interestingly, I could not help but notice that Jorge's religious devotion turned out to be just as fervent and pronounced as his father's communist revolutionary passion. On many occasions, Jorge told me that Christ was his personal savior, and that he cared little what happened to him in this life. Undeniably, Jorge practiced his faith, giving away a percentage of his income to the church and to those with greater need.

Fig 3.1 Che mural in Avenida Céspedes, Cárdenas, Cuba

Ernesto "Che" Guevara's humanist values of the "New Man," a pious being who worked tirelessly with little material incentive for the betterment of "mankind," had ideologically slipped and transferred into the Christianity that Jorge practiced.[3] Jorge did not drink, smoke, or, as far as I could tell, womanize. Unlike other Cuban friends who asked me to bring them music, watches, and brand-name-style clothing, he never asked for or accepted any gifts. In all our interactions, Jorge insisted on paying for his share of expenses, and occasionally for mine as well. It was unclear to me whether this asceticism was a way for him to maintain traditional gender boundaries or was part of his nonmaterialist and spiritual orientation to life.

Although Jorge and his parents disagreed on most things related to the Cuban government, Jorge was respectful of them and contributed most of his earnings to the household. It was true of Jorge, and other tourism workers as well, that their income supported multiple family members. In a multigenerational family, typical of most Cuban households, Jorge's salary represented the main source of convertible currency. This is one reason why workers are often eager to augment their earnings through gratuities and participation in illicit activities such as the sale of cigars or rum or the sex trade. Nevertheless, during an interview Jorge claimed that what made jobs in hotels so desirable was not so much the earning potential or the conditions of work as the prospect for romance, marriage, and migration. He explained, "My friends at the Polytécnico [tourism-training school] were only interested in getting married to a tourist and getting out. That is the goal for every one of them, to find *una española* [a Spanish woman] and to leave the country."

I asked him how workers, such as waiters, forged relationships with foreigners dining at the restaurant:

ALC: Are there opportunities for getting to know them while you are working?
J: Yes, you find a way. If they smile at you, you smile back even more. If they ask you for something, you get it right away. You sweat to bring them what they want. And if they want a monkey or an elephant, you invent it. The thing is that you find a way to please them. And that has nothing to do with tips.

ALC: But how do you get the relationship to a more intimate level?

J: That is not the problem. The issue is being able to get time alone with them.

ALC: How do you do it?

J: You try to get them away from the hotel. Go to a *discoteca,* a disco. Or invite them to your house and have them meet your family. ¡No es facíl! [It's not easy!]

This chapter is a case study of the organization of labor in the all-inclusive hotels of Varadero, a resort community a few miles from Jorge's home. First, I argue that Varadero's all-inclusive workers strive to create and exploit conditions of intimacy, to forge bonds with guests through pleasant conversation and subtle gestures. This exploitation of affect is principally orchestrated by foreign management through the implementation of training programs that encourage the fostering of pleasing and personal interactions and devoted servility—personal service—as a marker of quality service, but it is also appropriated by workers who use their graces and charm to befriend tourists for their own aims. Second, I examine the stratification of labor and the uses of affect, race, gender, and sexuality that structure the work process.[4] I contend that sexuality is an integral component of transnational all-inclusive resort corporations operating in the Caribbean, and that the provision of sex to guests can be a manifestation both of the eroticization of the work process and of a worker's agency. The eroticization of labor is thus a double-edged sword whose outcome cannot be predicted in advance.

My positionality in conducting field research is pertinent in relation to the enclosed compounds of Varadero's luxury hotels. I was privy to the work of all-inclusive resorts in Varadero as an assistant tour guide to U.S. travelers to Cuba. On various trips I accompanied U.S. travelers attending educational conferences and music festivals whose itinerary included half days in Varadero or overnight stays. On separate trips I conducted field research in Cárdenas, where I befriended resort workers, such as Jorge and his family, who provided valuable insights into the labor regime of Varadero's all-inclusive resorts. I visited the homes and places of work of tourism workers. For example, a few times I waited for Jorge to finish his shift at the hotel restaurant, and I traveled back to Cárdenas on the workers' transportation bus. As someone who looked like a tourist, I was able to hang out and walk through all-inclusive resorts in Cuba, bypassing the scrutiny—and racial profiling—of security personnel. Perhaps my tourist guise— sunglasses, hat, comfortable shoes, and a more relaxed style of cloth- ing than Cuban women wear—made me look like a foreigner and someone at leisure. If I did not speak a word, I could easily blend in as an innocuous, vacationing *española*. In other words, safeguarded by my age, gender, and ethnicity against discrimination and racial profil- ing, I wandered about freely in and out of resorts.

As someone who has lived in the United States for over thirty years—I left Cuba when I was ten years old—I know what it is to be the perpetual foreigner, *no soy ni de aqui, ni de alla* (I am not from here or from over there). As a tourist guide and a former "native," I could not enact "authenticity"—I am from here, but from over there at the same time. Ironically, in the deterritorialized spaces of all- inclusive hotels, I did not raise suspicion and my identity was never questioned. In contrast, one of my relatives, a young man from the countryside, *un guajiro,* was unceremoniously and violently removed from a luxury resort in Varadero as soon as he set foot on the lobby. In the Dominican Republic, a kind friend, a *mulato* law student, was chastised and treated like a *sanky panky* when he accompanied me to visit a compound of resorts in Puerto Plata. For one who is between insider and outsider, or an outsider within, the rage and humiliation of both of these experiences are difficult to put into words. Yet the com- monality of the exclusionary practices of transnational corporations, upheld and supported by state policies that privilege foreign invest- ment and the police apparatus that keeps these regimes in place, made me realize that it did not matter where I was from. The maintenance of all-inclusive resorts as deterritorialized spaces depends on the territori- alized exclusion of bodies marked by racial, class, and gender differ- ences.[5] Because these exclusionary practices are often associated only with Cuba, it further emphasized the homogeneity in arrangements of the all-inclusive regime.

All-Inclusive Resorts

Exclusive Caribbean resorts are established on the best beaches. In the Dominican Republic and Cuba, the best beaches are segregated. With privatization features such as fences and around-the-clock security personnel, luxury resorts resemble the free trade zones that are nearby. Foreigners stay in enclosed compounds that give them access to the most pristine coastline. Even in places where the beach is not privatized, beachgoers are segregated, with locals bathing in the less desirable waters. Most resorts are spatially isolated from local populations and face away from local populations. In Cuba, the all-inclusive-resort model predominates in Cayo Coco, in the north central region, as well as Varadero.

Currently, Varadero is Cuba's second most popular tourist destination, next to Havana, and the sixth most popular destination in the Caribbean. Visitors from Canada, Germany, France, Spain, Italy, and the United Kingdom account for 72 percent of foreign vacationers visiting the resort (*Havana Journal* 2005).[6] In the last fifteen years, most of the peninsula has undergone a process of urbanization with the development of all-inclusive resort hotels, offering lodging to as many as 22,000 overnight visitors per day. It seemed that almost overnight Varadero went from 5,299 hotel rooms in 1990 to 13,490 in 2001 (*Cuba in Figures* 2002). Transnational tourism conglomerates such as Super Clubs, Sol Meliá, Beaches, and Sandals dot Varadero's beaches.

Established in 1887, Varadero has been intimately connected to metropolitan centers for over one hundred years. Located in western Cuba, two hours east of Havana, the twenty-five-kilometer peninsula of Varadero has a resident population of approximately 18,000. After the Cuban Revolution, many of the opulent beach homes that belonged to North American and Cuban elites were nationalized by the government and redistributed to workers. Large mansions such as the Du Pont and Josone estates were converted into state-owned tourism-oriented enterprises.

During Cuba's height as a neocolonial destination for U.S. travelers, Varadero served as a holiday resort for wealthy and bourgeois Cuban families and for U.S. industrialists and mobsters. In the 1920s, most of the land in Varadero was purchased by Irénée Du Pont de Nemours of the Du Pont fortune. Du Pont built a mansion in Varadero, as did Chicago Mafia boss Al Capone. Cuban dictator Fulgencio Batista had a house in Varadero. Nobel laureate Gabriel García Márquez is known to vacation at Fidel Castro's Varadero beachfront compound.

The potential for international development was strong when, as early as 1988, Fidel Castro envisioned Varadero as a destination of growing demand (Castro 1988).

Varadero has become an enclave of luxury hotels, and the all-inclusive resort style dominates the market. Generally, the all-inclusive package offers a destination, where all of a tourist's expenses, often including airplane travel, have been paid for before the tourist leaves his or her country of origin. There are few opportunities for locals to make money directly from tourists in the all-inclusive economy because dollars and tourists seldom circulate outside the compounds. Proliferating in the 1990s, the vast majority of these all-inclusive Cancún-style beachfront resorts and high-rise hotels lie east of the city, removed from the residential areas and their inhabitants. Cuban friends and Varadero residents protest that Varadero is too expensive and affordable only to tourists, given that most of the businesses and new hotels cater exclusively to foreigners. Some exemplary workers, students, and Communist Party dignitaries are provided paid vacations at some of the resorts. However, Varadero has been marketed as a fantasy island that is exclusively for foreigners, an insulated space, complete with a mall, yacht harbor, convention center, and golf course. Cubans, in contrast, are routinely harassed on the beaches and at the entrance to Varadero by the ever-present tourism police force and by the private security personnel of the resorts.

Despite its heterogeneous class composition—bus drivers, hotel cleaners, chefs, and surgeons share neighborhoods—endemic racism characterizes Varadero. During an interview, a Black woman living in Cárdenas lamented that she could not live in the house she inherited from her father because that would expose her children to the racism prevalent in the schools and neighborhoods of Varadero. Only two of the *mulatas* whom I interviewed in Cárdenas had worked in the hotels of Varadero, and one had been fired under questionable circumstances. The government's redistributive practices that assumed that racism would eventually die out with the eradication of poverty proved that race could not be subsumed under class. Over forty years after the Cuban Revolution, light-skinned Cubans live in the small bungalow homes of Varadero, while Blacks live in the large housing projects in Santa Marta, a small working-class town across the bridge from the entrance to Varadero.

Selling Tropical Paradise, Selling Emotional Labor

The tourism industry is structured to sell hotel rooms, meals, entertainment, souvenirs, and other amenities, but tourists purchase more than these things. Tourists purchase an "experience," a set of feelings that is packaged and hence predictable. Tourism as a commoditization of experience permits people to "exercise their fantasies, to challenge their physical and cultural selves, and to expand their horizons" (Graburn 1983: 29). What is often stressed in the marketing of Caribbean locations is the tropical playground where tourists can "engage guiltlessly in sensuous abandon and bodily pleasures" (Sheller 2004: 178). In fact, the destination of the vacationer can be of little consequence in marketing a particular experience. J. Gerald Baillie explains that "one of the most successful advertising campaigns actually failed to mention the location of the resort: the selling of the holiday experience itself and not the destination was the important factor" (Baillie 1980: 19–20 as quoted in C.M. Hall 1994).

Mass-tourism travelers, who come to Varadero for its white sandy beaches and warm weather, seek a reprieve from monotonous, overworked, and structured lives. All-inclusive resorts offer a destination away from home, with a regimen of structured recreational activities and all the conveniences of home—and more. Central to the selling of the Caribbean and other former colonial destinations is the notion that metropolitan travelers can escape from the daily grind of alienating work while having their needs met by smiling, courteous "natives" who appear, and know when to disappear, to serve them. In marketing an island paradise, for example, so-called natives appear to exist only to fulfill the tourists' desires or to perform for them. Such reassuring images are especially pronounced in post- and neocolonial settings, where it is important to evoke the colonial past while reassuring travelers of the nonthreatening, subservient, and welcoming population that awaits them. In contrast, no such marketing effort is made to remind travelers of the friendliness of Parisians, even though Paris is the most popular tourist destination in the world with denizens that have a reputation for deriding tourists.

In travel and tourism, therefore, where the labor process aims to sell an experience, the quality of social interaction between workers and guests is of paramount importance to the profitability of the enterprise (Filby 1992). There is no room for unpleasantness and no tolerance for unhappiness. The "experience" sold has an important component that fabricates social relations, where the objective is for the worker to please the guest, creating a comfortable environment and providing fun, friendliness, and recreation (Filby 1992: 37). This McDisneyfication of the work process is highly scripted, but there is room for transgression when workers usurp the policies and tourist space for their own benefit.

In selling the tropical paradise, resorts strive to tend to all of a vacationer's needs—physical, emotional, sensual—within the resort enclave. Few spaces provide more intimate contact than resorts, where tourists and workers are in constant and intimate contact twenty-four hours a day (Adler and Adler 2004). Management expects workers to personalize service and "develop a social relationship based on warm, friendly, welcoming, courteous, open, and generous behavior" (Crick 2002: 101; Burgess 1982).[7] Increasingly, management encourages employees to nurture friendships with hotel guests, even to the point of maintaining contact with them after they leave as a way to attract and retain customers (Crick 2002). The aim is to turn hotel guests from visitors into friends. For example, in an interview with Maira, a light-skinned hotel cleaner and a single mother in her mid-twenties working at a resort in Varadero, she revealed how workers are trained to deliver personalized service to guests. Maira's supervisor instructed her to leave written, personal notes in each guest's room. Later, she took it on herself to place a fresh flower on the pillow and to create towel art—in this case, designs of swans made with towels. She purchased the flowers from one of the groundskeeping crew and nightly wrote notes to those staying in the rooms she was responsible for cleaning.

Consigned to staff and service positions, joint-venture hospitality workers must navigate the conflicted terrain plotted by the intersection of a transnational capitalist management model and a socialist ethos. In February 2005, Cuban tourism minister Manuel Marrero issued new regulations directing all tourism workers to minimize "mingling with foreigners" and accepting personal gifts. The regulations further stipulated that tourism workers restrict their contact with foreigners to only what is necessary for their work. The state's actions were motivated by concerns that interactions with foreigners might lead workers to question socialist principles and facilitate plots against the government. The new policy temporarily led to conflicting practices within hotel resorts. For example, Amaury, a massage therapist at a resort spa, explained that workers are required to attend a morning training meeting, led by a foreign management team that orients them in customer service. Their daily newsletter updates them on groups visiting the resort and new activities. The training meeting and the newsletter persuade employees to enhance and expand their interactions with guests in order to increase customer satisfaction. Meanwhile, the Cuban manager, a former military officer, warns against attempts on the government and reminds them to restrict their interactions with guests. Workers like Amaury are compelled to chart a path that enables them to work within conflicting policies while at the same time creating interactions that will tend to their personal objectives.

By establishing, maintaining, and enhancing personal relationships with guests, hotels aim to increase earnings in a highly competitive industry with narrow profit margins (Ryan 1991). For workers, therefore, the work process calls for the use of care and intimacy in an otherwise public space. In fact, Leidner (1999: 83) suggests that in frontline interactive service work, "it is impossible to draw clear distinctions between the worker, the work process, and the product or outcome, because the quality of the interaction is frequently part of the service being delivered and thus, in many cases, the product generating company profits." It becomes difficult to differentiate where the producer ends and the product begins (Macdonald and Sirianni 1996). Workers are expected to go beyond merely providing service with a smile. Indeed, management encourages the cultivation of intimacy and affectional bond. In this case, the use of emotional labor—the commercial manipulation of workers' emotions to produce and evoke feelings in customers—functions as a corporate strategy to increase return visitors, one of the most sought-out segments of the tourism market. In addition to the exhausting physical labor of their occupation, workers perform intimate labor to create "return customers," thus increasing the profit margin for transnational corporations.[8] This intimate labor is an important feature on which resorts capitalize, given the homogeneous nature of the Caribbean resort, where one beach destination resembles another.

The Structure of Labor

For those workers fortunate enough to have a job in a tourist resort, such as Maira, the work can be physically rigorous and emotionally demanding. The International Labour Organization (2001) explains that service work in resorts is considered unskilled, low paid, and lacking in job mobility. The hours are long, and in some of the more spatially segregated hotels in the Dominican Republic, for example, workers are required to stay overnight on the premises. As a consequence of seasonality, resorts create flexible labor arrangements, meaning that the workforce must adapt to the flow of visitors, shrinking during the slow season (fall and spring) and expanding during the high season (winter and summer). Seasonal and contingent work and low wages compel workers to seek other avenues for income on or off the job. Maira made sure to maximize the use of her time in the hotel in strategic ways.

Even though service work in hotels is low paid and labor intensive, workers are subject to a high degree of surveillance. Besides management policies that require workers to be amenable to the discipline and control of an immediate superior, workers are continually encouraged to perform a certain measure of servility that, combined with efficiency and friendliness, produces the ideal resort worker. The surveillance of workers also extends to the daily search that is conducted on all workers leaving the premises. For instance, it is a common policy and practice for all-inclusive hotels to have a designated area for the workers to exit. Upon leaving, their bags and other personal belongings are checked by a security guard.

Other limitations exist that point to the racial and citizenship hierarchies of the hospitality industry. Whether in Jamaica, the Dominican Republic, or Cuba, top-level positions are often restricted to foreign managers (UNDP 2005). In joint-venture investments, foreign entities provide their own management teams, or contract this work out, and the foreign team is "shadowed" by a national counterpart team with less authority, pay, and privileges. And even in Cuban enterprises that are 100 percent state-owned, the state uses hotel management contracts to run the businesses (Cerviño and Bonache 2005). Resentment develops about the role of foreign managers in these enterprises. Even when local people are employed in management positions, they are monitored by an expatriate. In this manner, they are infantilized and undermined in their administrative functions. In Cuba, workers complain about the lack of authority of Cuban managers, in contrast to their European counterparts who have more power.[9] Dominicans often condemn the practice of having to train their foreign supervisors even while earning many times less. Modesto Aponte, a Dominican hospitality worker employed by a Spanish hotel chain, complained about the unequal labor arrangements (Tuduri 2001: 31):

A Dominican that succeeds in achieving a position of responsibility makes less than half than a Spaniard doing the same job, which we consider unjust. Besides, on occasions when an employee is sent from Spain to take a position that he is not trained for, it is the Dominican worker who trains him. I left my last employment for that reason, because I was doing the job of a manager who made a lot more money than I did and he did not know how to do his job.

The transnational resort reinscribes a labor hierarchy that positions Europeans as always already superior to the local population.

In places such as Puerto Plata and Sosúa, in the Dominican Republic, with a large community of expatriates who own bars, recreational sports businesses, boutiques, and restaurants connected to the tourism sector, there is bitterness about the prosperity of foreigners in building businesses and "taking jobs" and opportunities away from locals. Much to the chagrin of local workers, resorts in Varadero often hire and import Europeans as head chefs and provide them with lodging within the premises. In one of the more lavish resorts, workers complained about a head chef living in one of the villas and rumored to make $4,000 a month, approximately forty times more than what tourism workers make in a year. These and other reminders of the many unequal exchanges that are evident in all spheres of the tourism process replicate broader geopolitical processes.

The competition is not only fierce for the low-paid seasonal employment that is offered in resorts; it is also limited to those who have the proper social characteristics (gender, race, age, "good looks," sexuality, and "personality"), in addition to some training and connections. Diffuse notions of "personality" can mean that a worker is friendly and eager to go along with the program; someone who is manageable. The notion of *buena presencia,* meaning light skin, of European descent and features, discussed in Chapter 2, is also paramount for entry into the work setting. Most hotel workers in Varadero are trained at the local tourism-training center, the José Smith Comas Institute of Hotel and Tourism Services. The school has strict regulations about physical appearance, with weight, age, and height requirements. Trainees must be young, attractive, and in good physical shape. Jorge explained that potential students are disqualified for "missing or ugly teeth, being short, overweight, having short arms and fingers, and being ugly." By fixing the appearance of workers—the fashioned aesthetic of "natives in paradise"—transnational tourism further creates a dimension of visual pleasure and satisfaction for the tourists who get to gaze upon "good-looking servants."

Racial and Gender Stratification of Labor

Hospitality businesses are dependent on gendered and racialized sexual constructions in their production and organizing of the labor process (Sinclair 1997; Kinnaird and Hall 1994; Enloe 1989). However, with the exception of Adler and Adler's (2004) study of Hawaiian hotel resorts, there are few studies of resorts and even fewer of the racial-ethnic stratification of the labor process in them. Adler and Adler's study supports the findings of other studies that suggest a convergence between occupation and racial-ethnic profile in hospitality services (Thompson 2002; Stepick and Grenier 1994).

The eroticization of race as a component and feature of colonial labor regimes, discussed in the work of Stoler (2002) and McClintock (1995), is operational in third-world hospitality settings where the conflation of race, sexuality, and the politics of exclusion facilitates the appropriation of labor and the regulation of sex. This "racial embeddedness of sexuality," as Stoler (2002: 45) shows, was a core aspect of the colonial project and of imperial regimes. Joint-venture resorts use race, color, sexuality, and gender to stratify the labor process in Cuban and Dominican resort hotels.

In Cuba, scholars and social observers alike have identified the absence of Black Cubans in hotel and tourism-related employment. However, the exclusion of Blacks from tourism jobs is not a monolithic form of discrimination. *Mulatos* and *mulatas,* for example, are often favored for certain jobs. Those with darker skin are less likely to be employed in frontline service positions with direct face-to-face customer contact. For instance, in the famous Hotel Nacional in Havana, all the public restroom attendants and janitors are Black, in stark contrast to the white and lighter-skinned workers who serve as receptionists and in other administrative functions in the lobby and the business center. In this sense, people of color provide invisible "backstage" services such as working in the kitchen and in maintenance, construction, and security jobs. Black Cubans can also be found in the less prestigious, state-run hotels, where they are also more likely to be employed in the lower echelons of services. Conversely, they are widely represented in the entertainment venues of hotels and resorts, where their hypervisibility and eroticization serve to enact Cuban culture. Through Black Cubans performing in clubs as musicians and dancers, Afro-Cuban talent, music, culture, and dance are made a prominent feature of what is "folkloric" and authentic about Cuba. Some of the dance revues, complete with pasties and G-strings, represent the performance of an eroticized racial fetish. Here, the Black body serves up the notion of the primitive, close-to-nature, racialized other. At one such show that I attended occasionally, the dancers, both men and women, partnered with audience members after the show for drinks,

Fig 3.2 Entertainment, lobby of the Hotel Meliá Santiago, Santiago de Cuba

conversation, and romance, further fusing lines between work and pleasure. Nonetheless, some of the performance venues in hotels offer quality entertainment by professionally trained artists, including various expressions of Afro-Cuban culture, such as dance, music, and religious ritual. It is ironic that what is deemed to be authentically Cuban and is otherwise absent from the structures of the all-inclusive resort is the presence and performance of Black Cubans in these shows. By both its absence and presence, the commodification of race is accordingly articulated at various levels of the organizational structure.

Within resorts, the training and distribution of work results in occupational segregation by race. Besides being relegated to entertainment in the cabaret shows and other performance venues, Black Cubans find work as hotel entertainment workers, known as *animadores* (animators): scantily clad young women and men with darker skin tones who instruct the guests in salsa dancing, games, sports, and other forms of recreation. This is also true of the Dominican Republic, as the story of Yolanda in the Introduction to this book indicates. Through work that is mainly physical and sensual and often involves suggestive and sexualized contact with guests, Afro-Caribbean people who work in resorts are incorporated into the organizational structure either as low-level workers or in highly sexualized arrangements.

Another area in which Black Cuban workers are also part of the laboring masses, and in which their contribution is particularly invisible, is resort construction. Men, bused in primarily from the eastern provinces to work as manual laborers and in construction work on the many hotel resorts built in Varadero in the 1990s, are an invisible army of laborers who toil under some of the harshest work conditions. During a scorching hot summer day in 2001, I visited construction sites at the end of the Varadero peninsula. There I spoke with a Black worker in his early twenties who had been brought from the province of Granma (approximately ten hours east of Varadero) to build new hotels. He explained that workers from the eastern provinces of Cuba, a part of the island with the largest concentration of Afro-Caribbean people, were brought into the area and housed in Santa Marta to work for several months building hotels. Eventually they are returned to the eastern provinces. Glad to have a job, he nevertheless complained about being away from home for so long and working at a job that paid only in pesos.

Hospitality services, as with other forms of service work, enact and re-create social hierarchies in the hiring process (Acker 1990). In an interview conducted with a Cuban hotel manager of a joint-venture resort about the lack of Black Cubans employed in the luxury hotel where he worked in Varadero, he claimed that the European managers tend to favor light-skinned Cubans and are reluctant to hire Blacks. However, a European manager with whom I spoke said that Cubans made all the hiring decisions. In hiring and designation of job duties, European and Cuban notions of white supremacy collude to articulate the reproduction of white supremacy. The organization of work, therefore, relegates dark-skinned workers to racialized and sexualized occupational categories. As Macdonald and Sirianni (1996: 15) argue, occupations in service industries "are so stratified that worker characteristics such as race and gender determine not only who is considered desirable or even eligible to fill certain jobs, but also who will want to fill certain jobs and how the job itself is performed." Work in the top-rated four- and five star hotels employs younger and lighter-skinned workers. Consequently, race scripts occupations and segments workers in the labor process.

Feminist research on the service economy reveals how gender and sexuality are also embedded in the organizational structure of work, informing the conceptualization of jobs, job specifications, control over workers, and relations between women and men (Macdonald and Sirianni 1996; Adkins 1995; E. Hall 1993; Filby 1992). I asked Beatriz, a receptionist at a large Varadero resort, if women were ever employed to open doors or carry bags. After giving me a bewildered look, she said firmly, "The doorman is always a male, chambermaids always women. Things are like that here." The labor process is gendered, and this is most likely a universal phenomenon, with women perceived as possessing innate skills that render them more adept at subservient roles or jobs that are an extension of their reproductive role and that duplicate women's traditional domestic and care duties (Tyler and Abbott 1998; Macdonald and Sirianni 1996). The majority of women are found in positions related to domestic maintenance, such as housekeeping, or in food service, reception, and retail sales (ILO 2001). The structure of occupations is such that higher earnings often go to male-defined positions, such as bartenders and baggage handlers. Furthermore, young and lighter-skinned males are given preference for jobs with high visibility, public contact, and supervisory functions.

Sexuality as a Feature of Labor

The prominence of sexuality is also an important component in the organization of labor. Job requirements are often predicated on images of women as objects of male desire and gratification, where physical attractiveness is the most important qualification. Sexuality, as feminist studies of the hospitality sector reveal, is used to commodify women's bodies, because a sexually attractive appearance is often indistinguishable from the product sold.[10] A number of service jobs, for example, require women to exhibit and use their sexual appeal as part of their work (E. Hall 1993). Adkins argues that "women are thus not only 'economically productive' but also 'sexually productive' workers" (1995: 147). Feminist labor scholars maintain that sexuality is an integral aspect of production and the organization of power relationships (Bank Muñoz 2007; Salzinger 2000; Filby 1992). Filby (1992) further points out that those references to "personality" often mask the functioning of sexuality in business relationships, making sexuality both an embedded and an open feature of women's work in hospitality services (Crick 2002; Adkins 1995).

In travel and hospitality services, jobs that require women to present themselves as sex objects are numerous, including the chambermaid (an inherently gendered and sexualized position), the flight attendant, the flirty cocktail waitress in a revealing uniform, and the entertainment coordinator, whose requisite displays of enthusiasm, sexiness, and friendliness render her vulnerable to sexual harassment. When sexiness is part of the job itself and flirting is encouraged, it becomes difficult to draw the line between "'selling the service' and 'selling sexuality'" (Gilbert, Guerrier, and Guy 1998: 50).

Sexuality is used by the hospitality industry to structure production and organize labor. Workers are recruited to provide sexualized care services, through flirting and displays of affection. However, sexuality also offers an opportunity for resistance. Some scholars maintain that the emotional labor that workers perform intensifies their alienation by infringing on sacrosanct parts of the self (Leidner 1999: 90; Hochschild 1983) and that "resistance to organizational demands seems the only self-respecting response open to workers" (Leidner 1999: 90). Others contend that context plays an important role and that emotional labor can be both pleasurable and difficult for the worker, depending on a host of other factors (C. Williams 2003: 513). Resistance to corporate norms of workplace sexualization is not a clear space of opposition, as this research indicates. Rather, it is complicit with diffused articulations of power while also challenging them. Through sex-for-money and other affective exchanges, resort workers are able to forestall the alienating practices within the organizational structure by nourishing relationships with hotel guests. The fact remains that once sexuality is unleashed, it can be unpredictable, generating contradictions and ambiguities for both workers and management (Filby 1992).

Sexuality and Relations between Resort Workers and Guests

If all work in resort organizations is sexualized to some degree, it should not come as a surprise that hospitality workers also provide sex to tourists. Studies conducted in the Dominican Republic of tourism's formal-sector workers found a striking prevalence of sexual relations between hotel workers and tourists (CEPROSH 1997). Studies revealed that workers in food and beverage services, maintenance, administration, entertainment, and reception were providing sex to tourists. One study reported that close to 20 percent of resort workers admitted to having had sexual relations with guests (CEPROSH 1997). Another study confirmed that 38 percent of male sex workers had regular jobs in hotels as waiters, porters, security guards, and other service occupations (CESDEM 1996). It was not uncommon to learn in Varadero that informants were traveling overseas because a tourist *amigo* had sent a visa for an extended stay in his or her country. Reports from Jamaica also indicate that socializing with tourists can lead to "future job offers or even marriage" (A. Crick 2001: 15).

Romance between workers and guests in the Caribbean tourism industry has been scrutinized in the U.S. media with the case of African American writer Terry McMillan, who was swept off her feet by a young, attractive Jamaican man, Jonathan Plummer, whom she met while on vacation in Jamaica. McMillan wrote about their affair and marriage, in her best-selling novel (1996) and film (1998) *How Stella Got Her Groove Back*. Both cultural productions depict Plummer as a resort worker.[11] In contrast, Laurent Cantet's film *Vers le sud (Heading South)* (2005), based on three short stories by Dany Laferrière, a Haitian author, depicts otherwise unemployed Haitian men who provide paid sex to middle-aged North American women in a beachfront resort. The film strikingly depicts moments of sexual-affectional intimacy even while representing the men as crushed by poverty and a brutal political regime. Unlike the exclusive resorts of Cuba and the Dominican Republic that keep out locals, the men in the film appear to wander about the resort and even sleep with the women in their rooms.

As a woman traveling alone in the Dominican Republic, I found myself accosted in public spaces by *sankys* offering companionship. This I expected. However, in 2005 I was particularly caught off guard when a twenty-something luggage handler, Santos, progressively made romantic overtures during my stay at a business hotel in Santo Domingo. After a few days in which he made increasingly more flattering comments, I decided that he was not just doing his job; he was crossing the line into what felt like sexual harassment. Santos quickly denied any impropriety and initially claimed that it was his courtesy and part of his job to pay compliments to the hotel's guests and to offer "lonely" women protection. The next morning he went out of his way to tell me that he always enjoyed friendships with older women. For instance, he had befriended a hotel guest from New Jersey, and since her departure, they had continued communicating every day via e-mail. As if providing further proof of the authenticity of his friendship with her, he said, "Estoy planeando visitarla." (I plan to visit her). It was unclear from our discussion what type of interpersonal connection Santos enjoyed with his New Jersey friend or with other hotel guests. Most likely, aspects of money and friendship were connected in complicated ways.

The transition into the sexual economy can be a smooth one for hospitality workers because of a number of factors. First, in providing service to hotel guests, workers comply with organizational expectations that commodify care. As Santos pointed out, workers strive to care for feelings, emotions, and bodies. Resorts provide not just meals and sleeping accommodations but entertainment, recreation, exercise, and medical facilities, all within easy reach. Hotel compounds in the Dominican Republic often function as minicities with spacious streets, sidewalks, nightclubs, theaters, restaurants, post office, banks, and all kinds of shopping and business amenities. As explained by Camilo in the Introduction, hotel management discourages guests from consorting with local people and degrades them as petty thieves and untrustworthy. Keeping travelers within these white ghettos restricts their exposure to the local people and culture by confining their experience to the tourist enclave. Workers are often the only locals whom guests meet during their stay, and their level of interaction is regulated through management's demands and organizational exigencies.

Second, because hospitality workers are trained to please their guests and to befriend customers, their move into the sexual economy is in an organizationally hospitable terrain, where they traffic in the same emotions called for in their work. The selling of tropical pleasures through billboards, magazines, the Internet, and newspapers entices would-be vacationers with images of sensual pleasures. Tourism is marketed as a sexualized experience, albeit to different degrees. Workers are trained to comply enthusiastically with constant demands and repeated requests from guests, from extra towels to special meals, but these requests also include requests for sex. With intimate access and proximity to hospitality workers, some tourists feel entitled to ask, entreat, and badger. Maira mentioned being exposed to various men in different phases of suggestive disrobing through her work as a chambermaid: "Maybe they think that all Cuban women are *jineteras*. But I have to say, that part of my job is the worst because you never know when you walk into a room if some guy is going to be there naked holding his thing in his hand." Although Maira felt exposed to high levels of sexual harassment from guests, she did not want to complain for fear of losing her job.

Even though Maira sustained some sexual exchanges with tourists for money, she preferred befriending couples with children and establishing a relationship based on mutual affinity for kids. Relationships that create long-term obligations and commitment are, for many resort workers like Maira, more beneficial and less risky than commercialized sexuality. Upon leaving, many of the guests gave her not only gratuities but also clothes, toiletries, and other gift items. Maira often asked for e-mail addresses of the guests she looked after and sent them messages after they had left Varadero. She even got a Canadian tourist to send vitamins for her son.

Another reason that hotels create an environment that sustains sex-for-money exchanges has to do with the description and requirements of jobs. The boundaries between work and play are blurred, especially for *animadoras,* entertainment directors, whose job features elements of leisure at work. The young woman or man getting you to shake your hips to a Latin beat is performing a function of her or his work that might not be agreeable to her or him. However, in leisure positions, it is not always clear that the person at play is also at work (Guerrier and Adib 2004a, 2004b). Workers must learn to navigate a thin line between encouraged behavior such as "safe flirting" and fraternizing with guests and more sexually explicit relations. In these latter cases, the worker risks being fired for crossing into unambiguous territory. In other words, claiming the circulation of their sexuality is grounds for dismissal.

Third, in the highly militarized resort enclaves, with around-the-clock security details, the local population is effectively kept out and guests are trapped in. In Varadero, this is particularly acute, given that the majority of luxury, all-inclusive resorts lie far from public transportation and isolated from the community (Tuduri 2001b). Much has been made of the so-called tourist apartheid in Cuba, where Cubans are not allowed to enter the hotel resorts and beaches. My experiences in Cuba revealed that this policy was inconsistently applied. But tourist apartheid needs to be contextualized within the practices and policies of the transnational all-inclusive complexes across the Caribbean. Whether in Cuba, Mexico, Jamaica, or the Dominican Republic, all-inclusive resorts generally restrict the entry of nonregistered guests. Plastic wrist bracelets control who wanders about freely and who is turned away at the front door; race and class also mark who gets in and who is escorted out of the compound. For tourists who come expecting to meet and consort with local denizens as part of their vacation experience, the all-inclusive scenario can be bleak, with the exception of resort workers. Maira explained how the expectations created in tourist-sending countries encourage this situation: "Look, the problem is that they come here—well, the Italians are specially the worst—they come here with the idea that Cuban women are hot, and they end up here in the middle of nowhere, and they get to the hotel, and they want a hot Cuban woman right away."

Certainly, other opportunities for sex include fellow vacationers staying at the enclave. However, for some tourists, sex with an "exotic other" is more of an adventure, is less compromising, and provides more control. In addition, a sexual encounter with a local person ensures a level of anonymity. As the marketing slogan for Las Vegas, a popular global sex tourism destination, claims, "What happens here, stays here."

Finally, guests turn to resort workers because police harassment, repression, and incarceration of citizens from the neighboring areas make it difficult for tourists to find companionship outside the resort.[12] In some ways, this resembles the common trend throughout the global North, where prostitution has moved indoors into business establishments, and only marginal segments of the population—transgender people, drug addicts, and women of color—are relegated to the streets. In this manner, hotel resort workers are protected from the prevalent social stigma attached to commercial sexual exchanges and are safe from police scrutiny by their formal-sector "indoor" jobs.

Hospitality workers can complement their low wages by participating in the sexual economy directly, by providing sexual services, or indirectly, by orchestrating interactions. For example, Juana, a resident of Puerto Plata, discussed how front-desk personnel allowed her to enter a tourist's room if they were given a cash payment of $20 to $40. Other Dominican women revealed how the security guards, locally known as the *wachiman,* also accepted cash to allow them to enter hotels. Furthermore, formal tourism workers facilitate sexual liaisons between tourists and locals, often at the request of the hotel guest. Alternatively, they provide sexual services directly to hotel guests. Along with room service and extra towels, hospitality workers perform sexual services within the hotels. These practices of the sexual economy implicate many different types of workers, most of whom do not identify with a sex-worker identity.

Many resort workers are eager to procure extra earnings while on the job. Solarba, a twenty-seven-year-old chambermaid working in a luxury resort in Varadero, related the story of a coworker whose goal was to build a house for herself and her mother:

> She slept with everything that moved that month. She would have fucked the shower curtain if it paid her in dollars. In a

short time she was able to make $2,000, and she built her
house. She does not do it anymore, because it was dangerous,
but she got what she wanted.

Access to tourists provides resort workers with opportunities that
would otherwise be unattainable. The sexual and affective economies
operating in the hotels effectively complement the low wages of hospitality workers and make possible the expansion of consumer desires
and needs. Within the tourist enclaves, the sexual economy operates
to subsidize the low wages of the formal-sector workers and redistribute the wealth of tourists more directly to hospitality workers. Jorge
summed up this new contingency: "*Camareras* [chambermaids] are
the legitimate and official *jineteras*."

As a waiter, Jorge met a Canadian woman ten years his senior who
frequented Cuba on business. They became fast friends after her first
stay at the resort. On her second trip, he invited her to visit his hometown of Cárdenas. Even though there are many visible signs of prosperity in Cárdenas, the city's major form of transportation is still the
horse-drawn carriage. Jorge's Canadian friend was charmed by the
rustic transportation and delighted to see the sights in Cárdenas, which
she felt was more authentic and the "real Cuba" than the resort where
she stayed.

On one of my return trips to Cárdenas, Jorge and I were traveling
one evening in a horse-drawn carriage to visit a mutual friend, another hotel worker in Varadero who also lived in Cárdenas. Jorge was
still wearing his work uniform, but without the smoking jacket. In
some ways we resembled the stereotypical couple in depictions of Caribbean sex tourism: the middle-aged traveler escorted by a young,
Cuban man. I noticed that Jorge's conversations about his friendship
with the Canadian tourist were more pronounced and incessant. He
mentioned that she might hire him to work for her and that he might
visit her in Canada. He asked what I thought of Canadian men and
North American men in general. Before I could answer, he asked if
I thought that North American men were cold and not as *cariñoso* (af-
fectionate) as Cuban men. His line of questioning perplexed me. Was
Jorge positioning himself within the international division of romance as a Latin lover? Was he developing a romantic relationship
with his Canadian friend? Did she invite him to visit Canada for work

or pleasure? Was he in love with her? The ambiguity of the situation left me perplexed.

Nothing in any of my interactions with Jorge positioned him as a hustler. Nevertheless, it became increasingly difficult for me to distinguish Jorge's work from his personal life. Jorge's dilemmas were magnified by the blurring between leisure and work in hospitality organizations and the ways in which relationships for hotel workers combined friendship with material exchanges. Relationships with tourists, myself included, were always ambiguous, intertwining opportunity and gain with genuine affection and care.

Conclusion

Although previous studies of the uses of emotional labor in a work setting argue that workers are harmed by the manipulation of private emotion for public use, this research challenges this dichotomy and suggests a more nuanced reading of emotional labor and worker agency. Instead of distinguishing a binary in workers' use of emotional labor where a public and private division of emotions takes place, I want to emphasize the thin line between manufactured intimacy, as suggested by management, and the ways in which hospitality workers use sentiment to break down boundaries between themselves and customers. In other words, they are able to appropriate the personalized dynamics of their work for their own strategic purposes.

The commodification of interaction between workers and customers, set in motion by corporate policies, provides an environment that favors the cultivation of friendship, but also of sex-for-money-exchanges, romance, and migration, which may ultimately benefit resort workers and improve their lives. Through corporate policies that manipulate affect, Caribbean hospitality workers are able to set in motion dynamics where subversion of and compliance with corporate policies are intertwined.

Called upon to provide intimate forms of labor by transnational corporations, hospitality workers in the Caribbean make use of affect and sexuality to cultivate friendships, romance, and other exchanges. This leaves room to exploit sexuality in creative, albeit limited, ways. Resistance for these workers can be found not in withdrawing from processes of sexualization, but in complying with the organization's exigencies and, in some cases, appropriating and benefiting from their sexualization. In the process, hotel workers erode hierarchical relations in occupations that render them invisible and subservient. Although it may appear to management that workers are complying with corporate customer service policies, their complicitous resistance circumvents (while reinforcing) these norms. These strategies push resistance to a new level as hospitality workers take back the circulation of their sexuality to further their dreams.

Transnational hospitality conglomerates operating in the Caribbean commodify bodies, emotions, and sexuality in ways that call on workers to be sexually available or at least appear so. The services performed by hospitality workers materialize notions of race, gender, and sexuality. Perversely, sexual-affective exchanges within resort compounds enjoy little social ostracism. However, in settings that draw on sexuality as a commercial organizational resource, sexuality can be a double-edged sword. Filby posits, "As a product itself partly of discursive practices, sexuality also contains the potential for creativity and development" (1992: 30). This potential for creativity, where sexuality is used for a worker's own gain, is also a form of resistance that, although temporary and partial, can bring rewards. This does not deny

Fig 3.3   Varadero visitors

the differential power imbalances that exist between hospitality workers and leisure tourists, with constraint and mobility, socialism and capitalism, and the geopolitics of North and South playing themselves out in these microlevel processes. Rather, this is to conclude, along with anthropologist Paula Ebron (2002: 188), that oppression does not erase agency.

4 / Daughters of Yemayá and Other *Luchadoras*

Never Whores or *Putas*

Naomi, a thirty-year-old, divorced mother of two, lives in a dilapidated section of Old Havana close to the Malecón, the seawall that borders the capital city. She recounts the circumstances that drove her into a relationship with a foreign man at the age of twenty-four:

> I have two children, one with birth defects. Their father abandoned them for another woman; he did not give me anything to help maintain them. Some mornings, I did not even have money for milk and bread. A neighbor was the one in charge of buying my bread and milk. It goes without saying that sometimes I did not eat all day long.[1] Besides, I was not able to work because of my sick child. I did not have anyone to take care of him. For someone to take care of a normal child costs a lot of money; imagine how much it would have cost to care for a child with defects! Then when I saw myself lost, I did not know how to feel, I wanted to cry. I could not sleep. It was very painful to see my children in that situation. I only weighed about ninety pounds, and one morning I went out like a crazy

woman. I went to the Malecón, and there I met an old woman who told me, "Why don't you tell your problems to the virgin of the sea, to Yemayá?" From that day on, I felt a belief in what that woman had said to me. I went back to the Malecón every day; I would cry and pray that Yemayá would find me something so that I could take care of my children, to help me find something to eat, money, a good job, anything. I had been there, crying, with my pain, for about an hour, when an Italian man approached me. He asked me what was wrong, but I could not answer because I was crying so hard. I was finally able to tell him about my situation, about my two boys, about the one with the problems. I told him how I could not feed them, and he said he was going to help, but that he wanted to be sure what I said was true. I took him to my house, which is not really a house, but a modest room with two little beds and a kitchen. I went to look for my boys, and when he saw my son, the boy with the problem, he was very . . . well, let's just say, he was very traumatized, to see him and the situation in which I lived. Just like that, he gave me money to buy something for the boys. After that, he visited every day. He gave me money and bought us food and many other necessities. This was a beautiful situation, but it only lasted for about twenty days because he had to return to Italy. Before he left, he gave me $500 so that I could continue to buy the things I needed for a while. When the time came to say goodbye, he came over, and I noticed that he was sad about leaving me and my children in such a critical situation. He left me the money, but knew that it would not last long. He told me that he was married, that he had a business back home, and that he did not want to leave me like this because he imagined his own children in the same situation.

Yemayá figured prominently in the narrative of Naomi and those of other mothers whom I interviewed. Many invoked Yemayá as guiding and protecting their path. One of the Yoruba orisha deities, Yemayá is part of a pantheon of divinities brought to Cuba by African slaves. West African slaves, from the region that is today known as Nigeria, faced religious repression and Catholic conversion. They syncretized

Fig 4.1   Sitting on the Malecón, Havana, Cuba

orishas with Catholic saints, creating La Regla de Ocha, or Santería, as it is widely known. Santería continues to be a religious and cultural system widely practiced in Cuba and in many other parts of the Américas.[2] Although frowned upon by elite elements of society, Santería informs many different artistic expressions, such as music, literature, art, and dance (Barnet 2001). Since the rise of tourism in Cuba during the 1990s, the state has promoted Santería as an integral part of Cuban culture (Hagedorn 2001). Katherine Hagedorn (2001) mentions that high-ranking priests of Afro-Cuban religious traditions such as Ifa, Santería, and Palo Monte are involved in government-sponsored tours for foreigners. These tours, for tourists seeking initiation into Afro-Cuban religions, "are called Ochaturs and *santurismo* by Cubans who perceive the many layers of irony in a Marxist government's sponsoring of religious initiations, and represent the culmination of the 'folkloricization' of Afro-Cuban religious traditions" (Hagedorn 2001: 9). For Cuban women, Santeria serves as a powerful tool for reworking relations with tourists.

According to Neltys, a single mother of two, Yemayá answered appeals to relieve economic hardship and affirmed her motherhood by bringing tourists from across the seas to provide support for her children. In this account, Neltys credited Yemayá, the deity that protects mothers, for bringing a benefactor to help:

> In 1993, when I was thirty years old, in the middle of the *Período Especial,* to tell you the truth I did not have anything, and I was going hungry like someone who is doing thirty years in prison and with two children—at that moment my daughter was ten and the younger was four, both from different fathers. The support between the two of them was 35 pesos; at that moment the dollar for me was impossible. During that time my friend and I talked how so-and-so married a *yuma* [a foreigner] and made *tremendo pan* [a lot of money]. And she had luck because the guy had a lot of money. We talked with a neighbor who had as much hunger and misery as we did. She stayed taking care of the children, and we went to Varadero. Imagine that I went with only the clothes that I was wearing and a little bag with a very bad toothbrush, without even underwear because I did not even have a pair of underwear. We hitchhiked and got there in the afternoon, but I think that God granted us good luck because I prayed so much for my children. When we got to the terminal, my friend and I were so hungry that we ate pizza from the trash bin. The next day, we washed up in the bathroom of the terminal and went to the beach because they told us that it was easier to find tourists there. Four hours later, when I thought I would die, I prayed to Yemayá, the virgin of the sea. A tourist passed by and said, "What beautiful green eyes you have. Why are they so sad?" Maybe it was so much hunger. Everything started like that. It was my salvation. I went to stay with him, and he was crazy about me. *El pobre,* poor guy, I think I worked him very hard because he was a widower. He even took me to Santa Clara in a taxi [a two-hour taxi ride]. That is how it started. He would write to me, but I think that he got scared of so much misery, and after three months time I did not hear from him again.

Naomi and Neltys narrated their paths and actions as guided by the divine and sacred mother, Yemayá, who understood their suffering as mothers and provided foreign men who brought alleviation. They described their experiences with tourists not as sexual exchanges or commercialized sexual services but as a form of spiritual deliverance. Yemayá's divine intervention aligned the spiritual with the exigencies of daily living. Mothers, in particular, conceptualized their interactions with tourists as part of an answered prayer.

Yemayá's hagiography characterizes her as the goddess of "universal motherhood," representing the feminine and maternal principle in Yoruba cosmology (Barnet 2001: 49). Unlike her younger sister Oshun, whose divinity is associated with love, money, marriage, and children, Yemayá is the "great mother" who not only raises her own children but also the children of others (Clark 2005: 18). She is the force or energy that protects women, especially mothers, and her elements are the oceans and salt waters (Brandon 1993). But Yemayá differs significantly from the asexual mother or maternal virgin of Christianity. Unlike Christianity, with its distrust and repudiation of sexuality (especially in the case of the Virgin Mary), Santería cosmology does not exclude or chastise sex and sexuality, for it posits that the "world of the flesh and the world of the spirit are not so distant, the spirit is often understood as a duplicate of the body—and of bodily needs" (Vidal-Ortiz 2005: 31).

Whereas Catholic mores expound on the dangers of sex unconnected to procreation and the dishonor of the unchaste, while generally condemning sexual acts outside procreation and marriage, Santería offers believers the possibility to renegotiate dominant gender and sexual norms.[3] For instance, Santería belief does not conceive of the universe, and sexuality, for that matter, as existing within binary fields of male/female, straight/gay, and good/bad. Instead, its cosmology allows for ambiguity and fluidity in gender and sexuality, with greater availability of gender options, deities that change gender identification, androgynies, and spirit possession that is interpreted as a "sexual metaphor of human intercourse with the divine" (Strongman 2002: 186).

Santería is an affirmation of the cultural, spiritual, and physical survival that people of African descent experienced in the Americas. It encompasses the life strategies that African slaves improvised, adopted, and enacted to resist dehumanization and to transcend an insufferable existence. The notion of syncretism, central to the understanding of Santería, unveils a counterdiscourse to the "either/or" analysis of sexuality and commodification. I borrow the notion of syncretism from Santería, the combination of various forms, ideas, and practices, because it is this spiritual universe that opens the path for many women to participate in monetized sexual-affective relations with foreigners. Bypassing Western polarities of "good" mothers versus whores, the worship of Yemayá allows for the possibility of reworking the boundaries between "good" sex and "bad" sex.[4] As Oerton and Phoenix (2001) ascertain, erotic, embodied, physically intimate acts "do not exist in and of themselves" (387); they gain meaning within frameworks of symbolically discursive terrains (388). Sex, and what counts as sex, does not have a universal meaning across cultures, generations, and cosmologies.

For single mothers without connections to the tourist economy and who lack relatives from abroad who can send remittances, relationships with foreigners, whether they include sex or not, often provide unmatched economic returns. Monetary considerations are important, but, as the women in this chapter indicate, so are affective and spiritual ones. In this chapter, I challenge the concept of sex work as an analytical tool for understanding interactions between tourists and locals. Instead, I offer the concept of *tactical sex* as a strategy used by women in Cuba and the Dominican Republic that does not rely upon essentialized notions of identity or labor. I propose an analysis of interviews that detail the incomplete and fungible nature of relations and the degrees of commodification that bring complexity to these arrangements. I am not interested in the commodification of sexual relationships as a way to determine whether it is "good" or "bad" for women, but rather as a way to shed light on how the meaning of sexual-affective exchanges is incomplete. Nor am I invested in finding "true and pure" love that supposedly exists outside market relations. I am far more interested in the spaces between love and money, where the negotiations that people make are more meaningful than saturated categories of analysis. This alternate reading calls into question the epistemologies and methodologies traditionally deployed by scholars and investigators when addressing the phenomenon termed *sex tourism*.

What Is Wrong With Sex Tourism?

Scholars and social observers tend to represent encounters between third-world women and foreign men, particularly if they involve persons with differences in race and ethnicity, socioeconomic class, and age, as a form of prostitution or sex work (Cabezas 1998; Kempadoo 1999). Other sexual encounters—between same-sex partners or people with similar forms of cultural capital, with matching racial-ethnic background, or of the same nationality—have not captured the imagination as much. The underlying assumption is that "true" love is about untainted intimacy, mutual pleasure, and emotional comfort; pure love is without monetary exchanges. When there are strategic behaviors that beget marriage offers, that beget visas, then these relationships become tainted, impure, and suspect. There seems to be no liminal space, only simplistic binaries, where women ultimately lose and men eventually gain. However, women's tales of their experiences are often riddled with contradictions that suggest agency, multivalent meanings, and fluctuating situations. These relationships can be ephemeral, amorphous, and strategic, combining affect, money, mobility, and yes, even pleasure.

Western intellectual history and ideology traditionally separate the world of the market (a masculine-gendered domain of supposedly impersonal, rational, and self-interested behavior) from the domestic realm (associated with women and the locus of sentimental economies untainted by commerce), making it difficult to understand the mixed motivations of transcultural social relations. This worldview of antagonistic and dichotomous spheres essentially erases agency, the economic dimensions of "legitimate" relationships, such as marriage, and the affectional ties that bind people in market settings and commodified relations (Zelizer 2006). Because researchers perceive all encounters in sex tourism as functioning in a world divided into separate spheres, all erotic relationships where there is an exchange of gifts and money become sex work. Without the clearly defined boundaries erected by more rigidly structured interactions, for example, those demarcated by brothels, people involved in these transcultural encounters strive for a more flexible approach.

Recent paradigms in the study of commodification prove useful in reaching a more complex understanding of sex tourism. For example, new work in feminist philosophy, legal criticism, and economics suggests that markets, monetary exchange, and strategic behaviors coexist with friendship, intimacy, closeness, security, and altruistic behaviors.[5] These scholars challenge the separation of the world into two separate spheres—the market, or that which conforms to rational self-interest, and the intimate realm that operates according to altruist principles—that underlies much of the work on sex tourism. Zelizer (2005) argues that people strive to match and negotiate intimacy and commercial transactions in everyday interactions that include marriage, child care, and domestic work. In arrangements that mingle intimacy and money, people "do relational work" to "match appropriate relations, transactions, and media" (53).

Williams and Zelizer (2005) argue for a differentiated reading of commodification that assumes that market transactions have "elements of emotion and sociability, and that many intimate transactions have economic dimensions" (368). Miranda Joseph's (2005) concept of "multivalent commodities" strengthens the notion that some relations are commodified, some are not, and still others combine commodified and uncommodified elements, depending upon the context and the particular meanings that emerge. The stories in this chapter suggest that intimacy coexists with incomplete commercialization in truncated, incomplete, and fungible ways. Thus the market, or the transfer of money, does not have a hegemonic effect but can serve a plurality of purposes.

Even in sex businesses, the notion of "multivalent commodities or "incomplete commercialization" is theoretically more productive in that it captures the affective ties cultivated by participants in the sex industry. For instance, De Gallo and Alzate's (1976) research in Colombian brothels found "incomplete commercialization" of the relationship between client and prostitute. Colombian prostitutes working in brothels had "*mozos*," a favorite boyfriend that they treated in a different manner than their regular paying clients. More recently, Sallie Yea (2005) documents the complex interactions between Filipina entertainers and GIs in the *kijich'on* clubs of South Korea, where women forge emotional ties and long-term relationships with their customers that transcend the sex worker-client relationship. In the Dominican Republic, I interviewed women who identified as sex workers but referred to their tourist acquaintances as *amigos* (friends), indicating an unwillingness to characterize them as customers or paying clients.[6] The term *amigo* challenges the notion that foreign acquaintances are simply clients; rather, it affirms the malleability of tourist-oriented relationships that can easily evolve and assume other diverse functions. Through this reluctance to completely commodify all their interactions with tourists, Dominican women expand and create multiple outcomes. The myriad arrangements exist along a continuum from informal ties of affection to commercialized heterosexual transactions that evolve and transform into socially "legitimate" arrangements over time.

Tactical Sex

Commodifying sex in freelance arrangements provides a provisional use of sexuality without a long-term commitment to sex work or to essentialized notions of identity. As the daughters of Yemayá reveal, young, single mothers employ sexuality tactically and diffusely in their relationships with foreigners. The tactical use of sexuality—what I call *tactical sex*—is part of a complex circulation of sex and affect to cultivate social relations with foreigners. Tactical sex alleviates the pain of economic hardship, but economic transactions and gifts do not foreclose the chance to find solace, companionship, and friendship. For some women, tactical sex is undertaken temporarily as a way to survive financial privations. In other words, tactical sex does not imply entrenched worker subjectivity or an established and permanent financial recourse. Rather, it speaks more to a flexible, contingent activity that can move into and out of sexual-affective relationships and that uses sexuality as a stepping-stone, a bridge, to permanent romantic attachments, economic support, and, at times, international migration.[7]

Tactical sex, therefore, captures the sporadic and strategic use of sexuality. There is a conscious use of sex and affect to relieve economic necessity, even if it is resorted to only intermittently. Tactical sex is one of various short-term strategies used to get by and to prosper.[8] The exchange of sexuality, however, does not encompass the entire experience in question. It is just one component that is present—inconsistently and differentially—in many situations, where it is difficult to distinguish the boundary between market and nonmarket transactions. The following section details how the Cuban and Dominican lexicon reflects this understanding of tactical sex.

From *Jinetera* to *Luchadora*

Cubans, since the fall of the Soviet bloc, have categorized a wide array of behaviors and activities under the terms *jineterismo* and *la lucha,* which marginalize the sexual component of interactions. In Cuba, the term *jineterismo* sought to distance people from hard-and-fast definitions of *jineteras* as prostitutes, or *putas*. At the beginning of the 1990s, when it entered the Cuban lexicon, the term *jinetera/o* was used to refer to people hustling in the tourist trade at multiple income-earning schemes. Over time, all other activities were annulled, and the term became focused exclusively on sexual behavior. Progressively racialized, the term *jinetera* now refers solely to Black women, historically inscribed as hypersexual and erotic, even though some studies conducted in Havana indicated that it was primarily light-skinned women who were involved in the sex trade (Fernández 1999).

As *jinetera* came to denote mainly commercialized sex, a new term emerged to acknowledge the multiple strategies and heterogeneity implicated in all kinds of social relations and activities: *la lucha* (the struggle), along with *luchadora* (one who struggles). By the end of the 1990s, the pejorative, racialized term *jinetera*, associated with a debased identity, was no longer widely in use. *Luchadora* slowly entered the Cuban lexicon to describe a wide range of activities and networks of exchange, which may or may not include the provision of sexual services. As with *jinetera*, the term *luchadora* deemphasizes the sexual dimensions of these struggles for daily living.[9] *La lucha* is understood not as sex work but as part of a communal struggle for livelihood. For example, a woman explained this slippery terrain to Tomás Fernández Robaina (1998):

> The ones who come [tourists] know the reality that we have and they give us a good gift, I don't always see it as a gratuity, it's not right to classify it as that, but they give you a gift and that's that. You are not going to be discourteous, or assume a false pride, when they give you something for your kid, or something that can help you resolve a material problem that you have at home. That cannot be *jineterismo*. Of course, sometimes in that *lucha*, struggle, the relationship deepens, you become a girlfriend or a boyfriend of the one you pay attention to, and the rest depends on how that link develops, you have to be very careful. (140)

Stressing the power to determine the meaning of social relationships, this woman explained how negotiating the meaning of the interaction is a crucial and delicate process. As the work of Fernández (1999) suggests, it is a process mediated by race, class, gender, and cultural capital. In other words, it is easier for those with more social and racial privilege to escape suspicion and disreputability. The term *luchadora* thus encompasses the struggle for self-making, social meaning, and the negotiation of identity.

In the Dominican Republic, it is also common to use *buscársela* in ways that connote struggle. *Buscársela* is a term similar to *luchar* and *resolver* in that it implies multiplicity and ambiguity in action. Padilla (2007), for instance, found that in the Dominican context people use *buscársela* to refer to informal income-generating strategies (58–59). Padilla elucidates the importance and meaning of this term:

> *Me la busco* often remains intentionally ambiguous in actual discourse, it is likely that it refers to the feminine of "life," or *vida*, yielding the semantic approximation, "I look for life." Yet perhaps the ambiguity of the term reflects its most important function in actual discourse, since the phrase *"me la busco"* immediately indexes a fundamental uncertainty about how to make ends meet in a difficult world.

This notion, he goes on to explain, is also used outside the pleasure industry as people forge a living through various strategies. It is the uncertainty of the situation that is relevant here because it allows people to negotiate practices and identities in the informal economy.

The woman interviewed by Fernández Robaina also spoke to the role of gifts in forging and defining intimate relations. Gifts are an important feature of exchange and solidarity in all relationships. While they have many functions in human interactions, they often underscore the affective foundations of social ties (Komter 2005). Thus it is no surprise they comingle with sex. But we cannot know in advance whether a gift is a thing or a commodity, for complex negotiations and the changing context of human relationships make it difficult to establish the precise meaning of the gift (Komter 2005: 21). Gifts can function to sustain the affective dimensions of a relationship, to enhance social networks, and to strengthen identities. In the next section, I consider how the use of gifts provides a foundation for relationships that makes them more expansive rather than reduces them to a direct sex-for-cash transaction.

Regalitos/Gifts

Gifts figure prominently in establishing the boundaries and dynamic nature of relationships.[10] Gifts, like other forms of monetary exchange, serve multiple purposes in signifying the type of relationship and the level of commitment. In many of the interviews, women referred to gifts not as payments in kind for services rendered but as a way to solidify and strengthen the affective connection. As Marilyn Strathern affirms, gifts can provide "enchainment with others" (1988: 139). Gifts not only present meaning to relationships but, in a context of poverty and global inequality, can also alleviate the gulf of disparities. Tourists, in particular, are keenly aware of the enormous inequalities between themselves and their hosts and often bring gifts, pay for meals, or send remittances once they return home. These forms of social solidarity are expressed even when sex is not involved in the relationship. This often complicates how relationships are perceived and how they are demarcated. For instance, in his ethnography of *pingueros* in Havana, Hodge describes how gifts and transfers of money complicate the terrain. Given the differences between Cubans and tourists, he makes clear that "there is no clear boundary between sex work and recreational sex" (2005: 207).

Gifts are used not only to mediate economic disparities but also to define relationships, create and affirm social ties, and maintain connections. Gifts serve to confirm and reflect identities, but they can also function to injure and disturb them (Komter 2005: 54). Barry Schwartz (1967), writing about the social psychology of gifts, refers to the function of gifts in imposing "an identity upon the giver as well as the receiver" (2). It is through gifts that "the pictures that others have of us in their minds are transmitted" (1). Mairelis's story exemplifies how combining gifts and sex creates dynamic social interactions.

Mairelis is a twenty-year-old resident of Cárdenas, of medium height and light skinned, reserved, and almost shy. Nonetheless, she approached many of her clients in the streets and beaches of Varadero and offered them companionship and sex. She often went unnoticed by the police because she had a cousin living in Varadero and used that as an excuse to travel there.[11] She managed to establish, from time to time, a steady infusion of cash to supplement her otherwise meager earnings. She explained how she met her current foreign boyfriend one day when she set out to meet a tourist to make some quick cash to *resolver* (to solve some problems):

> M: I was walking on the beach, and this Italian man fell in love with me. He was thirty-three years old, interesting; a different kind of man *se me acercó* [approached me]. He asked my name. I went with him, thinking it was to have sex, but this man was different. That night he did not ask me for anything. Not even to sleep with him or nothing. We just talked. *Muy romántico, cariñoso* [He was very romantic, very affectionate]. He is a wonderful person. We started a precious relationship from that moment on. We write to each other. He calls me on the phone almost every day. Before he left, he gave me a gift of $200. He went to my house. And he wants to marry me. And as soon as we get married, he will get me a visa to travel.
>
> ALC: Would you like to leave the country?
>
> M: Yes, of course.

Even though Mairelis set out to sell sex, her experiences were quickly eclipsed by romantic love. The man approached her; she did not have to seduce him. He was interested in companionship and not commodified sex. As with Yolanda, whom we encountered in the Introduction to this book, he left her a *regalito*, a small gift.

In this case, a sex-for-money transaction became peripheral to the larger, romantic relationship. Mairelis became equally interested in romance and marriage with this partner, without negating the economic aspect of the relationship. Rather, the gift helped solidify and strengthen the bond. The gift giving, in this case, allowed Mairelis and her boyfriend to define and affirm the relationship as one of courtship and love. The gift symbolically represented solidarity, care, and concern for her well-being. In addition, it appeared as a promise for a future together. Mairelis's relationship accommodated gifts, unidirectional exchanges of money, and romantic love. It evolved over time.

Another case, that of Miladis, exemplifies elements of tactical sex with gifts as forms of solidarity. When I met her in 2000, Miladis was also a single mother who learned that tourists could provide a little fun, cash, and friendship. A light-skinned native of Havana with a twelfth-grade education, she had two children, ages three and seven, when she traveled to tourist destinations in central Cuba for a short vacation. Even as she undertook sociosexual exchanges with an implicit financial goal, she found mutuality in her interactions with tourists. Her account reveals that even when motivated by financial gain, relationships cannot be reduced to impersonal, commercial transactions.

Miladis's relationships with tourists offered her company, leisure, friendship, and a way out of her economic troubles. After her first unplanned encounter with a sex tourist, she began to frequent the beach resorts of central Cuba:

> When I was twenty-nine years old I went to spend three days in Cienfuegos to relax at a friend's house, for my situation does not allow me to be away from home for very long. One night I went out to a disco, and I had a really good time. I danced, I drank, and I enjoyed myself. Around midnight, I met a foreigner, a person of fifty-three years of age, a Canadian from Toronto. He spoke some Spanish, and we understood each other. He offered me a relationship and offered me some money. I had financial needs; I did not know what I was going to do, but he offered me fifty dollars, and, well, it was the first time that I sold my body. I was with him for five days, in which he told me that he worked as a stevedore; he did not make a lot of money. He never offered me the possibility of traveling to his country, because he told me that he did not have a way to invite anyone to his country. I can say that he was a wonderful person and that, while we did not share love, we shared a friendship. After that, he traveled two more times to Cuba, and he always sent for me. He gave me gifts, and we shared more about ourselves. I told him that I was *aterriyada*, overwhelmed in this life with problems, with my children, and that I hardly had anything to eat. He took pity on me and gave me gifts, and when he left, he was anguished. He took pity on me for all the things I said to him—for being a single mother—and he thought I should not

be in this life [selling sex], and he left for his country very sad after knowing my history.

Miladis forged a bond of obligation and solidarity with her Canadian friend. The Canadian tourist showered her with gifts, and after each visit he left sufficient cash to last a few months. After this experience, she told a neighbor that she was going to find another tourist and asked that she look after her children. She met the second tourist on a trip to Trinidad that she undertook with a girl friend:

> I was with a fifty-two-year-old Spaniard. I was with him for fifteen days, and he paid me well. I did not have any problems with the police.

She stayed in Trinidad, and when the Spaniard left, she met another man, a sixty-year-old Italian tourist:

> He was also a very good person. He paid me well, and I hardly had to do anything. Imagine at his age! I did not have to expose my body. We also shared a friendship. He came to Cuba three more times, and I always saw him. He was a good person. He could have been my father. He gave me gifts. And we shared something of our frustrated lives. Maybe that is why we were committed to one another. We shared a friendship. He was the last character of this history. Although I did not meet any bad people in this world, I had already *levantado cabeza* (gotten ahead), and my kids were getting older, and I began to reflect. I got out of that life, and I started to do manicures *por cuenta propia* [self-employed]. After that, I became a hairstylist and I have been *luchando* [struggling]. Today my son has a degree in economics. And my daughter will finish twelfth grade. They never knew what I did for them.

Miladis was able to relieve her loneliness by establishing relations of reciprocity and intimate exchange. These monetized sexual exchanges did not foreclose intimacy and solidarity (Zelizer 2005). Ultimately she was able to support her children and start a private business, *por cuenta propia,* as a manicurist and hairstylist. When I last saw her in 2006, I asked how she was doing. She replied, "Aquí, en la lucha." Known as the *peluquera* in her neighborhood, she continues struggling.

In another case, Ysabel's narration of falling in love highlights the dynamic nature of relationships and the role that gifts play in establishing boundaries and defining the realm of affect. One afternoon in 1999, walking along the Malecón in Havana, Ysabel and her friend were stopped by a tourist asking if they wanted a ride. They quickly accepted, since hitchhiking is a common practice in transportation-strapped Cuba. Ysabel was sixteen years old at the time, and the man who befriended her was a forty-year-old Italian entrepreneur doing business in Cuba:

> I could tell that he was very educated and different from Cuban men. We had only traveled a few blocks when he invited us to go for some refreshments, and I accepted. He was very cordial, and I asked him where he was going. I could tell that he was very impressed with me. I will not lie to you: the same thing happened to me, because he impressed me with his character, with his way of being.

After going for refreshments, he invited them to go out that evening: "He asked us where we would like to go, and we agreed on a time and place to meet." After that evening, Ysabel and her Italian friend became exclusive. They enjoyed good times, seeing each other regularly during his stay. Before returning to Milan, he gave her $300, and within a few days he was calling, writing, and sending her money, gifts, and clothing.

It is difficult to call Ysabel a sex worker; certainly she had no history of or association with hustling tourists, and there was no direct exchange of sex for cash in her relationship with the Italian entrepreneur. Nevertheless, her relationship, marked by differences in age, citizenship, class, and race-ethnicity, fits the paradigmatic, asymmetrical interactions stereotyped in sex tourism. Thereafter, Ysabel had a relationship with a Canadian man. This, she explained, was because "foreign men are more attentive and refined than Cuban men." She preferred dating foreigners, she said, since she learned that they were not abusive and domineering like Cuban men. Ysabel's serial monogamy with foreign men did not define her as a sex worker but, rather, a woman wishing to challenge and escape local configurations of masculinity and gender relations.

Finally, in Cuba, Ludmila, a twenty-five-year-old light-skinned woman from Cienfuegos who started befriending foreigners when she was fifteen years old, further illuminates the fluidity between market and nonmarket interactions and the uses of tactical sex:

> I went out with my friends to a discothèque. And there I met someone. He came over to me and proposed a tryst for money, and I accepted because for one night he paid me $80. He was thirty years old and lived in Frankfurt and sang in a discothèque. This relationship did not last long because he was a crazy type of person who used drugs. He was not good for me. Later I met another; he was kind of old, lived in France—in Paris—and worked at the airport. He fell in love with me, but I did not with him. The relationship continued, and he would come to visit. He sent me money. He would call me and talk for up to three hours. It was monotonous—all that stuff about "I love you" and "I like you." We were going to get married, but it was all a farce. I, so young, married to an old man? I can't even imagine that. He came to Cuba without telling me. He wanted to surprise me. He came ready to marry me but found me with a twenty-eight-year-old Spaniard. This one I liked since he was my type. But he had a big problem. He was a drug addict.

Ludmila broke the Parisian's heart and had a long-running but tortured romance with the drug-addicted Spaniard. She was able to purchase things and experiences that most Cubans do not have access to: perfume, shoes, and good meals at fancy restaurants. She said, "I had to lie a lot to justify everything that I purchased. I had to pretend to have a relationship with a friend's brother who lives in Miami." In the long run, however, she kept studying, became a physician, and is now working in a medical clinic. In speaking about her stint with tourists, she said, "I buried it and I do not let it come out."

The contradictions and ambivalent linkages that Cuban women are able to craft were present in the Dominican Republic as well. Entanglements with foreigners in touristic spaces, however, more often than not were scripted along the lines of clear-cut sex work. In the Dominican Republic, it is a way of life for most women to be deprived socially, educationally, and economically across the generational spectrum. This is not the case in Cuba. There, lack of an organized sex industry that congeals identities provides more spaces of liminality and control than in the Dominican Republic.

The Dominican Case: Fusing Market and Nonmarket Interactions

The women interviewed in the Dominican Republic were familiar with the discourses surrounding the term *sex work*. Targeted by nongovernmental organizations in their safer-sex educational outreach programs, they were well informed about not only condom use but also how to transact sex-for-money exchanges with foreigners that were quick and profitable. However, what seemed particularly imperative for the majority of women was to create an affective connection with foreigners to transcend the commodified aspect of the relationship. Hence, when meeting tourist men, many women alluded to their economic situations or presented themselves in a less entrepreneurial role. For instance, Leonora, in her early twenties and from Sosúa, talked about sitting at a restaurant, buying her own drink, and waiting until a man approached her. Forging relationships with tourists that were more expressions of friendship than anything else allowed her to establish connections that emphasized other dimensions of her existence. Consequently, the dynamic of the interaction was not a singular act of sex in exchange for money. She could potentially establish transnational networks that were more fruitful in the long term.

Like the narrative of the Cuban Ysabel, many women in the Dominican Republic also spoke of a preference for foreign men, not only for their earning power but also for the preconceived notion of egalitarianism that accompanied them (Cabezas 1999). Just as foreign men imagine Dominican women as more subservient, Dominicans see European men as less domineering. For instance, her grandfather told Leonora that instead of getting pregnant by a Dominican man who was going to beat her and live off her earnings, she would be better off finding a foreign man. She explained that her grandfather said that "it was better for me to sleep with a *gringo* so that way I can support my kids."

Leonora in the Dominican Republic and Ysabel in Cuba imagined that alliances with tourists provided a way out of oppressive heterosexual arrangements and a method of contesting gender norms and circumventing local poverty. The transnational social imaginary effectively intertwined desire with sex, love, and money.[12]

While I was conducting research in the Dominican Republic, I found that some women left open the definition of their relationships, even while they commodified certain aspects. For example, I use the term "committed *amigos*" to denote partially commodified relationships in which bonds of affection are extensive and that develop into marriage (Cabezas 1999). The foreigner typically sends regular remittances or periodic infusions of cash when needed. The woman, in return, often pledges emotional and physical fidelity. Even women who identified as sex workers sought to distance themselves from commercialized sex by establishing stronger affective ties. Free from rigid emotional boundaries around commodification, they could enhance bonds of solidarity that were longer lasting. Zelizer (2006) differentiates between "narrow" and "broad" relationships, with prostitution being at the narrow end, meaning relationships that are short in duration and with few shared practices (308). Conceptually, it is difficult to apply categories of narrow and broad to the narratives in this chapter because they change over time. Thus some of the relationships operate in spaces of liminality. In using intimate labor that deemphasized the sale of sex, women were able to perform relational work that could open up the relationship to more stable and productive possibilities.

The many limitations imposed by the global economy and the meager role that the state plays in providing basic services prove painfully restricting, as Paloma's narrative indicates. When I met Paloma late one night in November 2007 in Boca Chica, she looked radiant with her *café-con-leche*–colored skin and short-cropped hair, red shorts, and a white tank top. She was sitting on a park bench under the light of an amber-colored lamp, waiting to get tested by an ambulatory STD clinic. She was a striking vision in this quaint public square. Full of charm and vivaciousness, appearing much younger than her twenty-three years of age, she told me that she was the mother of two young children. The older was two years old.

Paloma started out selling sex in her teens after she got pregnant at the age of sixteen by her neighborhood sweetheart.[13] The baby's father left town shortly after the birth, and she moved back in with her mother. Soon, however, her mother, a single head of household with young children to feed, told her that she had to support her daughter because the mother's own earnings were insufficient to provide for her three other siblings.

Most of Paloma's encounters with tourists were short term until she met a vacationing African American police officer from New York in his late thirties, John. Paloma and John became romantically involved during his vacation stay in the Dominican Republic. John left promising to return. True to his word, he revisited within a few months to spend two weeks with her. When she became pregnant, he promised to support their child. Paloma claimed that John returned regularly and sent approximately U.S. $60 a month to support their then eight-month-old daughter. Whenever she needed anything extra for her, all she had to do was call him. Yet Paloma sat on the park bench of Boca Chica most nights, a few blocks from the police station, and continued to seek out relationships with foreign and local men.

"Why do you still look for tourists?" I asked her. She looked at me in a languid manner: "Perro que no camina no encuentra hueso" (A dog that does not walk will not find a bone). She replied with a proverb or saying, implying that if she did not hustle, she would not eat. Then she employed another proverb in a more fearless manner: "De la suerte y la muerte, no hay quien se escape" (From luck and death no one can escape). She explained that her oldest daughter had liver disease, and the medications were costly. She could not afford to feed two children with $60 a month. Fear of abandonment kept her from telling John all the details of her situation: "I don't want to scare him away." Although her long-term strategy was to leave the Dominican Republic for the United States, presumably as John's wife, John had not yet proposed marriage. In the meantime, she had to continue commodifying sexual services on the side.

In Boca Chica, I also met Carmen, a twenty-eight-year-old single mother of one. She was working at an expensive *casa de cita,* or brothel, that catered to foreign men, men from the capital city, and Dominicanyorks.[14] The first night I visited the brothel with two members of MODEMU. MODEMU outreach workers in Boca Chica regularly drop in to distribute condoms to the women and talk to them about sexual health. During previous periods of fieldwork, I visited *casas de cita* and other sex industry businesses in Puerto Plata and Santo Domingo, but these catered primarily to Dominican men. They played loud merengue and bachata music across brightly painted walls. In contrast, the chalet in Boca Chica appeared more luxurious, subtle, but also more like a sterile military compound.

Carmen worked at this *casa de cita* for three months at a time. She returned to Puerto Plata for a few months to live with her mother and six-year-old child. "I tell them that I work in a hotel in Boca Chica. They do not really know what I do here. But I miss my son so much that this time I am thinking of leaving early."

The *casa de cita* is located in a residential area of Boca Chica, a few blocks from the police station and the park where Paloma sits. Except for the tall steel security gate and the extensive security detail at the entrance, the façade resembles all the other chalet-style houses in the neighborhood. We entered into a spacious entryway with marble floors, a small bar to the right of the entrance, and a main living room encircled by black couches. Three or four men were sitting on the black velvet couches along the living-room wall. Eight or nine young women in various stages of undress were either dancing on the stripper pole strategically placed in the middle of the living room or sitting cozily with the men. Seemingly, we looked so out of place that we were hastily ushered to the back kitchen. We walked into the back kitchen and were asked to return the next day. First, the manager said that it was because all the women were working. However, I got the sense that she felt uncomfortable with my visit. We left a notice for the day manager that we would return.

The following day we returned in the early afternoon, but it was difficult to get access to the working women on that day as well. There seemed to be some apprehension about my presence there and the request to conduct interviews. Miriam, a founding member of MODEMU in Santo Domingo, had accompanied me. She talked to the managers, explaining that I was "like one of them" and that I would not ask any question or report information that could harm the business establishment. This reassurance from Miriam seemed to assuage their fears a bit. Granted permission to spend half an hour each with two of the women in their dormitory rooms, I was feeling lucky until Miriam told me that I was asked not to return.

Carmen, a light-skinned woman from Santiago with large bright eyes, looked athletically fit but with a serious demeanor. Wearing tight black pants and a loose shirt, she graciously asked me to sit on her bed that took up the entire space. She made small talk about preparing for the long night of work while I settled into her room. She lived in one of the small cottages in the back of the property, where she shared a bathroom with another woman who had an adjacent room. With her earnings, she decorated the room in hot pink, with a flower bedspread and matching curtains. There was a red stuffed teddy bear on her bed. The owners of the brothel provided the furniture, a dark wood bedroom set and a color television—the latter, she mentioned, was important in helping her fall asleep in the early morning hours. With hair wrapped in a towel, and while applying nail polish to her long fingernails, she talked effortlessly about her life.

Unlike other spaces in tourist zones where foreigners and locals meet, a brothel inscribes identities with little ambiguity through male-controlled labor regimes that script every interaction to extract the maximum amount of profit from the workers. There is little doubt that the women are there for an explicitly commodified sexual experience, and there is little tolerance for uncertainly in these spaces. Nevertheless, even in these spaces women capitalize on the affective dimension of the commercial sexual exchange. They exploit a sense of social solidarity and masculine chivalry. Denise Brennan (2004), in her research on sex workers affiliated with sex businesses in Sosúa, demonstrates that many of the women who work in these establishments can parlay their interactions with clients into ongoing arrangements. Carmen described how men often fell in love with her and proposed projects, such as marriage, to "rescue" her from the brothel:

> Yo no como por lindura [I do not make money because I am beautiful]. I pretend to like these guys and to feel something for them that sometimes I do not want to pretend. However, it means that I make more money if they think it is for real.

Some tourist men asked for her telephone number and later called, even after leaving the country. Carmen used an affective sensibility in a commercial manner to transform an otherwise fixed and restricted arrangement. As with the resort workers discussed in Chapter 3, she capitalized on the affective dimension of the interaction to extract further value from the exchange.

Carmen explained how George, a Canadian tourist from Toronto, forged a strong emotional attachment to her. He brought her gifts and asked to meet her son. She was convinced that he would be a good marriage partner. Unlike her previous husband who cheated on her with a younger woman, George was in his early seventies and, in her estimation, unlikely to digress. He planned to return in December to marry her. "I do not know if that is going to happen. These guys come here and promise you everything." Few delivered, according to Carmen. "I count on what I earn, not on what they promise me." Even though Carmen had been disappointed in the past, she was ready to renegotiate her relationship with George, one where she could rework and better control the terms of exchange. Indeed, Carmen was ready to bargain with George and alter the arrangement between sex worker and client. She told me, "I will marry him, if he promises to take care of my mother and child."

Unlike many of the relationships in Cuba where blurring of the boundaries is possible, in contexts such as brothels and streetwalking in the Dominican Republic, it is difficult to leave the market nature of the interaction out of the arrangement. But men with whom I spoke understood that the women they were involved with were doing so out of economic desperation. A short, slight, Canadian man in his early fifties who purchased an electric fan for a Dominican woman told me, "I know that she has no other alternative. I try to help her whenever I come here." Repeatedly, men fell in love or in solidarity with the women. An engineer from the United States understood this much about his Dominican girlfriend: "I know she has other boyfriends. She has to do that to survive. I do not hold it against her. When I am away, she has to make a living, but I try to do everything I can to help her when I am here. I don't hold that against her." Tourists sent remittances and visas and promised returned trips, marriage, and love. They purchased refrigerators, electrical appliances, and clothes for the children. The commodified aspect of the initial interaction evolves over time, or it becomes one of partial commodification.

Using love, sex, and romance, the narratives of Cuban and Dominican women speak of how women from the working class have repositioned themselves as desiring subjects within the political economy of tourism. Thus far, I have focused on women in Cuba and the Dominican Republic who have suffered and endured the most under neoliberal reforms, women from the working class and racialized women. In contrast, in the next section, I examine how professional and middle-class women gain access to mobility through relations with foreign men.

Professional Women

Not just in Cuba, but in many parts of the Caribbean, professional women are finding it difficult to parlay a formal education into a decent livelihood. Work for educated women is difficult to find because of the lack of jobs with decent wages. Migration and marriage are often the recourse chosen for mobility. With the push to build the tourist economy and with the reduction in the state sector, professionals traditionally employed by the state cannot find work. Foreign investment that seeks to capitalize on women's low-wage labor has not only created employment for few but has also made it difficult even for those with high levels of education to get by under the new arrangements. Yvet's story exemplifies some of the contradictions inherent in the gains Cuban women have made during the past forty years.

At thirty-two years of age, Yvet is a Black lawyer employed by the state who lives in Havana and earns 320 pesos a month. This is roughly equivalent to U.S. $12, which goes to support her teenage daughter and assists her mother, who is retired and receives a small pension equivalent to $4 a month. Like many other professional women in Cuba, Yvet is independent and self-supporting. She has high expectations for her professional career and personal life and a difficult time reconciling these with her current path. Thus Yvet is rather deliberate in her use of tactical sex.

Yvet's strategy is to meet a foreigner who will help her migrate. She is not seeking love; this is strictly a business venture: "I want a foreigner to help me [migrate] so that I can work in my profession in some other country where I know I can make more money than here." She plans to pay back any costs she incurs in the process. Toward this end, Yvet has forged a deal with a woman, María, who rents rooms to foreign travelers in a *casa particular,* a private family home. Whenever a man traveling alone stays there, she informs Yvet, who gives her little gifts and cash as a token of appreciation. María tells her that she is doing this only to help her out of solidarity because she understands the *lucha* involved in providing for a better life.

Yvet provides companionship to foreign tourists. She acts as an escort who takes tourists sightseeing around the city, goes out to dinner with them, provides lively and intelligent conversation, and sometimes has sex with them—but only if she likes them. She is discreet and cautious, assessing whether the relationship will present her an opportunity to migrate and using sex tactically, to provide a bridge to a better life or a night of pleasure. Thus far, tourists have been courteous and generous, and the extra income and a few recreational experiences relieve her constant stress, but she has not been able to find a paper husband.

Jennifer had worked at a bank in Puerto Plata before coming to Boca Chica to work in the high-end brothel mentioned earlier. She got tired of the low wages at the bank and particularly the sexual harassment from her boss: "I was working long hours, making little money, and having to pretend that I was well-compensated because you have to spend money on your hair, nails, stockings, and on and on, to work in a bank." More than anything, she wanted her own home. At the brothel, she had been able to save enough to begin building a small house. When I asked her if she would leave with one of her foreign clients, she replied:

> Si, claro que si [Yes, certainly, yes]. There is nothing here for me in this country. To make a living here, besides this place [the brothel where she works], there is nothing. I do not even like it here because they abuse you too. They charge you for the room, the food, the hairstyling. I want to be able to marry and leave the country. I am educated and I cannot even make a living in my country. Why should I have to leave? But, it is true that here there is nothing but exploitation.

Jennifer had not found the right man. In fact, she complained about the men who visited the brothel as only wanting sex and nothing more. Consequently, the strategy for advancing her life involved the possibility of repositioning herself for an amorous arrangement with a foreign man. Being a sex worker in a brothel was just a stepping-stone to bring about other outcomes.

The dreams of women such as Jennifer and Yvet resonate with those of other formally educated women placed in the middle strata of societies in the global South with high levels of education and lacking social and economic mobility. The research of Rhacel Parreñas (2001), Laura Agustín (2007), and Pierrette Hondagneu-Sotelo (2001) all attest to the growing movement of formally educated women who use transnational migration, with stints of care work, in search of a better life. Many enter into various forms of care work (domestic and sex work) in Western Europe and North America mingling sex, money, and love to improve their lives.

Conclusion

The narratives in this chapter represent neither sexual slavery nor moral depravity but offer a glimpse into the intricate accommodations and negotiations that women make in the globalized economy, where a wide range of elements and a continuum of experiences with tourists offer the possibility of transforming their lives. Participants in these encounters are able to open a crucial space of liminality and engage in a discursive struggle over meaning. Given the stratification of economic opportunities in the tourism market, sexual-affective exchanges provide a way for some women to renegotiate their status and navigate the disparities of late capitalism. This is not a separate economy of intimate encounters and erotic labor. It involves dynamics similar to those operating in other, heteronormative contexts that are deemed more legitimate.

The narratives in this chapter also speak to disparities generated by the penetration of transnational capital—how transnational capital plays on and through women's bodies. In Cuba, the collapse of relatively egalitarian economic structures has left women scrambling for opportunities. Sexual-affective relations with foreigners help navigate the contradictions of free-market practices in a socialist context. Nevertheless, these relations do not have the appearance and scale of the sex industry before the Cuban Revolution, nor are they similar to the structure of commercialized sex in the Dominican Republic. Florence Babb's analysis of sex and romance tourism in Cuba and Nicaragua is instructive here for comparative purposes with the Dominican case. She comments that "Cuban sex workers tend to have greater control over these practices than their Nicaraguan counterparts—who are often targeted as highly vulnerable due to their youth, poverty, and lack of social support" (Babb forthcoming). The lack of human capital formation in the Dominican Republic and the many privations experienced by racialized women make for increased vulnerabilities.

The spectrum of experiences related in this chapter reveals that commodified sex can be a form of resistance to patriarchy, alternative spiritual epistemologies can provide meaning to relationships, and gifts and exchanges can "melt together" to provide definition to social interactions (Ertmann 2005). People creatively rework and establish the meaning of social interactions to negotiate improved life chances. Commodification in many relationships does not erase affect. And accounting for affect does not erase the market implications of intimate arrangements or the importance of sexual-affective relations to the generalized transfer of care from the global South to the North. Certainly, it appears that the extraction and exploitation of intimacy happen across a wide range of economic and social landscapes. However, any attempt to render these women victims crushed by poverty without choices erases the ways in which they are capable of managing multiple options and trying to find the most human way of getting through.

5 / Tourism, Sex Work, and the Discourse of Human Rights

> The master's tool will never dismantle the master's house.
>
> —AUDRE LORDE, 1984

I was sick of getting beaten by my husband all the time. He tried to burn me once and he cut my face. I told a friend of mine because she saw the way I looked with black eyes and bruises all over the place. He said he would kill me. I had nowhere else to go. She brought me here to Sosúa and she lent me some clothes and told me what to say and what to do. That's how I got here. I'm never going back to that life. If I stayed, he would have killed me by now.

This statement, from a twenty-three-year-old woman from Sosúa in the Dominican Republic, was echoed repeatedly in the accounts of other women I interviewed. In a neighborhood of Old Havana, a woman explained that she preferred to work with tourists because with Cuban men all she got were beatings:

I had a stepfather who used to beat me just so that he could feel good. Then I came here to live with my baby's father. He was good at first but he eventually started to beat me up. He even beat me when I was pregnant with the baby. Twice he put me in the hospital. They put him in jail for that, but I didn't care anymore about anything. I had to take care of my daughter. So I found me a Spaniard who gave me some money, and with that money I was able to stay in this room. I finally left [the baby's father]. Now I don't know where he is and I don't want him coming near me or my daughter. He's probably out of jail by now.

These women used sex work as a way out of troublesome heterosexual arrangements. Sex work with tourists offered a way to escape the violence of poverty, beatings, and life-threatening situations that too often take place in intimate relationships. Scholarship and policies that homogenize all forms of sex work as violence against women and that subsume the complex realities of a sexual-monetary exchange under narratives of patriarchy and oppression cannot fully account for such nuances in the sexual economy. This is not to minimize the abuse that women encounter at the hands of tourists, but rather to point out that undifferentiated theories of prostitution, those that erase contradictions and complexities, cannot account for the multiple uses of paid and unpaid sex. Many women escaped intimate forms of partner violence through sex work only to bear the brunt of state-inflicted violence against women. Ironically, the state was rapidly becoming the arbiter in issues of violence against women. The globalization of the human rights agenda on violence against women had set up the state as the protector and rescuer of women.

Previous chapters have explained how adverse situations in Cuba and the Dominican Republic, compounded by the adoption of neoliberal policies, have exacerbated gender and racial inequalities. In teasing out the multiple ways in which women define and negotiate encounters with tourist travelers, I demonstrate how women circumvent the sex-worker identity. In contrast, this chapter reveals the ways in which the state establishes and imposes that identity under the pretext of protecting tourists from immoral women, imposing a revolutionary ethic, or controlling the mobility of women in public spaces. Fundamental to the narratives in this chapter is the extent to which physical violence and structural violence converge on the bodies of working-class racialized women.

I am guided by Antonia Castañeda's (1993) and Andrea Smith's (2005) deconstruction of sexual violence against Native women and women of color as an instrument of "sociopolitical terrorism" (Castañeda 1993: 29). Specifically, Castañeda (1993) argues that sexual violence is inherent in the process of conquest, colonialism, and imperialism. I extend this analysis to Cuba and the Dominican Republic. Castañeda's examination of how gender and sexuality were pivotal in the imposition of colonial, military, political, and economic rule in the Américas and Smith's analysis of current processes reveal how sexual violence is at the root of empire-making. These feminist scholars propose an analysis of sexual violence that cannot be disengaged from structural violence and the circuits of global capitalist accumulation. For, as Catherine Lutz (2004) also proposes, violence is not just a tool for the pursuit of a state's political interests; rather, violence in the twentieth century is intertwined with the "widening international and intra-national gap between the rich and poor, and with the searches of old and new forms of racism" (320). Gender- and race-based violations of personal integrity take place not only through direct corporal violence but through a macro-level political economy that feeds an empire of transnational capital. Configurations of gender and sexuality figure prominently in militaristic modes of containing women's uses of their sexual labor.

This chapter examines the many forms of violence against working-class women of color and the globalized remedies created by the human rights framework. I begin by analyzing state-sponsored violence against women in the Dominican Republic and Cuba. I then turn to an examination of whether the human rights discourse could transgress this ordering. I conclude by examining the emergence of new modes of tourist-local liaisons in Cuba.

State-Inflicted Violence

In the Dominican Republic, law enforcement uses mass arrests to keep women from "bothering" tourists. Nightly, police arrest women as they exit discos or congregate in the streets and restaurants of tourist resorts. Young women (and men) are particularly vulnerable to police harassment, are subject to disciplinary tactics and restrictions on their freedom of movement, and face violence at the hands of the police. These tactics were documented by many women. In 1997, a woman in Puerto Plata told me, "When you exit the disco, they come and grab you. Many times, they have hit me. Once they slapped me and gave me a black eye because I told them that there was no justice here. There is justice when it is convenient for them."

Mari is a twenty-three-year-old woman born in the capital city of Santo Domingo who works in one of the parks of Boca Chica offering tourists companionship and sexual services. She supports her family and pays for her sister's university education. In 2007, she told me about the police arresting women when a tourist was found dead:

> Whenever a tourist is robbed or beaten they come here and arrest all the women. They take you and don't give you a reason why you are being arrested. They say it's for bothering tourists and later they start asking us questions about murder.

The testimony of other women repeated and elaborated Mari's experiences with the police. Carmen, a Dominican forty-year-old former sex worker, said:

> When women here are arrested, they are thrown in buses like pigs. You understand? Tourists don't like to see that. Right now, there are a lot of problems because they don't let women into the discothèques, except the ones that they want. So one goes to the discothèque and gets mistreated, and they send you to jail for five days. They just tell you, "You're arrested." They put you in jail with prisoners who have been arrested for killing or for selling drugs. That's who they put you in there with! If you say anything to recriminate them, they hit you.

When asked if she had ever been arrested, a sex worker in Boca Chica answered:

> That's part of the life here. They arrest you whenever they want. If you are sitting around the park they take you in, if you are walking the streets they arrest you. That is what they are here for, to arrest us. But they are good for nothing else.

In the Dominican Republic, women are subject to arbitrary arrest and detention and to bodily harm, sexual violence, and verbal abuse from police officers. The women remain incarcerated until they can pay a hefty fine. A woman in Puerto Plata stated after being arrested three times, "That's 1,500 pesos that I did not eat or drink." More important, however, is that the police use extortion and rape in return for impunity. In Sosúa, Isabel was raped by a police officer. When I interviewed her in 1997, she had a six-year-old daughter from that rape.

The tourist-based economic reordering of the state has increased repression and violence against local women through stigmatization, harassment, coercion, extortion, robbery, and sexual violence. The state regulates the mobility of women and access to tourist spaces. Low-income women working as informal vendors in tourist spaces are routinely stopped in identity checks. This process marks them as *mujeres de la calle* (streetwalkers), and delinquents, while simultaneously criminalizing them (Gregory 2007: 58–59). The process is productive for subsidizing the state police apparatus. These arrests serve not only to control the number of women on the streets but also to generate bribes and sexual favors for the police and, through fees and fines, income for the state. In Puerto Plata, a woman described this practice:

The police are always arresting the women that do not steal. I have to pay them some 500 pesos [U.S. $36.00] I just earned, spend five days in jail, and then I end up owing the food and other expenses for being in jail. I am alone here without someone to bring me a plate of food or to run my errands. So I end up in further debt. All that after being arrested!

Women who sell sexual services are particularly vulnerable to multiple forms of abuse, from social ostracism, discrimination, extortion, and harassment to beatings, rape, and murder. Since the police are sanctioned to use force with impunity, they stand to benefit from extortion and sexual and monetary favors without facing the risk of being accused of atrocities.

A comparable situation takes place in Cuba, where state violence against women exists in a continuum that encompasses everything from harassment and verbal abuse to rape. Elizabeth, a young woman living in Cárdenas, Cuba, often travels to the nearby beach resort of Varadero on the weekends to find tourists. As a single head of household, she supports her two children and sixty-seven-year-old mother. She lives in an old, dilapidated tenement, where this interview was recorded:

In Varadero, the police persecute you. They don't let you walk the streets. It's persecution. They are right there after you, right there. Right there, persecuting you! The police are persecuting you, and the tourist is calling out to you. The tourist calls you because he wants to be with you, but you can't. You feel inhibited because if you stop to talk to him on a street corner, the police will be after you, not after the tourist. Not the tourist. The tourist is untouchable. Then they send you a letter of warning. They take you to prison, the prison is called La Cumbre, and it has these huge bugs that are disgusting. There in that prison there are these disgusting insects that suck on you and these other small insects with a lot of legs that stick to you. They treat you like a dog, like a whore. They call you bad names, many offensive words. That is the biggest problem that Cuba has at this time, if we had all the things we needed to have, we would not have this problem because we are not demanding luxuries, only an economy.

Extortion and bribes were reported to be a regular practice in Havana, Varadero, Sosúa, Boca Chica, and Santo Domingo. Elizabeth explained:

ALC: Do you think the police are violent toward women?
E: They hit them, they call them whores, they push them, they throw them. Yes, yes, it's horrible.
ALC: Do you know of women who pay the police so that they can work?
E: Absolutely, you have to go out and work. Because I have two kids in my house, I'll call my sister or my brother, and I tell them I have $100 saved. Let's give him [the policeman] $50 dollars to let me out of here automatically. I give him $50 and another $50 to the other policeman who is guarding the station. They both get a share, and they let me out. It's like that.

Over the years, I have heard many versions of this particular story from Cubans working and living in or near the tourist areas. The police routinely harass unaccompanied women. Young women walking alone are asked for identification, and searched for valuables that may be confiscated. Many of the local women are afraid to visit places like Varadero at night because they are sure to be carded and harassed.[1] A Canadian male tourist reported that the persecution of women had facilitated and increased male-to-male sexual services in Varadero. Being an employee of the resorts does not necessarily shield one from police harassment, as Nena, a chambermaid in Varadero, explained:

> The police are terrible. I am not registered with the police and am not a prostitute. I pass through the bridge among the *jineteras*, but I do not have a problem because I work there. Most of my relations with tourists have been inside the hotel where I work. But the police really bother you. If you are walking the street, they ask for your identification, and if they do not like you, the police will right away put you in one of their cars and take you in. And when they see you with the tourist, perhaps at that moment they don't bother you, but if you are separated from the tourist for one second, they will put you in their car and take you in.

Yet being with a tourist does not always offer protection. A University of Havana student recounted how she was stopped when she was leaving a hotel with a tourist. She also described a typical pattern that traps women in a cycle that necessitates further hustling in order to recover lost earnings:

> I met this Spanish man in Old Havana, and he told me he was staying at the [hotel name]. I went over there. When we were leaving, the police got there and arrested me. Then I explained to them that I was helping him to find an address. But they did not believe me, and I had to bribe them, giving them $25 each so that they would not take me. This was the money I had earned the night before. When I paid them, and he saw this situation, well, I lost him. Then I had to find another to recover the money I had lost. I did not find anyone that night, but I kept insisting the next day. I went to the Hotel Inglaterra, where I had luck, and I found a forty-eight-year-old Frenchman. He was not to my liking, but I had to resolve the economic problems and my situation.

This system of state regulation and criminalization creates a vicious cycle where women are forced to find new tourists to recover the bribes that they have paid to the police. The state-military apparatus functions to push women further into selling sex and thus creates a productive cycle of criminality.

The hustling that goes on in the tourist-sexual economy implicates a vast array of social-economic actors, from taxi drivers to hotel concierges, but women constitute the easiest targets for continuous and repeated state intervention. Periodic crackdowns serve to ease social anxieties about the rapid and turbulent changes taking place in society, the inversion of power and control that the women evince, and they enforce exclusionary in the tourism market. Ultimately, however, the crackdowns reinforce state domination over women's bodies. The private violence and patriarchal control that women experience are shifted to the public sphere. Working-class women of color are denied protection against rape, battery, robbery, and murder. The state sets up the patriarchal regulation of female sexuality, resulting in the control and repression of surplus labor in the interest of transnational capital.

Rehabilitation Centers in Cuba

In Old Havana, I interviewed a young, self-identified *mulata,* Yonilys, the mother of a six-year-old. Her child's father had beaten her so severely that she had twice ended up in the hospital. The second time she was in a coma for several days, and he was eventually arrested.

Yonilys was incarcerated in June 2001. She attributed her arrest to the way she was dressed, with white spandex pants and high heels, and to the fact that she was walking alone late at night in the Prado. She was going home from a party around midnight when some Spanish tourists called out to her. The police were watching nearby. When the tourists walked away, she was arrested for "harassing foreigners" and taken to prison. For the next three days, she was subjected to police interrogations, a gynecological exam, blood tests for sexually transmitted diseases, and psychological counseling.[2]

In jail Yonilys met what she called "decent girls," meaning non-*jineteras;* some were lesbians who had been arrested en masse for being out in the street late at night. In fact, community activists in her neighborhood were outraged at the police sweeps that targeted so many and had started to complain that everyone was getting arrested. Yonilys was eventually released and given a *carta de advertencia,* or a letter of warning. If she receives three such arrests and warnings, Yonilys could be incarcerated in a rehabilitation center for up to four years.

The state's sporadic campaigns against visible forms of sex work culminated in the creation of "rehabilitation centers" for women. The state's crusade targeted women from rural areas (*guajiras*), the working class, *mulatas,* and those from Oriente subjecting them to gynecological exams, surveillance, arrest, incarceration, and forced labor. Men hustling in tourist spaces, particularly Black men, were harassed, routinely stopped for identity checks, and often fined and incarcerated for minor violations (Hodge 2005; Fosado 2004; Allen 2003). However, the training and rehabilitation camps were only for women.

As part of its efforts to intervene and mediate the negative impact of tourism on Cuban society and culture, beginning in 1998, Cuba implemented a system to criminalize and rehabilitate women of "questionable morality"—in other words, dissident sexual citizens. Rehabilitation centers were established with the assistance of the Federation of Cuban Women (FMC), Cuba's state-sponsored women's organization. Judicial authorities institutionalized so-called dangerous women in rehabilitation camps for up to four years. Under Cuban law, a person deemed to have a proclivity to commit an offense in contradiction with the norms of socialist morality may be arrested under highly variable circumstances and conditions. Since prostitution is not illegal, the state uses a law in which it defines a "state of dangerousness" to incarcerate women.[3]

The length of stay at the rehabilitation center depended on the degree of risk to society that the women represented and their likelihood of rehabilitation.[4] Once a woman has been incarcerated, she must prove through her attitude and behavior that she has been rehabilitated. Radhika Coomaraswamy, the United Nations special rapporteur on violence against women and the first UN human rights official to be invited by the Cuban government to visit the island, questioned the arbitrariness of leaving a sentence open until officials determine that the person no longer poses a social threat (UN Economic and Social Council 2000). In her report, Coomaraswamy noted that "anti-social behavior and causing disturbance to the community are considered manifestations of such dangerousness" (UN Economic and Social Council

2000: 13). When someone is determined to be dangerous in accordance with this provision, the Penal Code permits the imposition of pre-criminal measures resulting in reeducation for periods of up to four years. Coomaraswamy emphasized that this leaves room for abuse and subjective treatment and is inconsistent with fair judicial procedure (UN Economic and Social Council 2000: 14).

In her report, Coomaraswamy documented visits to several of the rehabilitation centers throughout the island, where women receive training in gender-stereotyped careers. The women were subjected to work from six to eight hours a day, mostly in the agricultural sector, picking fruits and other crops. Those incarcerated were not allowed to move freely outside the facility, but every fifteen days, they were permitted a two-hour visit from a limited number of family and friends on a pre-approved list. Although Coomaraswamy's report for the United Nations was critical of the rehabilitation camps in Cuba, no women's or human rights organizations stepped forward to denounce these policies. Even the Cuban American community in Miami, typically hyper-vigilant in reporting any alleged human rights violation in Cuba, remained silent on this topic.

In 2000, I interviewed one of the rehabilitation center trainers, a forty-year-old engineering professor who had been recruited by the FMC to conduct classes and work with the prisoners. She felt that many of the women were not selling sex because they lacked basic necessities. Rather, they were interested in acquiring consumer goods that were otherwise unavailable to the population. "If it were for real necessity," she commented, "than the entire country would be *jineteando*." "The problem," she asserted, "is that these women do not value their bodies and do not love themselves." Radhika Coomaraswamy noted in her report on Cuba a concern that the women are held for "'behaviour [sic] modification,' as a result of their involvement in prostitution" (UN Economic and Social Council 2000: 6). In an interview in 2001 in New York City, Coomaraswamy commented on the irony of seeing banners with messages on the walls of the centers exhorting women to love themselves. This reliance on liberal humanist values, or possessive individualism, as propagated through an odd mix of Western-based self-help psychology and revolutionary rhetoric, is difficult to reconcile with either Cuba's otherwise progressive history of sex education (Smith and Padula 1996) or with tenets of socialism. The FMC's trust in posses-sive individualism as a way to circumvent sexual agency is divorced from an analysis of the role of the state in inflicting myriad forms of gender-based violence, including the obvious and unrelenting poverty that characterized women's lives during this period.

When Che Guevara first instituted rehabilitation for prostitutes in the early 1960s, they were retrained as textile factory workers. In con-trast, the goal of the FMC in instituting the rehabilitation camps was to move women away from selling sex to foreigners by providing them with training in other, more "appropriate" work such as hairstyling. But the position of the FMC has been to implement policies and norms that are out of touch with the reality of Cuban women's lives. At a 1997 conference on *jineterismo* in Cárdenas, for instance, a functionary from the FMC revealed an element of rehabilitation that not even Guevara could envision. What *jineteras* needed, she asserted, was to find Cuban intimate partners as a way out of their predicament.

The use of rehabilitation centers in Cuba had mixed success. Kar-ina, a dark-skinned woman who was arrested for being with tourists in Varadero, was not rehabilitated during her incarceration in a labor camp. She talked of her experience and determination to continue as a *jinetera*:

> I am single, with two kids, and I went to Varadero to look for a
> tourist. I have no shame whatsoever in saying this, because it's
> my body and because my mother died and I was left to care for
> my two brothers and I had no one to help me. I left the kids
> with a neighbor and went to Varadero. In Varadero I was with
> a tourist who paid me very well, a Spanish man who paid me
> $100, and after that the police caught me. I was sentenced to a
> year but released after six months due to my good conduct. I
> was there for being with a tourist, but I don't understand it
> because, after all, it's my body, and one can do with it what one
> pleases. I spent six months picking fruit, and they paid me, but
> very little.

Karina had no intention of ceasing trying to meet tourists. In her inter-view, she explained that being with Cuban men does not "pay" both literally, because of their failure to provide financial resources, and figuratively, because of the ways in which society devalues women:

> I am not ashamed to say that, because Cuban men give you nothing. When a Cuban gives you something, it's a beating. They are not all the same, but practically. I have to go out and find money. Hay que buscaserlo [You have to look for it].

The rehabilitation camps were part of a campaign, a social panic, through which the state reaffirmed its control over women's sexuality, establishing a terrain of uncertainty and terror for women. The campaign further empowered police to harass and coerce women into sexual favors and bribes and thus served to further institutionalize state-inflicted forms of violence against women. In Cárdenas, I asked a thirty-year-old mother of two about her experience and that of her friends:

ALC: Do you think there's sexual abuse?

M: I tell you, I have a friend called Betty who they arrested in Varadero on Calle 29 in the back of the park. There was a police officer there, and he told her that it was the only way she could free herself—because she had a warning letter. If you don't have a warning letter [on file], it does not matter, you can go and that is it. But before you go, they check you in automatically, and they register you and then you can go. But she had a letter of warning. She had to make love with him, and she had to give him the $50 that she had earned that night and a gold chain that she had around her neck.

ALC: How many letters of warning does a woman get before she goes to jail?

M: Well, it should be three letters of warning. There are many *jineteras* that are prostituted, but they work for the police, for the state security. There are some that have five letters of warning, and they are still out in the street, and they keep doing their stuff. Why? They work for someone, for example, Deonicio.

ALC: Who is Deonicio?

M: Deonicio is a boss who heads up a Special Brigade that only persecutes *jineteras*.

ALC: Do the women pay him?

M: Yes, they pay him. It's a bribe. But they have to do it in order to work.

The campaign allowed the FMC to assert its role as protectors of its "fallen" sisters who not only were victims of capitalism and the lure of meaningless consumption but also needed rescuing from their own oppression.[5] As in many cases of social hysteria, once the panic subsided, so did interest in maintaining the camps. Eventually, the rehabilitation camps met the same fate as the UMAP camps of the 1960s that incarcerated religious and political dissidents and gays, and the AIDS sanatoriums of the 1980s and 1990s that isolated and institutionalized all people diagnosed with HIV/AIDS. By 2003, the rehabilitation centers had disappeared from Cuba altogether. One Communist Party official whom I interviewed said that they were too expensive to run and that they never did contain the problem. By this time sexual-affective encounters with tourists were mediated by male brokers or had moved not only "indoors" but also into more circuitous modes.

Radhika Coomaraswamy's report for the United Nations raised awareness and concern about the rehabilitation centers in Cuba. Obviously, this form of transnational advocacy was successful in bringing the issue of gender-based confinement to a global forum. Given that the state is implicated in gender- and class-based violence against women, can the state be relied on to resolve these same types of human rights violations? Given that the UN discourse of human rights is intertwined with the vast expansion of global capitalism, can it provide resolution to the violence perpetrated by that same system? In the next section, I examine the applicability of the human rights framework to the violence discussed in this chapter.

Women's Rights

Can the concept of human rights intervene and serve as a recourse to ameliorate the conditions of oppression for women who confront multiple forms of violence? We have ample reason to be wary of international human rights instruments. After all, it was not until the last twenty years that the discourse of human rights became associated with emancipation and progressive social movements. Before that, it was often maligned for its complicity with U.S. geopolitical interests, the Cold War, and hegemonic capitalism. Although for some, the discourse of human rights "fill[s] the void left by socialist politics" in the wake of globalization (Santos 2002: 39), for other feminist and postcolonial scholars the efficacy of using the discourse of human rights is problematic, given its association with "androcentric, classist, western, and racialized" ideologies (S. Alvarez 2000: 48). Corinne Kumar (2005), for example, contends that the foundational premise for conceptualizing human rights—the liberal-democratic rights characteristic of the European Enlightenment—does not accommodate other definitions of rights, cultures, and value systems but allows for only the narrowest interpretation of difference within its logic and imposes a worldwide regime that excludes other epistemologies. Further, she argues that redress within this system comes from the nation-state, which is too often the most violent offender of human rights. The language of human rights, nevertheless, became increasingly important as a globalized value for subaltern subjects at the end of the twentieth century (Gott 2002). The rhetoric of human rights has also been fruitful for Dominican sex workers, providing a language for movement organizing, coalition building, and political action. In the following section, I examine how the hermeneutics of human rights becomes a malleable tool that can favor collective agency for Dominican sex workers.

Violence Against Women

Global organizing around the issue of human rights gender violations has been a significant victory for women's advocates, culminating in the 1993 UN World Conference on Human Rights in Vienna, where violence against women was included on the international agenda for the first time (Merry 2006; Bunch and Fried 1996). The framework, while purporting to be inclusive, revealed an orientalist and class-based signification. The focus on the various forms of gender-based violence was couched in narratives that fit into existing configurations of power. Disparate issues such as female circumcision and dowry death were combined with rape and wife battery under the rubric of "violence against women." Thus the agenda was once again set to reinscribe the discourse of rescuing third-world women from their perceived non-Western, backward cultures.

The campaign to include gender issues as part of the human rights rubric did not address sex work except as a monolithic form of violence against women, regardless of context. When female prostitutes enter human rights discourse, they usually do so only as clearly defined victims. Conceived as victims of patriarchy in feminist discourses that define all forms of prostitution as violence against women, or victims of either trafficking or "forced" prostitution,[6] women who sell sexual services to complement low wages, raise funds in a financial crisis, migrate, leave violent husbands, or achieve economic mobility do not fit the model of woman-as-victim, worthy of protection and deserving of salvation. Sex work is disconnected and isolated as essentially deviant and different from óther transactions that combine monetary exchange and intimate relations.

One of the problems with the "violence against women" instruments and the rhetoric of human rights is that they are couched in narrow terms of female victimhood. For instance, although the issue of violence against women has been an important one for Latina feminists for more than twenty years, the conceptualization of the female subject within this discourse has largely focused on domestic battery, a heteronormative bias that overlooks women who sell sex.[7] Women who sell sex are outside the bounds of patriarchal protection, religious mores, and legality. They violate norms of respectable femininity by soliciting and accepting money for sex. Women engaged in commercial exchanges with tourists invert relations of power. They are explicitly and aggressive in the pursuit of tourist *amigos* (friends) and thus disrupt the boundaries of submissive femininity.

A second issue relevant to the passive-victim model is that violence against women has been configured within a racialized agenda that excludes women of color (A. Smith 2005). Women who openly participate in the sexual economy as street-based workers are marked by race and class. For instance, indoor forms of sexual exchange are often invisible and hidden. Middle-class call girls, or "beeper girls," as they are called in the Dominican Republic, are generally university students and office workers who participate in the sex trade through relatively privileged and concealed arrangements that approximate heterosexual romance (MODEMU 2002). Those with cell phones, automobiles, and full-time jobs are able to bypass the state's disciplining practices. In contrast, public forms of sexual commerce are subject to surveillance, police harassment, criminalization, punitive measures, and violence. Speaking about the inadequacy of the human rights instruments in addressing class issues, Puerto Rican feminist Yamila Azize Vargas asks, how is it that "two aspects so connected to women's private sphere as domestic work and sex work, have not received the same attention as, for example, domestic violence in the context of discussions of women and human rights" (Azize Vargas 1997). The script of the passive victim is not readily afforded to working-class women because the human rights episteme restricts the represential means through which the subject gains access and sets what Randall Williams (2006: 31) discusses as the erasure of the "other scene of politics" and "in the process work to reproduce the State's monopolization over the means of violence." It is not just that violence against sex workers does not fit into the class- and race-inflicted conceptualizations of "private" violence, but that the paradigm does not accommodate and make visible state-inflicted and sanctioned sexual violence.

Globally, the many forms of violence against sex workers are readily tolerated, and normalized violence against sex workers is met with social indifference. As a result, sex workers not only are subjected to the state's terrorizing practices but also seldom receive police protection when they are raped, beaten, robbed, or killed by their clients, husbands, or intermediaries. Miriam, a leader in the sex worker organization in the Dominican Republic, MODEMU, incensed by the lack of attention that the killings of sex workers receive, communicated:

In La Romana in 2007, five *compañeras,* comrades, were killed. Lucy Rodríguez and Elcilia Guerrero were asphyxiated in a hotel. Yomarky Castillo was dismembered. Yeny Cordero was shot and Seleste Aquino was stabbed to death. In Boca Chica a woman walking with a tourist who was about to be assaulted by three men intervened to protect him. The men had machetes and the woman put her hand out to prevent them from hurting the tourist and they cut her hand off. In our country they protect the tourist a lot. It is not that I am against that. It is just that when a tourist gets killed they round up all the sex workers. We also have the case of a sex worker who was constantly beaten by her husband. He even broke a bottle over her head. To defend herself, she took a knife and threw it at him, killing him. Now they are looking for her and she is not about to turn herself in. I don't want her to do it because here the justice system is *machista* [male dominated]. There is no justice for us. No one cares when a sex worker is killed.

The issue of violence against women has gained more traction and is more prominent in the Dominican Republic than in Cuba. Radhika Coomaraswamy, the United Nations special rapporteur on violence against women, noted in her report that in certain Cuban bureaucratic spheres, violence against women was not considered a social problem because socialist doctrine prevented recourse to violence (UN Economic and Social Council 2000: 5). There was no need to alter laws or create programs. However, other entities, such as the FMC and the Women's Studies Centers, were more adamant about the need to raise awareness of violence and to conform to the Beijing Plan of Action. The FMC has created 175 houses nationwide, or Casas de Orientación de Familia, that provide services to women within a given community.

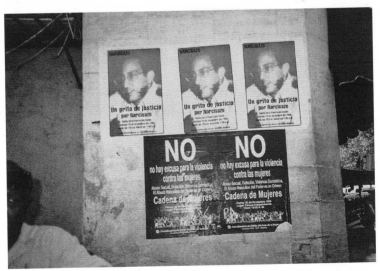

Fig 5.1   No Excuse for Violence against Women, Dominican Republic

The Dominican Republic has a longer history of raising awareness of violence against women. For example, the UN day to commemorate violence against women, November 25, is named in honor of three Dominican sisters who were killed by the Trujillo dictatorship in 1960. Attention to their plight has reached a frenzy of state purposive action. Buildings, parks, schools, and a province have been named after the *Hermanas* (sisters) Mirabal.[8] On November 25, 2007, all the newspapers carried major stories about the problem of femicide in the country and other forms of gender violence. Still, there was no coverage of the deaths of sex workers. Yaniry, a leader in the sex worker movement in the Dominican Republic, explained that sex workers have not received assistance when they have sought redress from the Secretaría de Estado de la Mujer, the state's women's affairs office. "We are ignored if we go there with a complaint. They don't pay attention or care about our problems," she says with indignation. The level of awareness in the Dominican Republic is important but remains limited. Only private forms of violence are addressed—the doings of evil men—and only injustices against specific women are recognized.

The absence of sex workers' experiences in the human rights dialogue of violence against women raises significant questions about what voices are heard, what counts as violence, and what assumptions are made about women's sexuality in legal reforms. Underlying the juridical framework in the Dominican Republic are essentialist notions of gender subordination that erase differences and diversity in women's conditions in the interest of conformance to UN conventions and imperial feminisms. Nevertheless, the irony remains that sex workers are using the human rights discourse for mobilization and consciousness-raising. The usefulness of human rights language for MODEMU is the subject of the next section.

Sex Workers' Rights as Human Rights

Sex workers have gained a particular kind of prominence with the advent of the HIV/AIDS pandemic. They were one of the first groups to enter the system of global surveillance, classified as "reservoirs of infection" (Schoepf 2004). The global surveillance of sex compelled the study of commercial sexual practices using a gendered rubric. Funding agencies stepped forward to finance projects that only targeted women

Fig 5.2   MODEMU conference, Dominican Republic

for training in safer-sex education and condom use—not their clients or any of their other sexual partners. As a consequence of this international surveillance and funding priorities, the sex-worker organization in the Dominican Republic emerged. A nongovernmental organization providing health and education to marginal communities in Santo Domingo, the Centro de Orientación e Investigación Integral (COIN), initially trained a team of sex workers to conduct peer-to-peer education for the prevention of HIV/AIDS and sexually transmitted diseases (Kempadoo 1998).[9]

From the initial group of peer educators grew an autonomous organization led by sex workers. Again, the role of the human rights regime was crucial in establishing the movement (Salas 1996). At a 1996 UN conference on the traffic in women and forced prostitution, sex workers were brought together from throughout the Latin American and Caribbean region. Marina Torres, one of COIN's original peer educators, was present at the meeting and recalls that a sex worker organizer from Brazil first gave them the idea of forming a sex-worker union: "It was Jacqueline Leite who told us that we should be independent. This is how we started to think about it. We went on to form our organization and now it's been over ten years."

Since the inception of the organization, MODEMU has employed the human rights framework to articulate demands for recognition of sex workers' rights and to gain social respect. MODEMU is dedicated to the fight against the social, political, and economic marginalization of sex workers.[10] Presently, the organization is composed of former and current sex workers. MODEMU also works to organize gays and transvestites who work in the sex industry. There are approximately two thousand Dominican and Haitian sex workers who participate in the various projects of the organization. Most of the members work in brothels, streets, and other organized sex industry businesses. They have not been able to organize women whom they call "*muchachas beeper*," referring to, for example, the women who work in casinos and five-star hotels.

MODEMU as an organization does not condemn sex work but instead encourages women to know their rights and to practice safer sex, "We cannot offer our members alternatives to sex work because this is a poor country. There are no jobs here," says its current president, Jacqueline Montero. Therefore, MODEMU members, like sex workers in Mexico City in the 1920 and 1930s, face a paradox, developing a collective identity based on the right to have pride in their labor even as they find ways to leave the occupation (Bliss 2004: 167).

The term *sex worker* and the international rhetoric of human rights have been crucial in expanding the authority and legitimacy of MODEMU. For example, in 1997, the new Minister of Tourism, Félix Jiménez in an attempt to deal with the bad publicity generated by a British Broadcasting Corporation report that portrayed the Dominican Republic as rampant with sex tourism, resurrected legislation to concentrate sexual commerce geographically through zoning laws (Bonilla 1997). In other words, in response to the damaging report he proposed a "redlight" district to contain all forms of prostitution. MODEMU, with support from COIN, quickly responded with a press release that stated, "The solution cannot be based on condemning our women through discriminatory policies and violation of human rights." The proposed legislation, it asserted, would victimize women working in prostitution. It added that the problem of prostitution is a global phenomenon that affects all nations in social and economic crisis. It called for a meeting with the Minister of Tourism and sent him a list of issues to discuss, including alternatives to sex work and the creation of jobs for women in the Dominican Republic and for Dominican women working in the sex trade overseas. In addition to literacy and job-training programs, they requested medical, legal, and psychological services (Placencia 1997). Finally, MODEMU demanded that tourism and migration officials be trained so as not to violate the human rights of Dominican women. The Minister of Tourism did not respond to their challenge, but plans for a red-light district have not been mentioned since MODEMU's intervention.

The state's response to international scrutiny and MODEMU's retaliation illuminate how state policies to control and regulate the sex trade can be challenged by use of the moral legitimacy and activism of the human rights discourse, even by sexual subalterns. Using the term *sex worker,* a new globally dispersed subjectivity, MODEMU repositioned its members from fallen women to legal-juridical subjects worthy of protection. Often invoking the moral weight of human rights language, it has continued to demand the end of violence against sex workers at the hands of the police and business owners, protection of their labor rights, and access to free and high-quality health care (Feliz 2000; Hoy 2000; Suazo 2000).

Elsewhere, I have argued that the language of human rights provides women in the sex trade with a discourse to assert their rights as citizens (Cabezas 2005). I make a case for the use of human rights language to further the appeals for social justice of people working in commercial sex. However, I insist that the next wave of activism must come from the expansion of sexual rights—a concept that needs further elaboration in human rights instruments and feminist circles, and one that could encompass a broader set of actions besides and beyond "work." Using "sexual rights" as a rallying tool can serve the interests of all people—not just those who identify with the "sex-worker" label but also other "sexual outlaws" (Petchesky 2000; Petchesky and Correa 1994). This is a limited sphere, given that sex is not a universal category. However, as Emma Pérez (1998) suggests, the use of essentialism can be crucial for political action. In appropriating the human rights discourse, MODEMU usurps a space (*un sitio*) and a language (*una lengua*) to gain legitimacy and bring about social change (E. Pérez 1998).[11] The adaptation of human rights language to sex workers' lived situation has produced an analytical framework for political mobilization and social change that can effectively bypass the stigma traditionally associated with prostitution. The human rights *lengua* is made pliable in this *sitio,* thereby transforming the otherwise exclusionary practices of the human rights regime.

Cuban Sex Workers?

In contrast to the Dominican Republic, the language of human rights, particularly first-generation rights, is a distrusted discourse that the Cuban state experiences as a disciplining tactic used by the United States. Given the long history of U.S. attacks on Cuban sovereignty using the ruse of human rights, it is unlikely that the language of human rights will gain the same kind of relevance for civil society or governance that it has in the Dominican Republic. Cuba is more aligned with second-generation human rights, meaning social, economic, and cultural rights. At the level of the United Nations, Cuba often invokes its role as the injured party in relation to the United States. The negative effect of the economic embargo on the country, for example, is blamed for the curtailment and elimination of programs to promote equal opportunities and to eradicate gender stereotypes (UN Committee on the Elimination of Discrimination against Women, Concluding Observations: Cuba 1996).

In Cuba, the notion of a "sex worker" is slowly entering the language of epidemiologists, AIDS activists, and some feminists.[12] But few are ready to embrace the discourse of "sex workers' rights" or "sexual rights." Unlike the situation in the Dominican Republic, where brothels, as well as other outlets for sexual entertainment, cater to nationals, Cuba lacks an organized domestic sex industry that could secure a "sex-worker" identity, and women who attach themselves to foreigners have a difficult time identifying their actions as "sex work." As the MODEMU case in the Dominican Republic illustrates, it is through collective action that this term can gain relevance and legitimacy and provide a framework to facilitate advocacy for what is an otherwise marginal and dispossessed group. Furthermore, Cuba has been slow to recognize organizations that operate independent of the state and the Communist Party apparatus. There is no current framework to accommodate actors and practices similar to those operating in the Dominican Republic.

The heterogeneity of sexual-affective and economic attachments to foreigners makes it difficult to inscribe an identity that Cuban women do not want. Liminality in identity and action remains a powerful tool in allowing women to shape gender and sexual expressions, even while this closes off contacts with transnational advocacy networks that, as the case of MODEMU illustrates, can provide spaces for women's empowerment.

Old Tactics, New Modes

Repressive policies in Cuba instigated a move for male control of the sex trade where none had previously existed. Repression facilitated new brokers who arranged encounters between tourist men and Cuban women, taking a cut from both the women and the men. After 1996, sex work in Cuba moved indoors, either to *casas particulares* or to other arrangements, such as the use of cyber dating. In other words, women no longer publicly propositioned tourists. Women who originally sought tourists on their own accord were forced by the crackdowns to use an intermediary. Repressive tactics, such as the ones employed in Cuba, and state-sanctioned violence are effective in creating and expanding a network of middlemen, or male brokers, in tourism's sexualized entertainment and thus in maintaining patriarchal control over the sex trade.

A young doctor whom I interviewed in Old Havana had managed to create multiple income schemes under the new regulations. During the day he worked as a doctor; in the evening he served as director and choreographer for a nightclub dance revue in a hotel. Although he claimed to have received invitations to travel to Europe to work as a choreographer, he was content to make money by providing foreigners with access to the women of his dance troupe. His elaborated business scheme called for dancers to pose for a photo album that he presented to prospective clients—men he met at the nightclubs. He coordinated the rendezvous and often took a gratuity from the men and a cut of the dancers' earnings.

The development of new forms of intermediaries is made possible in Cuba by the repression of women in public spaces. It is now more difficult for women to approach men directly in public. A man who approaches a tourist with offers of a sister, a girlfriend, his neighbor, or his friend is manifesting an archetypal relationship between men and women, with women being trafficked between men. The state has set up this dynamic by establishing control over working-class women's sexuality through protective custodial and regulatory forms. The front-desk clerk who takes an extra $40 to allow a woman to go up to a tourist's hotel room, the taxi driver who provides a contact to pleasant company and a good restaurant, the U.S. attorney who lives part of the year in Havana and introduces his Cuban girlfriends to visiting compatriots, and those who run *casas particulares* and let women know of new tourists who might need an escort around the city are all implicated in a continuous system of networking and procurement. However, the facilitators cannot be easily classified as "pimps," because, as with the term *sex worker,* race, class, and gender dynamics mark this category more than the actual exchange taking place. The "pimp" category, therefore, serves to police those actors whose dynamics and social location lack ambiguity.

The Internet also provides new possibilities for foreign men and local women to meet (Johnson-Hanks 2007). Many of the cybercafes that have sprung up all across Cuba since 2003 now provide opportunities to develop friendships and to find a marriage partner overseas. Many women post photographs on Internet websites looking for romance, travel, friends, and new opportunities or visit chat rooms frequented by presumably single men from different countries. Others use the services of intermediaries such as Yosbany, an English-language instructor who works as a professional interpreter and translator. I met Yosbany in 2006 in the city of Santa Clara in central Cuba. He explained that he is sought by women who want to meet foreign men through the Internet. His English-language skills have made possible the arrangement of many meetings, some of which have been successful in generating *una invitación,* a letter of invitation for a European visa. His work as a translator also facilitates meeting foreign men interested in local women. This works opaquely, with the men asking questions such as "Where can I go to meet women here?" Yosbany does not receive direct payment for his work as an intermediary; instead, he is able to procure gratuities and gifts of recognition while building a relational network that he can call upon to *resolver,* to resolve problems.

When I asked a Cuban friend about the new Internet arrangements, she alluded to the shifts in the sexual culture after the repressive campaigns against *jineteras.* She commented:

Ya no es la jinetera de la saya corta [It is no longer the case of the *jinetera* with the short skirt]. She no longer has a trademark. She does not have to go to Varadero anymore. She is not the girl with a different look every fifteen days; the one who no one knows how she makes her money. Instead, now she puts her picture on the Internet. She does not have to leave the town. Like a friend of mine who met a Chinese man on the Internet. He came to Cuba and they got married. Now she is trying to figure out if she wants to leave the country. He comes regularly and leaves her money and takes care of her family. The family is saying that they knew him, that he was already a family friend, from before. But I don't know. To me it's *jineterismo* but more *solapado* [hidden]. It is the same *jinetera* that cannot go out. It is the same as before, though, you do not know which relationship is real and which one is based on material interest.

The state's enforcement of a repressive sexual system has created new forms of distrust and hostility toward working-class culture and cross-cultural, transnational relationships. As Fosado's (2004) ethnography of *pingueros* in Havana points out, there is a general deep concern with the state of love in Cuba, where people are suspicious of relationships between foreigners and locals because they are now considered to be economically motivated, *relaciones de interes*. There is a new distrust of hypergamy that did not exist before. There is intense concern for managing representations particularly in the mingling of intimate relations and economic transactions (Zelizer 2005). There is a certain anxiety about the state of love. However, the new uneasiness is often motivated by a deeper concern about the crossing of racial and class lines that is involved in transnational relationships. For instance, a young Cuban man carrying on an amorous relationship with an older foreign woman is vexed by suspicion. In contrast, when both people in a romance share the same racial background, as when white Cuban Americans travel to Cuba for sex and romance with their compatriots, there is little talk of financial gain. Another example is that of a white Cuban chemist from Cárdenas who studied for her Ph.D. in Germany, where she met her husband, a Spanish doctoral student who was studying at the same university. Marriage to a Spaniard made it possible for her to stay living and working legally in Europe while helping finance her frequent trips to Cuba. No one I spoke with regarding this relationship felt uneasy or questioned the love and marriage arrangement, despite her obvious gains in mobility and assets. After all, they both have doctorate degrees, they share the same ethnic background, and no one expected that she would "marry down," understood here as marriage to a Cuban man.

Conclusion

This chapter started by examining state forms of sexual violence against women involved in trading sex. The underlying argument here is that tourism development has increased violence against women along racial and class divides. This is a form of structural violence that needs further recognition. The global movement to end violence against women has ignored the violence that is directed against an entire population of women because being accused of prostitution seemingly renders women deserving of abuse. This is a huge fissure in the women's movement in both the global South and North. Although violence against women is a global matter that has received international attention, violence against sex workers is often not taken seriously.

In addition to elucidating the ways in which the state and the police benefit from the abuse, this chapter shows how verbal battery, robbery, and rape at the hands of the police implicate national governments in gender-based violence. It is not an easy proposition when women seek redress from the state and end up caught in the paradoxical discursive parameters framed by the state (Alexander 1994). These are salient issues that confirm the multiplicity of uses of women's human rights discourse and why the discourse of human rights appeal to subordinated groups.

This chapter indicates how the global informs the local and vice versa. The human rights framework is part of the repertoire of strategies available to sex workers in the Dominican Republic. Yet it is a construction never envisaged by the international discourse of women's rights. Within this locality, human rights are modified, reinterpreted, and rearticulated by Dominican sex workers to negotiate their relations with the state and other patriarchal structures. Equally as important is that many of the women are able to connect to ideas that serve to strengthen their determination to organize, fight back against abuse, and redirect their lives. That the human rights framework can serve to temporarily bring forth ideas, identities, and issues that were heretofore absent and invisible is a strategy for change, but not one that can "dismantle the master's house."

Epilogue

One of the many public works that Trujillo built is an outdoor mall situated in the colonial area of Santo Domingo, called El Conde. Now considered too touristy by many highbrow Dominicans, El Conde attracts foreign tourists, lower-middle-class shoppers, street vendors, cruise-ship travelers looking for deals on Haitian art, and informal workers affiliated with the stores and restaurants of the mall. Among these are the young *dominicanas* who sit in the outdoor cafés and parade up and down El Conde.

When one is studying sex tourism, it is hard not to notice the young women sitting at the outdoor cafés talking to foreign men. "Why not organize them into the sex-worker union?" I asked Miriam, one of the members of MODEMU. She looked at me in surprise and responded in an almost despondent manner, "They are university students who do not identify as sex workers." "They don't identify with us," she emphasized.

Initially, I read her comments as indicating something about the stratification and hierarchy that operates in the sexual economy of the Dominican Republic and that separates sex workers across class lines. Women who work in the sex businesses with Dominicans tend to be of lower socioeconomic background, for instance, than those who work with foreigners. However, I started to rethink my observations, guided by experiences in Cuba that exposed the limits of prevalent theoretical frameworks.

While working as an assistant tour guide in Havana, I kept reframing and expanding my analysis of what tourist-local liaisons looked like. For instance, one particular experience significantly expanded my thinking. A cotraveler and academic from the United States, an older man with a head of graying hair, recommended his Cuban friend to me as a research assistant. He kept emphatically raving about her, "She is so smart, talented, and knows everything and everyone in La Habana! She can help you with your research. You can count on her for everything!" He was adamant about her knowledge and talents. An engineer and pianist, she worked at the nearby school, close to the hotel where we were staying.

For a few days I forgot about my friend and his Cuban researcher friend as I dashed about the city ushering U.S. travelers on their excursions and shopping trips, until one day when I ran into him. He was enjoying a drink in the lobby of a quaint boutique hotel in Old Havana. Sitting across from him was a beautiful, young, dark-skinned woman, wearing a tight, short skirt and laughing a lot. They were both visibly having a good time. I was stopped in my tracks and stood motionless, wondering if she was a possible research subject. For a few seconds I stood theoretically displaced.

"Amalia, come and meet Carmen." My fellow traveler introduced me to Carmen, whom I have now known for over five years. He was right. She is charming, witty, and extremely knowledgeable. She is known for her resourcefulness and graciousness, and numerous U.S. scholars and travelers have benefited from her assistance over the years. U.S. friends send her remittances and clothes, invite her to dinner when they are in Havana, and employ her whenever possible.

The transcultural liaisons that have attracted the most attention in sex tourism research are those that are marked by the most visible differences, people who are noticeably of different racial-ethnic backgrounds, age, class, cultural capital, and nationality. This has rigidly focused the research on cross-racial sex, assuming that the exchange of sex for money is the most important and demarcating aspect of the relationship. We know little, for example, of Cuban Americans' and Dominicanyorks' participation in the marriage, romance, and sexual economy. What are the dynamics and possibilities for these relationships?

In the same way, we know less about the phenomenon called "spring break" in the United States, which increasingly involves transnational travel and sexual relations.

Other forms of transcultural arrangements have also been ignored. These do not get marked or stigmatized because they do not include sex or romance. Consequently, in this study I have challenged the dichotomy that marks some relationships as automatically oppressive, devoid of tenderness and solidarity, while assuming that those that conform to social norms are somehow free of cruel dynamics, dubious intentions, and financial gain.

This book has called into question our compulsion to dichotomize relationships as "good" when the economic exchange is shrouded in patriarchal social institutions and "bad" when they represent a more direct form of monetary exchange. The narratives in this book challenge what up to now have been easy assumptions about these alliances.

In both Cuba and the Dominican Republic, there are a multiplicity of arrangements that are used to travel outside the island and to connect with the global economy, including marriage, work contracts, relatives living abroad, work in joint ventures, friendships, and other contacts with foreigners, that involve some commodified aspects blended with intimacy. Although sex-for-money exchanges have garnered the most attention internationally, money and sex are just two of many factors that motivate people, and not necessarily consistently the most significant ones. There are many other kinds of relationships where financial exchange does not simply indicate commodification but also communicates support and solidarity as a sign of obligation and love.

Notes

Introduction: Affective Economies of Sexualized Tourism

1. The elimination of prostitution is one of the foundational and proudest accomplishments of the Cuban Revolution. As Gisela Fosado (2004) explains, in a database of Castro's speeches there are over one hundred pronouncements on the eradication of prostitution in Cuba. Cubans also proclaim their accomplishments in the area of women's education. For example, in 2000, 51 percent of Cuban scientists were women, as were 52 percent of medical doctors and 50 percent of attorneys (Núñez Sarmiento 2004). Nevertheless, Núñez Sarmiento points out that Cuban men still hold most management positions (68.5 percent), even while their percentages as professionals and technicians are diminishing (2004: 26).

2. Cuban tourism was at its height in 1957, with 350,000 visitors. By 1968, the number of international tourists had dwindled to 3,000, recuperating by 1990 to reach 340,300 (Miller and Henthorne 1997).

3. See, for example, Cooper (1995); Darling (1995). Also, by 1995 the Italian travel magazine *Viaggiare* bestowed on Cuba an award for becoming the "paradise of sexual tourism."

4. There is little consensus on the origins of the term *jinetera*. A *jinete*, according to *The Oxford Spanish Dictionary*, is a horseman or horsewoman, and *jinetear* is to ride and to break a horse. *Jinetear* also means to jockey for a position. As I discuss further in Chapters 2 and 4, *jineterismo* is a colloquial term that refers to the broad range of activities and behaviors associated with

hustling, including, but not limited to, tourist-oriented sex work. *Jineteros* trade on the margins of the tourist economy; they are often seen soliciting foreigners in the streets of Havana, peddling everything from cigars and rum to sexual services. They act as tourist guides, escorts, brokers of sexual services, and romantic companions. Many Cubans speculate about the allegorical and historical origins of this term. One version postulates that since *jinetes* were the soldiers on horseback who fought against the Spaniards during the War of Independence, and because Spain was one of the principal tourist-sending countries in the early 1990s, the persons chasing after Spanish tourists were denoted *jineteros* or *jineteras*.

5. For recent research on sex tourism in the Dominican Republic, see Padilla (2007); Gregory (2007); Brennan (2004); Herold, García, and de Moya (2001); Sánchez Taylor (2001) and Cabezas (1999; 1998).

6. Many of the initial writings on Cuban women emphasized issues of agency (Stout 1996 Fusco 1996).

7. See the work of César Ayala (1999) for further elaboration of the term *unifying tendencies*.

8. The notion of a Great Caribbean has inspired revolutionary leaders and intellectuals alike throughout Caribbean history. Historian Philippe Zacair (2005) argues that the notion of Caribbeanness inspired Antonio Maceo, Cuba's foremost major general of the anticolonial liberation army. Zacair establishes that Maceo's philosophical thought in the second half of the nineteenth century refers to a conviction found among significant intellectuals, statesmen, and military figures of the different islands of the region. José Martí, Ramón Emeterio Betances, and José María de Hostos, among others, held the ideological belief that they belonged to a single people who shared a common history and a common identity and aspired to a common future. This expression of Caribbeanness emanated from two increasingly intertwined political battles. One related to the struggle to free Cuba and Puerto Rico from Spanish colonialism. The second pertained to the fight against the United States' imperial ambitions in the area.

9. I use the terms *sex-affective* and *sexual-affective* interchangeably throughout this book to refer to those relationships that combine elements of friendship, romance, sex, and solidarity. I concentrate more on these interpersonal relations than on clearly demarcated commercial transactions that are short-term, anonymous, and emotionally distant exchanges of cash for sexual services.

10. I was assisted by MODEMU and a nongovernmental organization, the Centro de Promoción y Solidaridad Humana (CEPROSH), which made the initial contact with informants and provided a space for the interviews. I am grateful to them for all their generous facilitation. See Cabezas (1999, 1998) for further reading. In both countries, I also held informal conversations with

hotel workers, tour guides, taxi drivers, restaurant workers, hotel guests, tourists, travel agents, academics, entertainers, and religious leaders. In addition, I conducted interviews with fifteen men from California who traveled to Cuba between 2000 and 2002.

11. I use pseudonyms and have changed the name of some locations throughout the book.

12. Indeed, before boarding a plane for Cuba from Miami International Airport, I suffered an aggressive confrontation by a Cuban American immigration agent who interrogated me about traveling to Cuba. Her hostile behavior was extreme, prompting one of her coworkers to intervene on my behalf.

13. I became keenly aware of this after the passage of the Track II portion of the Helms-Burton Act, which heightened tensions between the two nations and made my informants more fearful of sharing information. See Chapter 2 for further discussion of the Helms-Burton Act.

14. Scholars have struggled with the remarkable resemblance between tourists and anthropologists. See, for example, Crick (1995) and Minca and Oakes (2006). Are anthropologists simply "pretentious tourists" (Graburn and Barthel-Bouchier 2001)? The borders between ethnographic fieldwork and tourism are often fluid and porous, even as scholars astonishingly deride tourists as simple-minded sightseers. Bourdieu's (1990) critique of subjectivism and objectivism and the other binaries of Western thought that these reify is useful for thinking about the implications of research methods.

15. Scholarship on sex tourism reflects its traditional association with the economies of Southeast Asia (Bishop and Robinson 1998; M. Hall 1994; Truong 1990), where the U.S. military created rest and recreation (R&R) areas for military personnel on breaks from the Vietnam War. Key features of the R&R economies were sexualized forms of diversion, such as brothels, bars, and striptease shows. The R&R sector grew after the end of the Vietnam War, attracting male travelers from Western Europe and Japan. Consequently, it developed into a key sector of the national economies of Thailand and the Philippines, with the full support of their governments (Bishop and Robinson 1998; Lim 1998; Hall 1994; Truong 1990).

16. For an analysis of the term *sex tourism*, see Ryan (2000), Oppermann (1999), and Ryan and Hall (2001). See also Carter and Clift (2000) for scholarship on tourism on sex tourism and Crick (1996) for the political economy of sex and tourism.

17. The liminality of tourist-related relationships is best captured in cultural productions from the United States, Spain, and Cuba. See, for example, Jordi Sierra i Fabra's *Cuba: La noche de la jinetera* (1997), Pico Iyer's 1995 novel *Cuba and the Night,* and the Cuban/Mexican film *¿Quien diablos es Juliette?* (1998). In these works, the relationships between foreign men and Cuban women are ambiguous and fraught with contradictions. See Fosado (2004) for further

elaboration on the notion of ambiguity. For discussions of liminality see Turner (1982) and for liminality in sex tourism see Ryan and Hall (2001).

18. Folbre and Nelson (2000), maintain that all relationships involve forms of exchange, with some activities having complex significance and others motivated solely by payment. They suggest that there are elements of altruism and care in commodified relationships.

19. The International Labour Organization (ILO), in a 1972 report on the Kenyan economy, first conceptualized the informal sector. It is defined as income-earning activities that take place outside the state's regulatory framework. The structuralist approach to the informal sector, also termed the ILO-PREALC approach (International Labour Organization–Programa Regional de Empleo para América Latina y el Caribe or Regional Program of Employment for Latin America and the Caribbean), has been concerned with examining the exploitation of labor and how imperialism has expanded this via global economic restructuring (Rakowski (1994); Sassen (1994); Portes and Schauffler (1993); and Portes, Castells, and Benton (1989). Studies of these processes of capital accumulation reveal how forms of production are vital to the structure of local, regional, and international economies (Rakowski 1994). See Itzigsohn (2000) for a study of the informal economy in the Dominican Republic.

20. There are major differences between Cuba and the Dominican Republic concerning the sale of goods and services that are outside state control. One is that these activities in Cuba are against the socialist tenets of the revolutionary process and the ideological thought of Che Guevara and Fidel Castro, who instituted the nationalization of the majority of private enterprise and the near abolition of private property. In the Dominican Republic, some forms of informal entrepreneurial activities are incorporated and absorbed by the state. However, these are also closely regulated through a process of state-issued licenses to vendors, and those without licenses are subject to fines and other forms of criminalization (Gregory 2007). Nevertheless, at the ideological level these activities are celebrated and promoted by the state. For example, the Dominican Republic has received loans and grants to promote microenterprise projects. Microenterprise is also a formula sponsored by the U.S. Agency for International Development (USAID) and by nongovernmental organizations operating in the Dominican Republic. The Cuban underground economy, or second economy, as it is known, offers some flexibility and correctives to an otherwise inefficient, wasteful, and mismanaged state system of production and distribution (Michalowski and Zatz 1990). However, with the exception of some activities that were legalized during the 1990s, selling services and goods is ideologically repudiated and deemed illegal. Chapter 2 discusses the process of incorporating small enterprises into the Cuban economy. See also Ritter (2005, 2004), and Perez-Lopez (1995) for studies of Cuba's underground economy.

21. In a study for the ILO, Thomas (2002) maintains that employment in the urban informal sector in Latin America grew from 52 percent in 1990 to 57 percent in 1996. Informalized labor practices account for 60 percent of the urban labor force in Latin America. See Ferber and Waldfogel (1999) for an account of the growth in contingent labor practices in the United States, Western Europe, and Japan.

22. *Sankys* provide a wide range of services, from acting as tour guides to providing sexual services to foreign tourists during their vacation stay. See Padilla (2007) for research on gay sex tourism and the *sanky panky* phenomenon in the Dominican Republic. For a Dominican cultural production depicting the sanky panky phenomenon, see the video *Sanky Panky* (2007).

23. I use the terms *prostitute* and *sex worker* interchangeably and as historical referents. For instance, the term *sex worker* comes out of the sex workers' rights movement and the reformulation of prostitution as a form of labor. See, for example, Bindman (1997); Nagle (1997); Kempadoo and Doezema (1998); L. Bell (1987); Delacoste and Alexander (1987). I use the term *sex worker* to denote practices and identities that are associated with the sex-worker movement for political rights and recognition. When I use the term *prostitution*, I refer to practices associated with stigmatized forms of sexual labor, for example, brothels in Cuba before the revolution.

24. For innovative approaches in reconceptualizing the "prostitution" paradigm, see also Lucas (2005); Nussbaum (2005); and Wolkowitz (2002).

25. For example, women in the U.S. labor force are horizontally and vertically segregated in the job market, with most women working in clerical and sales positions. These "pink-ghetto" jobs are low paid and lack benefits such as medical insurance and paid holidays. All so-called labor choices, therefore, conform to the logic of capital.

26. Van der Veen (2001) refers to Marx's "Economic and Philosophic Manuscripts of 1844." See also Tucker (1978).

27. See also Pateman (1988) and O'Connell Davidson (2002) for similar formulations.

28. For further discussion of the "sex-work" category, see Wardlow (2004).

Chapter 1. Tourism in Cuba and the Dominican Republic

1. For a description of community participation in tourism development in Cuba, see Milne and Ewing's (2004) account of the La Moka Ecolodge project in Pinar del Río.

2. See D'Hauteserre (2004) for a discussion of colonialism in the tourism industry. For further discussion of the political economy of tourism see Shaw and Williams (2002) and (1988); Urry (1996) and (1995).

3. The most economical trip to the Dominican Republic, for example, is the all-inclusive hotel and air transport package controlled by tour operators. Independent travel is discouraged by higher prices.

4. Tourism services are increasingly purchased on the Internet via three mechanisms: (1) Global Distribution Systems (GDS), formerly Computer Reservation Systems (CRS); (2) third-party websites such as Orbitz and Travelocity; and (3) hotel- and airline-owned and operated direct booking. Tour operators and travel agents in destination countries use GDS to book travel, accommodations, and other tourism products as well. The cost of GDS fees and technology is prohibitive for small service suppliers. Orbitz, one of the two biggest online travel agents, is owned by the five largest U.S. airlines—American, Continental, Delta, Northwest, and United. Travelocity is owned by Sabre Holdings, the world's largest travel agent reservations system, and by GDS (PSTT 2004).

5. Wiarda and Kryzanek (1992: 76) comment, "Private capital, foreign aid, technical assistance, military training missions, and the long arms of its embassy give the United States a vast range of levers with which to manipulate the Dominican Republic."

6. Ferguson (1992: 11) notes that in 1985 Gulf and Western sold its Dominican holdings to an association of investors headed by the Cuban-Lebanese Fanjul family.

7. Rafael L. Trujillo was dictator from 1930 to 1961. His regime was extremely violent, with repression and the massacre of 12,000 to 18,000 Haitians in 1937, and was marked by the accumulation of immense personal wealth. He created state structures and placed his cronies in offices within these institutions to uphold his power (Betances and Spalding 1995).

8. The Dominican Republic has the lowest levels of education expenditures as a percentage of gross domestic product (GDP) in the Latin America and the Caribbean (UNDP 2005).

9. Foreign investment in the form of joint ventures has been allowed in Cuba since Law-Decree no. 50 was enacted in 1982.

10. Over 60 percent of world travel takes place within Organization for Economic Cooperation and Development (OECD) or European Union (EU) countries (UNWTO 2003).

Chapter 2. Neoliberal Times in Cuba and the Dominican Republic

1. See Brennan (2004), Cabezas (1999; 1998), and Roorda (1998) for accounts of Sosúa.

2. This is not to suggest that neoliberal reforms have been a homogeneous process in Latin America. See Arceneaux and Pion-Berlin (2005) for a discussion of factors involved in the variation of outcomes.

3. IMF-prescribed austerity measures were supposed to reduce the national debt and alleviate the country's financial crisis. To ease the discrepancies in its economy, including inefficient government enterprises, a large foreign debt, and widespread corruption of public officials, the government was forced to reach an agreement with the IMF that restructured its heavy loan debt. The standard of living dropped precipitously with the implementation of IMF measures as civil jobs were eliminated, along with food subsidies. Reductions in education and health expenditures caused social instability and widespread international migration.

4. In Latin America, the privatization of state and collectively owned assets accounted for the largest privatization proceeds in developing countries (World Bank Privatization Database 2006). The IMF claims that the Caribbean countries are some of the world's most highly indebted emerging market countries (Sahay 2004. In essence, the cumulative effect of neoliberal policies is to transfer the wealth from the global South to the North.

5. Cuba received 86 percent of its raw materials, 98 percent of its fuel, 80 percent of its machinery and equipment, and more than 70 percent of its manufactured goods from COMECON (Spadoni 2008; Judson 1992).

6. Ritter (1998) explains that the new laws effectively decriminalized most of the activities that were part of the underground economy.

7. Use of the dollar had previously been penalized by up to a fifteen-year sentence. Officially, the international exchange rate is one peso to one U.S. dollar, although the state adjusts the exchange rate for domestic use. In 1995, the Casas de Cambio (CADECA) were established with an exchange rate of twenty-five pesos to the dollar. Beginning in November 2004, Cuba ended the circulation of the U.S. dollar and made the *peso convertible,* also known as the *chavito,* the official exchange rate. U.S. dollars must now be changed to the *peso convertible* at an 18 percent loss. One U.S. dollar is equivalent to 0.82 *peso convertible.*

8. The rationing system was implemented in 1961 to provide all the population with the basic necessities at low prices in order to achieve an equitable level of consumption (Ritter 1998). In a line-item analysis of the *libreta,* Symmes (1996: 59) comments, "Cubans are hungry and unhappy, but they endure because the ration system is the center of a tattered but intact social safety net that includes education and health care at levels unknown in most of the Third World—or even in Washington, D.C., which has an infant-mortality rate nearly twice that of Havana. From the perspective of a dirt shack in Chiapas or a Haitian shanty, the Cuban system looks like an egalitarian success." Ritter (1998) claims that the *libreta* produced a system of minicapitalists because the items guaranteed under the *libreta* could be traded or sold to others.

9. Staples of the Cuban diet are rice and beans, with some meat protein; these could no longer be adequately provided through the ration card. The

only protein available on the ration card during the Special Period was the infamous *soy picadillo,* or ground soy, which Cubans unequivocally detested. The rations of rice and beans, when available, did not last for more than one week. In fact, most daily staples were no longer available in state stores. Instead, Cubans sought to replace and complement the loss through the underground economy, bartering, and purchases in the dollar stores.

10. López Vigil, a Cuban living in Nicaragua, reasons that "many do not understand this 'above board' state tactic, which creates some equality at the cost of other inequalities. What many see today is that it is not like it was before; the playing field is not at the same level for everyone. And in Cuba's political culture, nothing is as irritating as inequalities" (1999: 75).

11. Remittances from the Cuban community in the United States enter the island via three methods: (1) personal delivery, (2) *mulas,* or mules, are people who transport dollars, and (3) direct transfers. Direct transfers were modified by the Bush administration in June 2004 to permit only $1,200 to be transferred yearly to immediate family members.

12. Overseas Cubans are said to number more than 1 million, with about 700,000 Cubans in Miami, Florida, alone. The migratory movement of Dominicans to the United States is both legal and illegal, and they are said to number approximately 700,000, most of whom reside in New York. For an excellent discussion and comparison of remittances from Cubans and Dominicans, see Eckstein (2003).

13. The irony, of course, is that anti-Communist Cubans in the United States helped the government survive the crisis.

14. The nationalization of the private sector in the dawn of the revolution eliminated most private-sector enterprises. Small-scale agricultural producers and other microenterprises such as food vendors, bars, handicraft makers, and auto repair shops were shut down or driven underground by the Revolutionary Offensive campaign of 1968 (Ritter 1998). Nonetheless, the informal sector, although banned, thrived and continued to meet the demands of the population. The economic changes during the Special Period also included the introduction of private cooperatives and farmers' markets.

15. Ever since the United States broke off diplomatic relations with Cuba in 1961, it has sought to isolate it socially, politically, and economically. The Kennedy administration, for example, promised $1 billion in aid to Latin American countries to break off diplomatic relations with Cuba. In 1964, Cuba was expelled from the Organization of American States (Murray 1992). Only Mexico continued to have diplomatic and commercial relations with Cuba.

16. One of the provisions of this bill is to fund Cuban dissident groups.

17. For a documentary video that details a Cuban American's change of heart in relation to the embargo, see the story of Silvia Marini, *Our House in Havana* (2000) by Stephen Olsson.

18. For further discussion, see Eckstein (2003) and Kaplowitz (1998).

19. The Helms-Burton Act was impugned for its lack of humanitarianism, assault on Cuban sovereignty, and disregard for international trade agreements, but the harsh measures called for in the law did not permit U.S. presidents to make revisions or changes. Originally, President Clinton opposed the Helms-Burton Act, but he was compelled to sign it after two counterrevolutionary airplanes that violated Cuban airspace were shot down on February 24, 1996, killing four men. One of the airplanes was piloted by Martín Pérez and José Basulto. Basulto, a Bay of Pigs veteran, claimed that at one point he was on the CIA payroll. The sponsoring organization, Brothers to the Rescue, also operated a rescue mission for Cubans leaving by sea. However, the missions had violated Cuban airspace more than a dozen times between 1994 and 1995 (Fedarko 1996: 37). According to Miguel Alfonso Martínez of the Cuban Foreign Ministry, the group's planes violated Cuban airspace twenty-five times during the prior twenty months, dropping leaflets that called for civil disobedience. Cuba formerly protested to the U.S. government, warning that the planes risked being shot down.

20. Under Title IV, Helms-Burton targets firms that traffic in property confiscated by the Cuban government: "Foreign companies that owned or had commerce with Cuban properties expropriated from a U.S. citizen—even if that person had not been a citizen when the property was seized—would no longer be eligible for U.S. bank loans" (Brenner and Kornbluh 1995: 38; López 1998). The United States estimates the amount of property confiscated in the 1960s at $1.8 billion. About one thousand claimants are now entitled to sue Cuba under the Helms-Burton law (López 1998: 61). "By expanding the group of claimants," Brenner and Kornbluh assert, the estimated claims would reach $100 billion, "an amount, analysts pointed out, that Cuba would need more than 100 years to pay off" (1995: 38). Title IV also denies entry into the United States to executives dealing with Cuba and their families. Title II, one of the most controversial provisions, supports Cuban dissident groups, including a plan for U.S. backing to a transitional and "democratically elected" government in Cuba. However, this law excludes Fidel Castro and his brother Raúl from political office.

21. Ironically, under the Helms-Burton regulations, Ry Cooder, a jazz musician who gained international prominence with the *Buena Vista Social Club* and who was enjoying a huge success with the film, album and concerts in the United States, was fined $25,000 for traveling to Cuba. President Clinton pardoned him before leaving office.

22. Note, for example, that the U.S. Government Accountability Office (2007) reports that "democracy building" support for "regime change" in Cuba was misused to purchase such items as crabmeat, Godiva chocolates, Nintendo Game Boys, cashmere sweaters, and Sony Play Stations. Nevertheless, funds for dissidents in Cuba increased to $45 million in 2007.

23. Most emigration from Cuba took place from 1965 to 1973, with approximately 250,000 people fleeing the island. The Mariel exodus in 1980 involved approximately 125,000 people. In the last few years, *balseros* have become a media staple, making it seem as if the emigrations are constant and extensive.

24. In July and August 1994, various vessels were hijacked by Cubans attempting to leave for the United States. In July of that same year, a Cuban fireboat rammed a hijacked tugboat, drowning thirty-one people. Cuban authorities called it an accident, but President Clinton characterized the drowning as an act of "brutality" (Brenner and Kornbluh 1995).

25. The Cuban government accused the United States of not providing the allotted visas to Cuba and having a backlog as a way of creating pressure and dissent in the island. It also argued that since the 1960s the United States has had in place policies that push Cubans out and pull them to the United States. For example, the Cuban Adjustment Act of 1966 regarded all Cubans as political refugees, provided assistance in relocation, and granted permanent residency status to Cubans. Cubans also contend that the United States aggravated the migration problem by denying temporary visas to Cubans wishing to visit their relatives in the United States. Between 1990 and 1994, the United States denied between 40 and 60 percent of the requests to travel (Aja Díaz 2001).

26. Cuba has argued that the "dry feet, wet feet" policy continues to encourage Cubans to attempt the perilous journey to Florida. For example, in 1998, the U.S. Coast Guard intercepted 1,047 would-be immigrants (Fletcher 1999). Indeed, *balseros* continue to come to U.S. shores through their own ingenuity. Others are taken away from Cuban coastal waters by smugglers charging up to $8,000. For an Oscar-nominated documentary that details the experiences of *balseros* in Cuba, the Guantanamo military base, and the United States see *Balseros* (2003).

27. Economist Paolo Spadoni (2008: 2) states that by 2006 even the CIA and the Economist Intelligence Unit "put the island's growth, respectively, at 9.5% in 2006 and 6.5% in 2007." Hamilton (2002: 24) suggests that Cuba's "performance must be considered in the context of the economic crisis out of which the Cuban economy emerged in the early 1990s, the continuing crippling effects of the U.S. blockade, the fall in the world price of sugar, and the economic costs of natural disasters, particularly hurricanes."

28. For a detailed discussion of entrepreneurship in Cuba, see Ritter (1998).

29. Indeed, Ritter (1998) speculates that by 1996 the repressive polices toward the private sector had driven *cuentapropia* workers away from registering.

30. Progressive taxes ranging from 5 to 50 percent were implemented on "wages, salaries, interest, dividends, and income derived from currency ex-

change" (Barberia 2002: 20). The state implemented taxation as a way to curtail the accumulation of capital and to discourage growth of the merchant class.

31. As Marshall Beck (2001: 199) explains, "The consequence of using a universal standard intended to reduce enrichment of this hypothetical 'maximum earner' to a modest limit is that those with lesser abilities and/or greater financial need are pushed by this tribute system below a minimum survival level."

32. The problems with overpopulation in Havana have to do with sewers, the aqueduct, transportation, and educational, social, and health services, which are all compromised and do not meet the demands of an expanding population. Most important, Havana has 560,000 housing buildings, half of which are in bad condition, with many beyond repair. In addition to overcrowding, the city has approximately 7,000 *ciudadelas*, or shantytowns (Gutiérrez 1997: B10). Approximately 345 buildings collapse partially or totally every year. Old and Central Havana, the most densely populated areas of the city, have some of the oldest and most dangerous buildings in the province of Havana.

33. Cuban sociologist Marta Núñez Sarmiento points out that women workers have higher educational levels than their male counterparts, and these figures have remained constant since the 1979 census. Nevertheless, in 2000, only 33.5 percent of all managers in work centers were women (Núñez Sarmiento 2004: 26).

34. This refrain is captured in the title of the book by Spanish anthropologist Isabel Hodalgo Fernández (2000).

35. For a discussion of racially motivated criminal prosecution and enforcement, see Hernández (2000) and de la Fuente (2001). For related findings in the Dominican Republic, see Gregory (2007).

36. For instance, Black Cubans, who represent more than 40 percent of the residents in Old Havana and Central Havana, tourist-attracting zones, are unable to start a *paladar* or *casa particular* because they are more likely to live in tenements or in buildings with structural damage and where private bathroom facilities are not available, certainly unfavorable spaces for such enterprises (de la Fuente 2001).

37. Indeed, the level of discrimination toward Blacks is particularly acute in tourist zones. An African American informant revealed how, while waiting for a tour bus outside the Habana Libre Hotel, he was approached by security personnel and told to move on. The guard did not realize that he was a tourist. African American friends have revealed similar experiences of discrimination in hotels and other tourist-oriented businesses.

38. Cuban American economist Mesa-Lago (2002) estimates that remittances to Black Cubans are $31 per capita annually, compared with $103 for the rest of the population. Without access to dollars and formal employment, Blacks

turned to informal activities, where they were more likely to be involved in illicit dealings that are subject to persecution and that are criminalized.

39. In a study conducted in Venezuela and later replicated in the Dominican Republic, light skin pigmentation, preferably blond, was chosen as an indicator of *buena presencia*. In the Venezuelan study, for instance, 80 percent of interviewees perceived Blacks as common laborers and messengers, while 80 percent thought that the whiter-looking person was the spokesperson for the firm. Comparable findings were found in the Dominican study conducted by Valdéz (2005).

40. For many Cuban artists, musicians, and performers, the second half of the Clinton administration, when travel restrictions for Cuban artists were eased, provided the opportunity to earn dollars and travel to the United States.

41. Padilla (2007); Sánchez Taylor (2006), (2001); Herold, García, and De Moya (2001); Hodge (2001); De Albuquerque (1998); Meisch (1995); Pruitt and LaFont (1995); and Press (1978).

Chapter 3. Eroticizing Labor in All-Inclusive Resorts

1. In 1999, Cárdenas gained international fame as the hometown of Elián González, the boy who left with his mother in an inner tube for the Florida Straits. Elián was held captive in the United States by his Miami-based relatives until he was released to his father and returned to Cuba in June 2000.

2. Although Methodist and Presbyterian missionaries have been active in Cárdenas for more than one hundred years, during the early 1990s, places of worship gained a prominent role in people's lives as many sought refuge in the churches. The Protestant church in Cuba is regarded as more socially progressive and involved in public social works than the Catholic Church and other denominations. Indeed, the Protestant church in Cárdenas held two conferences on jineterismo during the 1990s. In addition, a few members of the National Assembly, the highest organ of the Communist Party, are openly Protestant. Other church leaders enjoy long-standing relationships with Fidel Castro. During the Special Period, many Cubans sought spiritual solace in the church, but the church also played an important role in distributing medications, meals, and other provisions at a time when the state was in full retrenchment. U.S., Canadian, and European-based Protestant churches made this possible with generous contributions and donations. I am grateful to Yvette Gomez for sharing with me her knowledge of the Protestant church in Cárdenas.

3. See Guevara (1975) and Löwy (2007) for further discussion of the New Man.

4. I conducted interviews in Havana and Varadero annually from 2000 to 2003 and in Santa Clara and Havana in 2006 for this chapter.

5. For a discussion of resort complexes in the Puerto Plata area of the Dominican Republic see T. Cole (2004). For a discussion of deterritorialization in the Caribbean all-inclusive resort see Titley (2004).

6. These countries represent the principal sources of visitors in the rest of the island (*Cuba in Figures* 2002).

7. Leidner (1999) defines personalized service as when an employee smiles, makes eye contact, and uses a customer's name. Reck and Reck (1996) define it as taking care of the unique needs of the individual customers. Along these lines, Crick (2001: 3) explains that personalized service contains at least two common activities: "emotional labor and customization."

8. Hochschild's (1983) concept of emotional labor in her celebrated work on flight attendants is pivotal in elucidating the commercialization of workers' feelings. Hochschild distinguishes between private and public emotions and shows how private feelings "fall under the sway of large organizations, social engineering, and the profit motive" (1983: 19). She suggests that emotional labor has negative consequences for workers because of the stress of performing inauthentic emotions.

9. In Cuba, management positions often go to those with extensive affiliations to the Communist Party and military apparatus.

10. Tyler and Abbott (1998); Adkins (1995); Filby (1992); and E. Hall (1993).

11. When Plummer eventually confessed having same-sex desires to Mc-Millan, she accused him of marrying her to leave Jamaica and obtain a green card.

12. Visitors enter Varadero by crossing a bridge. This makes it easy for police to conduct surveillance on the number of Cubans who enter the Varadero isthmus.

Chapter 4. Daughters of Yemayá and Other *Luchadoras*

1. The state provides and subsidizes basic daily provisions such as bread and milk. Milk is available to children and the elderly. Picking up the daily ration of bread is a way of helping a neighbor. These and many other forms of daily solidarity mark the Cuban daily social experience even in a rapidly changing context.

2. Santería in all its heterogenic manifestations, is widely practiced in Cuba. Santería literally means the way of the saints and is also known as La Regla de Ocha. Ocha is a contraction of oricha and is a more formal name for Santería. African slaves renamed Catholic saints with the names of their Yoruban orichas, or gods that they workshipped. Thus it is referred to as "the

way of the gods." The Regla de Ocha means the "law of the gods," or the "way of the saints."

3. For scholarship that analyzes gender and sexuality in Santería, see Clark (2005), Vidal-Ortiz (2005), Conner (2004), Fernández Olmos and Paravisini-Gebert (2003), Strongman (2002), and Fernández Olmos (1997).

4. See Gayle Rubin's (1993) for an analysis of forms of sex that are deemed perverse and those that are considered acceptable.

5. See, for example, Zelizer (2005, 2006), Williams and Zelizer (2005), Folbre and Nelson (2000), and Radin and Sunder (2005). For an excellent discussion of commodification, see Ertman and Williams (2005).

6. Encounters between tourists and locals include factors also present in other social relations. It is difficult to differentiate them, given that elements of affection, courtship, friendship, marriage, leisure, and various forms of reciprocity are present. Most researchers have been perplexed about how to classify these cross-cultural relations, particularly when the relationships are not clear-cut prostitution. As Dahles and Bras (1999: 287) affirm for what they term "romance entrepreneurs" in Indonesia, "If prostitution is not the right concept to characterize these relationships, love is not the right concept either." For discussions of *jineterismo* and sex work in Cuba see Berg (2004); Pasternostro (2000); Facio (2000); Wonders and Michalowski (2001); O'Connell Davidson (1996); and Pattullo (1996). For a historical analysis of sex work in the Caribbean see Kempadoo (2004).

7. Tactical sex is similar to what Jennifer Cole (2004) calls transactional sex. Writing about sex-for-money exchanges, Cole (2004) contends that young women in Madagascar engage in a broad spectrum of relationships that range from short-term encounters to long-term liaisons, ultimately hoping to use their youth and beauty to acquire a husband and migrate overseas. Partially commodified sex, for these women, provides support to households and generations.

8. Although the majority of Cubans suffered scarcities during the crisis of the early 1990s, as I detail in Chapter 2, not all the uses of sexuality are survival sex. *Survival sex* is a term defined in connection with sub-Saharan countries of Africa as "sex work [that] is about making money to remain alive, making money to feed one's children, and, in extreme cases, finding a place to 'hang out' or negotiating some modicum of physical safety and protection." Where, as Preston-Whyte et al. (2000: 165) maintain "It is better to die in fifteen years' time of AIDS than to die in five days' time of hunger." The contours of poverty in Cuba are different. Although its social safety net was threadbare during the height of the crisis in the early 1990s, Cuba managed to maintain a social infrastructure, albeit a minimal one. There were periods of acute scarcities of food and shortages of basic provisions, along with epidemics and diseases. But by the end of the 1990s, there was no premature mortal-

ity, widespread undernourishment (especially of children), illiteracy, persistent morbidity, or lack of access to medical care to indicate a basic deprivation of elementary capabilities (Sen 1999). This is not to deny Cuba's poverty or the temporary phases of shortages in resources and deprivations of various kinds. Rather, this challenges monolithic conceptualizations of prostitution and sex work that erase differences and hierarchies in the uses of sex.

9. See also Constable (2003) for a discussion of the overemphasis on the sexual dimensions of relationships in the mail-order-bride industry that ignores other significant dimensions.

10. *The Gift*, Marcel Mauss's classic work on gifts and commodities, established that exchange can take the form of the gift that appears to be voluntary but in reality is "given and reciprocated obligatorily" (1990: 3). Simply put, pure or free gifts are impossible. For important studies of gifts and commodities, see Carrier (1995, 1997) and Yan (1996).

11. Sex work is not illegal in Cuba. Rather, it operates in a gray area of the law, as I discuss in Chapter 5. During the late 1990s, Cubans were regularly stopped at the entrance of the bridge to Varadero as a way to curtail street vending, sex tourism, and other illicit activities.

12. This is not a space free of contradiction. Elsewhere I elaborate on how foreign men perceive Dominican women as hypersexual domestics (Cabezas 1999).

13. It is common for pregnant women to sell sexual services. For example, in November 2007, when I interviewed Paloma, there were two other visibly pregnant women selling sex in a park in Boca Chica. One of the women from MODEMU told me that some men prefer pregnant women for sex.

14. This term refers to Dominicans living in the United States, mainly in New York.

Chapter 5. Tourism, Sex Work, and the Discourse of Human Rights

1. See Hodge (2005) for descriptions of police harassment of young men in Havana.

2. See the work of Walkowitz (1980), Bliss (2004), and Guy (2000) for the historical precedents of medical inspection of prostitutes in Latin America and Britain. The case of rehabilitation centers in Cuba also has a history in its colonial past (Estévez 1976). In 1746, prostitutes were placed in a jailhouse re-education center in Havana. The young women from lower socioeconomic backgrounds were jailed as a way to cure them of "lasciviousness."

3. Women charged with a "state of dangerousness" are sentenced under Article 72 of the Penal Code, which states, "A dangerous state is considered the special proclivity in which a person is found to commit crimes shown by

their conduct in observed contradiction manifested with the norms of the socialist morality" (*Código Penal* 1998: 106).

4. Cuba has a history of incarcerating sexual dissidents in rehabilitation camps. In 1965, the state established military units to aid production (Unidades Militares de Ayuda a la Producción, UMAP), camps in which homosexuals and dissidents were forced to work in agricultural labor. There is no evidence that the camps were set up with the sole aim of incarcerating homosexuals, but some observers claim that as many as 60,000 gays were forced into them. Conscientious objectors to military service, Jehovah's Witnesses, and Seventh-Day Adventists were also jailed (Lumsden 1996). See Castro (1995) for a discussion of sex work during a meeting of the FMC.

5. The middle-class feminist phenomenon of being moral crusaders for their fallen working-class sisters took a new turn in the Dominican Republic when a women's NGO assisted in formulating legislation to eradicate violence against women, which, despite its good intentions, further excludes sex workers from juridical protection. For instance, in compliance with the UN Convention to Eliminate Discrimination against Women (CEDAW) and a regional convention to end violence against women (Convención Interamericana para Prevenir, Sancionar y Erradicar la Violencia contra la Mujer o Convención de Belem do Pará), various penal codes were modified in 1997 to promote the elimination of violence, including prostitution and trafficking. Two women's organizations worked to modify the Penal Code to conform to CEDAW and to implement and promulgate the tenets of the movement to eliminate violence against women without consulting women in the national sex-worker organization. For example, Article 334 penalizes those who assist men and women in the exercise of prostitution, those who receive benefits from the practice of prostitution, and those who contract, train, and maintain men or women in prostitution, even with their consent (Ley no. 24-97). These extraterritorial laws can be used to penalize those who violate them in foreign countries. These laws seek to penalize a fictitious "pimp" figure who allegedly lives off a woman's earnings. But investigations in this area reveal that sex work is used primarily to support families and specifically women's children. The contractors are often part of the kinship network that women use to migrate. Also, these laws erase women's ability to give consent, rendering them prone to further abuse. By subsuming all forms of prostitution under the monolithic framework of "violence against women," Article 334 creates a group of noncitizens who are not entitled to the same rights as other women.

6. Some of the UN conventions have moved to accept a distinction between forced and voluntary forms of prostitution (Hernández-Truyol and Larson 2002). The Beijing Platform for Action condemns only forced prostitution (Meillón 2001).

7. Caribbean and Latin American feminists began organizing against violence against women at the first Encuentro (Encounter)—the regional meetings of Latin American and Caribbean feminists—held in Bogotá, Colombia, in 1981. At the Encuentro, November 25 was declared the Day against Violence against Women to honor the Mirabal sisters, three Dominican women activists killed by the Trujillo dictatorship on that day in 1960 (S. Alvarez 2000). This proclamation initiated regional observance of the problem of gender-based violence.

8. The story of the sisters' political activism against the Trujillo regime was portrayed in Julia Alvarez's novel *In the Time of the Butterflies* (2001) and in the subsequent film (2004) featuring Salma Hayek, Edward James Olmos, and Marc Anthony.

9. See Gall (2006) for sex-worker organizing in Western Europe.

10. In 1995, COIN organized a sex-worker congress, where peer educators demanded rights from the state and civil society. At their congress, they discussed issues of violence against women, which was put at the forefront of their campaign. In 1996, they constituted their organization and planned for future conferences. In 1998, they held their first congress as MODEMU to address sex workers' rights as human rights.

11. Emma Pérez (1998) extends Gayatri Spivak's notion of strategic essentialism to argue for a political tactic that gives voice to marginalized groups in a process that is not fixed or permanent but "bonded temporarily at a specific historical moment" (88).

12. This information is based on a personal communication from Leonardo Chacón Asusta, January 6, 2006. Chacón Asusta is a Cuban sexologist who for many years was involved in the HIV/AIDS prevention programs in Havana and throughout the country.

References

Acker, Joan. 1990. "Hierarchies, Jobs, Bodies: A Theory of Gendered Organizations." *Gender and Society* 4: 139–58.

Ackerman, Holly. 1996. "The Balsero Phenomenon, 1991–1994." *Cuban Studies* 26: 169–200.

Adkins, Lisa. 1995. *Gendered Work: Sexuality, Family, and the Labor Market.* Philadelphia: Open University Program.

Adkins, Lisa, and Celia Lury. 1996. "The Cultural, the Sexual, and the Gendering of the Labour Market." In *Sexualizing the Social: Power and the Organization of Sexuality,* edited by Lisa Adkins and Vicki Merchant, 204–223. New York: St. Martin's Press.

Adler, Patricia A., and Peter Adler. 2004. *Paradise Laborers: Hotel Work in the Global Economy.* Ithaca, N.Y.: Cornell University Press.

Agustín, Laura Maria. 2007. *Sex at the Margins.* London: Zed Press.

Aja Díaz, Antonio. 2001. "La emigración cubana entre dos siglos." *Temas* 26 (July–September): 60–70.

Alexander, Jacqui M. 1994. "Not Just (Any) Body Can Be a Citizen: The Politics of Law, Sexuality, and Postcoloniality in Trinidad and Tobago and the Bahamas." *Feminist Review* 48 (Autumn): 5–23.

Allen, Jafari Sinclaire. 2003. "Counterpoints: Black Masculinities, Sexuality, and Self-Making in Contemporary Cuba." Ph.D. diss., Columbia University.

Alvarez, Julia. 1994. *In the Time of the Butterflies.* Chapel Hill, N.C.: Algonquin Books of Chapel Hill.

Alvarez, Sonia. 2000. "Translating the Global: Effects of Transnational Organizing on Local Feminist Discourses and Practices in Latin America." *Meridians* 1 (1): 29–67.

Anderson, Tim. 2001. "Island Socialism: Cuban Crisis and Structural Adjustment." *Journal of Australian Political Economy* 49: 56–86.

Arceneaux, Craig, and David Pion-Berlin. 2005. *Transforming Latin America: The International and Domestic Origins of Change.* Pittsburgh: University of Pittsburgh Press.

ASONAHORES (Asociación Nacional de Hoteles y Restaurantes, Inc.). 2005. Interview. Santo Domingo: Dominican Republic.

Atkins, Pope G. and Larman Curtis Wilson. 1998. *The Dominican Republic and the United States: From Imperialism to Transnationalism.* Athens, GA: University of Georgia Press.

Ayala, César J. 1999. *American Sugar Kingdom: The Plantation Economy of the Spanish Caribbean, 1898–1934.* Chapel Hill: University of North Carolina Press.

Azize Vargas, Yamila. 1997. "Latinoamericanas y caribeñas en el trabajo doméstico y sexual." Paper presented at the Reunión de ONG "Las mujeres y el desarrollo en América Latina y el Caribe," Santiago de Chile, 18 de noviembre.

Babb, Florence. Forthcoming. *The Tourism Encounter: Fashioning Latin American Nations and Histories.*

Báez, Antonio Carmona. 2004. *State Resistance to Globalisation in Cuba.* London: Pluto Press.

Baillie, J. Gerald. 1980. "Recent International Travel Trends in Canada." *Canadian Geographer,* 24 (1): 13–21.

Ballantyne, Tony, and Antoinette M. Burton. 2005. *Bodies in Contact: Rethinking Colonial Encounters in World History.* Durham, N.C.: Duke University Press.

Balseros. 2003. Directed by Carles Bosch and Josep Maria Domenech. Barcelona, España. HBO/Cinemax Documentary Films, Seventh Art Releasing

Bank Muñoz, Carolina. 2007. "The Tortilla Behemoth: Sexualized Despotism and Women's Resistance in a Transnational Mexican Tortilla Factory." In *The Wages of Empire: Neoliberal Policies, Repression and Women's Poverty,* edited by Amalia L. Cabezas, Ellen Reese, and Marguerite Waller, 127–139. Boulder, CO: Paradigm Press.

Barberia, Lorena. 2002. "Remittances to Cuba: An Evaluation of Cuban and U.S. Government Policy Measures." Working Paper 15, Harvard University, September.

Barnet, Miguel. 2001. *Afro-Cuba Religions.* Princeton, N.J.: Markus Weiner Publishers.

Barry, Kathleen. 1995. *The Prostitution of Sexuality*. New York: New York University Press.

Barry, Tom, Beth Wood, and Deb Preusch. 1984. *The Other Side of Paradise*. New York: Grove Press.

Beck, Marshall. 2001. "Cuenta-Propismo and Reform in Cuba: A Case Study." *Canadian Journal of Latin American and Caribbean Studies* 26 (52): 179–222.

Beck, Ulrich. 2000. *The Brave New World of Work*. Malden, Mass.: Polity Press.

Bell, Laurie, ed. 1987. *Good Girls/Bad Girls: Feminists and Sex Trade Workers Face to Face*. Seattle: Seal Press.

Bell, Shannon. 1994. *Reading, Writing and Rewriting the Prostitute Body*. Bloomington: Indiana University Press.

Benería, Lourdes, and Martha Roldán. 1987. *The Crossroads of Class and Gender: Industrial Homework, Subcontracting, and Household Dynamics in Mexico City*. Chicago: University of Chicago Press.

Benítez-Rojo, Antonio. 1992. *The Repeating Island: The Caribbean and the Postmodern Perspective*. Translated by James Maraniss. Durham, N.C.: Duke University Press.

Berg, Mette Louise. 2004. "'Sleeping with the Enemy': *Jineterismo*, 'Cultural Level' and 'Antisocial Behavior' in 1990's Cuba." In *Beyond the Blood, the Beach & the Banana*, edited by Sandra Courtman, 184–204. Kingston, Jamaica: Ian Randle.

Betances, Emelio, and Hobart A. Spalding Jr. 1995. "Introduction: The Dominican Republic; Social Change and Political Stagnation." *Latin American Perspectives* 22 (3): 3–19.

Bindman, Jo. 1997. *Redefining Prostitution as Sex Work on the International Agenda*. London: Anti-Slavery International.

Birkbeck, Chris. 1978. "Self-Employed Proletarians in an Informal Factory: The Case of Cali's Garbage Dump." *World Development* 6 (9–10): 1173–85.

Bishop, Ryan, and Lillian S. Robinson. 1998. *Night Market: Sexual Cultures and the Thai Economic Miracle*. New York: Routledge.

Bliss, Katherine Elaine. 2004. "A Right to Live as Gente Decente: Sex Work, Family Life, and Collective Identity in Early-Twentieth-Century Mexico." *Journal of Women's History* 15 (4): 164–169.

Bonilla, Juan. 1997. "Jefe de turismo estudiará fórmulas para control de la prostitución." *Periódico Hoy*, June 23.

Boorstein, Edward. 1968. *The Economic Transformation of Cuba*. New York: Modern Reader.

Bourdieu, Pierre. 1990. *In Other Words: Essays Towards a Reflexive Sociology*. Translated by Matthew Adamson. Stanford: Stanford University Press.

Bowman, Glenn. 1996. "Passion, Power, and Politics in a Palestinian Tourist Market." In *The Tourist Image: Myth and Myth Making in Tourism*, edited by Tom Selwyn, 83–103. New York and London: John Wiley & Sons Ltd.

Bradley, Colin. 1994. "U.S. Cuba Fulfilling Migration Deal." *Chicago Sun-Times,* September 14.

Brandon, George. 1993. *Santeria from Africa to the New World: The Dead Sell Memories.* Bloomington: Indiana University Press.

Brennan, Denise Ellen. 2004. *What's Love Got to Do with It? Transnational Desires and Sex Tourism in the Dominican Republic.* Durham, N.C.: Duke University Press.

Brenner, Philip, and Peter Kornbluh. 1995. *NACLA* 29 (2) (September–October): 33–40.

Britton, Stephen. 1982. "The Political Economy of Tourism in the Third World." *Annals of Tourism Research* 9: 331–58.

———. 1996. "Tourism, Dependency, and Development: A Mode of Analysis." In *The Sociology of Tourism: Theoretical and Empirical Investigations,* edited by Yiorgos Apostolopoulos, Stella Leivadi, and Andrew Yiannakis. New York: Routledge.

Buena Vista Social Club. 1998. Directed by Wim Wenders. Producer Ulrich Felsberg. Produced by Road Movies Filmproduktion. Berlin, Germany.

Bunch, Charlotte, and Susana Fried. 1996. "Beijing '95: Moving Women's Human Rights from Margin to Center." *Signs* 21 (3–4) (Autumn): 200–204.

Burgess, John. 1982. "Perspectives on Gift Exchange and Hospitable Behaviour." *International Journal of Hospitality Management* 1 (1): 49–57.

Butler, Judith. 1990. *Gender Trouble: Feminism and the Subversion of Identity.* New York: Routledge.

Cabezas, Amalia Lucía. 1998. "Pleasure and It's Pain: Sex Tourism in Sosúa, the Dominican Republic." Ph.D. diss., University of California, Berkeley.

———. "Discourses of Prostitution: The Case of Cuba." In *Global Sex Workers: Rights, Resistance, and Redefinition,* edited by Kamala Kempadoo and Joe Doezema, 79–86. New York: Routledge.

———. 1999. "Women's Work Is Never Done: Sex Tourism in Sosúa, the Dominican Republic." In *Sun, Sex, and Gold: Tourism and Sex Work in the Caribbean,* edited by Kamala Kempadoo, 93–123. Boulder, Colo.: Rowman and Littlefield.

———. 2004. "Between Love and Money: Sex, Tourism, and Citizenship in Cuba and the Dominican Republic." *Signs: Journal of Women in Culture* 29 (4): 987–1015.

———. 2005. "Accidental Crossings: Tourism Sex Work and Women's Rights in the Dominican Republic." In *Dialogue and Difference: Feminisms Challenge Globalization,* edited by Marguerite Waller and Sylvia Marcos, 201–229. New York: Palgrave MacMillan.

———. 2008. "Tropical Blues: Tourism and Social Exclusion in the Dominican Republic." *Latin American Perspectives* 160 (35): 21–36. May 2008.

Cantú, Lionel. 2002. "De Ambiente: Queer Tourism and the Shifting Boundaries of Mexican Male Sexualities." *GLQ* 8 (1): 141–168.

Carnoy, Martin (with Amber K. Gove and Jeffrey H. Marshall). 2007. *Cuba's Economic Advantage: Why Students in Cuba Do Better in School.* Palo Alto, CA: Stanford University Press.

Carranza Valdés, Julio, Luis Gutiérrez Urdantea, and Pedro Monreal González. 1996. *Cuba: Restructuring the Economy—A Contribution to the Debate.* London: Institute of Latin American Studies, University of London.

Carrier, James G., ed. 1997. *Meanings of the Market: the Free Market in Western Culture.* Oxford, England: Berg.

———. 1995. *Gifts and Commodities: Exchange and Western Capitalism Since 1700.* London and New York: Routledge.

Carter, Simon, and Stephen Clift. 2000. "Tourism, International Travel, and Sex: Themes and Research." In *Tourism and Sex: Culture, Commerce, and Coercion,* edited by Stephen Clift and Simon Carter, 1–22. London: Pinter.

Castañeda, Antonia. 1993. "Sexual Violence in the Politics and Policies of Conquest: Amerindian Women and the Spanish Conquest of Alta California." In *Building with Our Hands: New Directions in Chicana Studies,* edited by Adela de la Torre and Beatríz M. Pesquera, 15–33. Berkeley: University of California Press.

Castellanos de Selig, Grethel. 1981. "Bases para una política nacional de desarrollo turístico y estrategia para este desarollo." Paper prepared for the II Convención Nacional de Turismo, Puerto Plata.

Castro, Fidel. 1988. "Castro Discusses Tourism Plans, Medical Issues." http://lanic.utexas.edu/project/castro/db/1988/19880927–1.html.

———. 1995. *Salvar la justicia conquistada.* Clausura del VI Congreso de la Federación de Mujeres Cubanas, March 3. Havana: Editorial Política.

Censo Nacional de Población y Vivienda. 2002. Havana, Cuba.

Centers for Disease Control. 1994. "International Notes Epidemic Neuropathy—Cuba, 1991–1994." *MMWR Weekly* 43 (10) (March 18, 1994): 183, 189–92. http://www.cdc.gov/mmwr/preview/mmwrhtml/00025761.htm.

CEPROSH (Centro de Promoción y Solidaridad Humana). 1996. *Infosida* [newsletter]. Puerto Plata: COVICOSIDA, July.

Cerviño, Julio, and Jaime Bonache. 2005. "Hotel Management in Cuba and the Transfer of Best Practices." *International Journal of Contemporary Hospitality Management* 17 (6): 455–468.

CESDEM (Centro de Estudios Sociales y Demográficos). 1996. "Encuesta sobre conocimientos, creencias, actitudes y prácticas acerca del SIDA/ETS en trabajadoras sexuales y hombres involucrados en la industria del sexo en las localidades de Puerto Plata, Sosúa y Monte Llano." Mimeo. COVICOSIDA, Puerto Plata.

Chapkis, Wendy. 1997. *Live Sex Acts: Women Performing Erotic Labor.* New York: Routledge.

Chester, Eric Thomas. 2001. *Rag-Tags, Scum, Riff-Raff, and Commies: The U.S. Intervention in the Dominican Republic, 1965–66.* New York: Monthly Review.

Clark, Mary Ann. 2005. *Where Men are Wives and Mothers Rule: Santería Ritual Practices and Their Gender Implications.* Gainesville, FL: University of Florida Press.

Código Penal. 1998. Havana: Editorial de Ciencias Sociales.

Cohen, Jeff. 1991. "Cuba Libre." *Playboy* 38 (March): 69–74.

Colantonio, Andrea. 2004. "Tourism in Havana During the Special Period: Impacts, Residents' Perceptions, and Planning Issues." *Cuba in Transition*— Association for the Study of the Cuban Economy, ASCE, Miami, (14): 20–43. http://lanic.utexas.edu/project/asce/pdfs/volume14/colantonio.pdf.

Cole, Jennifer. 2004. "Fresh Contact in Tamatave, Madagascar: Sex, Money, and Intergenerational Transformation." *American Ethnologist* 31 (4) (November): 573–88.

Coles, Tim. "What Makes a Resort Complex? Reflections on the Production of Tourism Space in a Caribbean Resort Complex." In *Tourism in the Caribbean: Trends, Development, and Prospects,* edited by David Timothy Duval, 235–256. New York: Routledge.

Conner, Randy P., with David Hatfield Sparks. 2004. *Queering Creole Spiritual Traditions: Lesbian, Gay, Bisexual, and Transgender Participation in African-inspired Traditions in the Americas.* New York: Harrington Park Press.

Constable, Nicole. 2003. *Romance on a Global Stage: Pen Pals, Virtual Ethnography, and "Mail Order" Marriages.* Berkeley: University of California Press.

Cooper, Marc. 1995. "For Sale: Used Marxism." *Harper's Magazine* March: 54–66.

Crick, Anne P. 2002. "Glad to Meet You—My Best Friend: Relationships in the Hospitality Industry." *Social and Economic Studies* 51 (1): 99–125.

———. 2001. "Personalised Service in the New Economy: Implications for Small Island Tourism." *Journal of Eastern Caribbean Studies* 26 (1): 1–20, (March).

Crick, Malcolm. 1992. "Life in the Informal Sector: Street Guides in Kandy, Sir Lanka." In *Tourism and the Less Developed Countries,* edited by David Harrison, 135–147. London: England: Belhaven Press.

———. 1995. "The Anthropologists as Tourist: An Identity in Question." In *International Tourism: Identity and Change,* edited by Marie-Françoise Lanfant, John B. Allcock, and Edward M. Bruner, 205–223. Thousand Oaks, Calif.: Sage Publications.

———. 1996. "Representations of International Tourism in the Social Sciences: Sun, Sex, Sights, Savings, and Servility." In *The Sociology of Tourism:*

Theoretical and Empirical Investigations, edited by Yiorgos Apostolopoulos, Stella Leivadi, and Andrew Yiannakis. New York: Routledge.

Cuba in Figures. 2002. National Office of Statistics. Havana: Cuba.

Dahles, Heidi. 1998. "Of Birds and Fish: Street Guides, Tourists, and Sexual Encounters in Yogyakarta, Indonesia." In *Sex Tourism and Prostitution,* edited by M. Oppermann, 30–41. New York: Cognizant Communication Corporation.

Dahles, Heidi, and Karin Bras. 1999. "Entrepreneurs in Romance: Tourism in Indonesia." *Annals of Tourism Research* 26: 267–93.

Darling, Lynn. 1995. "Havana at Midnight." *Esquire* (May): 96–104.

De Albuquerque, Klaus. 1998. "Sex, Beach Boys and Female Tourists in the Caribbean." *Sexuality and Culture* 2: 87–111.

De Córdoba, José. 1992. "Cuba Embargo Is Tightened in House Vote." *Wall Street Journal,* September 25.

Deere, Carmen Diana, Peggy Antrobus, Lynn Bolles, Edwin Melendez, Peter Phillips, Marcia Rivera, and Helen Safa, eds. 1990. *In the Shadows of the Sun: Caribbean Development Alternatives and U.S. Policy.* Boulder, Colo.: Westview Press.

Delacoste, Frederique, and Priscilla Alexander, eds. 1987. *Sex Work: Writings by Women in the Sex Industry.* Pittsburgh: Cleis Press.

de la Fuente, Alejandro. 2001. "Recreating Racism: Race and Discrimination in Cuba's 'Special Period.'" *Socialism and Democracy* 15 (1): 65–91.

del Olmo, Rosa. 1979. "The Cuban Revolution and the Struggle against Prostitution." *Crime and Social Justice* (Winter): 34–40.

D'Emilio, John. 1993. "Capitalism and Gay Identity." In *The Gender/Sexuality Reader: Culture, History, Political Economy,* edited by Roger N. Lancaster and Micaela di Leonardo, 169–179. New York: Routledge.

D'Hauteserre, Anne-Marie. 2004. "Postcolonialism, Colonialism, and Tourism." In *A Companion to Tourism,* edited by Alan A. Lew, C. Michael Hall, and Allan M. Williams, 235–245. London: Blackwell Publishing.

Díaz, Alvaro. 1997. "New Developments in Economic and Social Restructuring in Latin America." In *Politics, Social Change, and Economic Restructuring in Latin America,* edited by William C. Smith and Roberto Patricio Korzeniewicz, 37–52. Boulder, Colo.: Lynne Rienner Publishers.

Díaz, Ileana. 2000. "Cuba: Igualdad de oportunidades." Paper presented at the 22nd Congreso de Latin American Studies Association (LASA 2000), Miami, Fla., March 16–18.

Diaz Tenorio, Mareelen. 2000. "La familia Cubana antes la crisis de los 90" Paper presented at the 22nd Congreso de Latin American Studies Association (LASA 2000), Miami, Fla., March 16–18.

Duany, Jorge. 2005. "Dominican Migration to Puerto Rico: A Transnational Perspective." *Centro Journal,* (XVII) 001: 242–269.

Duval, David Timothy, and Paul F. Wilkinson. 2004. "Tourism Development in the Caribbean: Meaning and Influences." In *Tourism in the Caribbean: Trends, Development, and Prospects,* edited by David Timothy Duval, 59–80. New York: Routledge.

Ebron, Paula. 2002. *Performing Africa.* Princeton, N.J.: Princeton University Press.

————. 1997. "Traffic in Men." In *Gendered Encounters: Challenging Cultural Boundaries and Social Hierarchies in Africa,* edited by Maria Grosz-Ngaté and Omari H. Kokole. New York: Routledge.

Eckstein, Susan Eva. 2003. *Back from the Future: Cuba under Castro.* New York: Routledge.

Ehrenreich, Barbara, and Arlie Russell Hochschild. 2003. *Global Woman: Nannies, Maids, and Sex Workers in the New Economy.* New York: Metropolitan Books.

Enloe, Cynthia. 1989. *Bananas, Beaches, and Bases: Making Feminist Sense of International Politics.* Berkeley: University of California Press.

Ertman, Martha M. 2005. "What's Wrong with a Parenthood Market? A New and Improved Theory of Commodification." In *Rethinking Commodification: Cases and Readings in Law and Culture.* edited by Martha M. Ertman and Joan C. Williams, 303–323. New York: New York University Press.

Ertman, Martha M., and Joan C. Williams, eds. 2005. *Rethinking Commodification: Cases and Readings in Law and Culture.* New York: New York University Press.

Espina, Mayra. 2008. "Viejas y nuevas desigualdades en Cuba: Ambivalencias y perspectivas de la reestratificación social." *Nueva Sociedad* 216: 133–149. (julio-agosto).

Espinal, Rosario. 1995. "Economic Restructuring, Social Protest, and Democratization in the Dominican Republic." *Latin American Perspectives* 22 (3): 63–69.

Espino, María Dolores. 1991. "International Tourism in Cuba: An Economic Development Strategy?" In *Cuba in Transition.* Association for the Study of the Cuban Economy, 1: http://lanic.utexas.edu/la/cb/cuba/asce/cuba1/espino.html

Facio, Elisa. 2000. "*Jineterismo* during the Special Period." In *Cuba: Transitions at the End of the Millennium,* edited by Eloise Linger and John Cotman, 55–74. Maryland: International Development Options.

Fanon, Frantz. 1963. *The Wretched of the Earth.* New York: Grove Press.

Farias Monge, Aquiles O. 1973. "Fuente de financiamiento nacionales y extrajeras." Paper presented at the Convención Nacional de Turismo República Dominicana, Puerto Plata, March 31–April 3.

Fedarko, Kevin. 1996. "Cold War Is Back." *Time* March 11, 37–38.

Feinsilver, Julie. 1993. *Healing the Masses: Cuban Health Politics at Home and Abroad.* Berkeley: University of California Press.

Feliz, Raysa. 2000. "Trabajadoras sexuales se organizan." *El Pais* (Santo Domingo, Dominican Republic): March 12.

Ferber, Marianne A., and Jane Waldfogel. 1999. "Contingent Labor." In *The Elgar Companion to Feminist Economics,* edited by Janice Peterson and Margaret Lewis, 77–82. Northampton, Mass.: Edward Elgar.

Ferguson, James. 1992. *Beyond the Lighthouse.* London: Latin American Bureau.

Fernández, Nadine. 1999. "Back to the Future? Women, Race, and Tourism in Cuba." In *Sun, Sex, and Gold: Tourism and Sex Work in the Caribbean,* edited by Kamala Kempadoo. Boulder, Colo.: Rowman and Littlefield.

Fernández Olmos, Margarite, ed. 1997. *Sacred Possessions: Vodou, Santería, Obeah, and the Caribbean.* New Brunswick, N.J.: Rutgers University Press.

Fernández Olmos, Margarite, and Lizabeth Paravisini-Gebert. 2003. *Creole Religions of the Caribbean: An Introduction from Vodou and Santería to Obeah and Espiritismo.* New York: New York University Press.

Fernández Robaina, Tomás. 1998. *Historias de mujeres públicas.* Havana: Editorial Letras Cubanas.

Filby, M. P. 1992. "The Figures, the Personality, and the Bums." *Work, Employment, and Society* 6 (1): 23–42.

Fletcher, Pascal. 1999. "Human Tide Ebbs Softly from Cuba's Shore." *Financial Times Limited,* August 3.

Folbre, Nancy, and Julie A. Nelson. 2000. "For Love or Money—or Both?" *Journal of Economic Perspectives* 14 (4) (Autumn): 123–40.

Fosado, Gisela. 2004. "The Exchange of Sex for Money in Contemporary Cuba: Masculinity, Ambiguity, and Love." Ph.D. diss., University of Michigan.

Freeman, Carla. 2000. *High Tech and High Heels in the Global Economy: Women, Work, and Pink-Collar Identitites in the Caribbean.* Durham, N.C.: Duke University Press.

Freitag, Tilman G. 1994. "Enclave Tourism Development: For Whom the Benefits Roll?" *Annals of Tourism Research* 21 (3): 538–54.

Fusco, Coco. 1996. "Hustling for Dollars." *Ms. Magazine* (September–October): 62–70.

Gall, Gregory. 2006. *Sex Worker Union Organizing.* New York: Palgrave Macmillan.

Gilbert, David, Yvonne Guerrier, and Jonathan Guy. 1998. "Sexual Harassment Issues in the Hospitality Industry." *International Journal of Contemporary Hospitality Management* 10 (2) (February): 48–53.

Gilfoyle, Timothy J. 1999. "Prostitutes in History: From Parables of Pornography to Metaphors of Modernity." *The American Historical Review* 104 (1): 117–141

Glazer, John, and Kurt Hollander. 1992. "Cuba's New Economy: Working for the Tourist Dollar." *Nation,* June 15, 820–824.

Golden, Tim. 1993. "Castro's People Try to Absorb 'Terrible Blows.'" *New York Times,* January 11.

González, Deena J. 1999. *Refusing the Favor: The Spanish-Mexican Women of Santa Fe, 1820–1880.* London: Oxford University Press.

Gorz, André. 1999. *Reclaiming Work: Beyond the Wage-Based Society.* Cambridge, U.K.: Polity Press.

Gott, Gill. 2002. "Imperial Humanitarianism: History of an Arrested Dialectic." In *Moral Imperialism: A Critical Anthology,* edited by Berta Esperanza Hernández-Truyol, 19–38. New York: New York University Press.

Graburn, Nelson H. 1983. "The Anthropology of Tourism." *Annals of Tourism Research* 10: 9–33.

Graburn, Nelson H. with Diane Barthel-Bouchier. 2001. "Relocating the Tourist." *International Sociology* 16 (2): 147–158.

Greenwood, Davyd J. 1989. "Culture by the Pound: An Anthropological Perspective on Tourism as Cultural Commodification." In *Hosts and Guests: The Anthropology of Tourism,* edited by Valene Smith, 171–186. Philadelphia: University of Pennsylvania Press.

Gregory, Steven. 2007. *The Devil behind the Mirror: Globalization and Politics in the Dominican Republic.* Berkeley: University of California Press,

Guillén, Nicolás. 1974. "Tengo."¡*Patria o Muerte! The Great Zoo and Other Poems by Nicolás Guillén,* edited and translated by Robert Márquez, 190–195. New York: Monthly Review Press.

Guerrier, Yvonne, and Amel S. Adib. 2004a. "Gendered Identities in the Work of Overseas Tour Reps." *Gender, Work, and Organization* 11 (3) (May): 334–50.

———. 2004b. "'No, We Don't Provide That Service': The Harassment of Hotel Employees by Customers." *Work, Employment, and Society* 14 (4): 689–705.

Guevara, Ernesto Che. 1975. *El socialismo y el hombre en Cuba.* Barcelona: Editorial Anagrama.

Gutiérrez, Pedro Juan. 1997. "Migración internal: Prevenir el caos." *Bohemia,* July 18.

Guy, Donna J. 2000. *White Slavery and Mothers Alive and Dead: The Troubled Meeting of Sex, Gender, Public Health, and Progress in Latin America.* Lincoln: University of Nebraska Press.

Hagedorn, Katherine J. 2001. *Divine Utterances: The Performance of Afro-Cuban Santeria.* Washington, D.C.: Smithsonian Institution Press.

Hall, Elaine. 1993. "Smiling, Deferring, and Flirting: Doing Gender by Giving 'Good Service.'" *Work and Occupations* 20 (4): 452–71.

Hall, Michael. 1994. "Gender and Economic Interests in Tourism Prostitution: the Nature, Development and Implications of Sex Tourism in South-east Asia." In *Tourism: A Gender Analysis,* edited by V. Kinnaird and D. Hall, 142–163. Chichester: John Wiley and Sons.

Hall, Michael R. 2000. *Sugar and Power in the Dominican Republic: Eisenhower, Kennedy, and the Trujillos.* Westport, Conn.: Greenwood Press.

Hamilton, Douglas. 2002. "Whither Cuban Socialism? The Changing Political Economy of the Cuban Revolution." *Latin American Perspectives* 29 (3): 18–39.

Havana Journal. 2005. "Varadero Cuba since 1887." http://havanajournal.com/travel/entry/varadero_cuba_since_1887/

Herdt, Gilbert H. 1980. *Guardians of the Flutes: Idioms of Masculinity.* New York: McGraw-Hill.

Hernández, Tanya K. 2000. "An Exploration of the Efficacy of Class-Based Approaches to Racial Justice: The Cuban Context." *University of California Davis Law Review* 33 (4): 1142–51.

———. 2005. "Sex in the [Foreign] City: Commodification and the Female Sex Tourist." In *Rethinking Commodification: Cases and Readings in Law and Culture,* edited by Martha M. Ertman and Joan C. Williams, 222–242. New York: New York University Press.

Hernández-Truyol, Berta, and Jane E. Larson. 2002. "Both Work and Violence: Prostitution and Human Rights." In *Moral Imperialism: A Critical Anthology,* edited by Berta Esperanza Hernández-Truyol, 183–211. New York: New York University Press.

Herold, Edward, Rafael García, and Tony de Moya. 2001. "Female Tourists and Beach Boys: Romance or Sex Tourism?" *Annals of Tourism Research* 28 (4): 978–97.

Hilario, David. 2004. "Tragedia estremece familiars de yoleros: El noreste llora a los Muertos del frustrado viaje." *El Caribe.* August 12.

Hirsch, Jennifer S., and Holly Wardlow. 2006. *Modern Loves: The Anthropology of Romantic Courtship and Companionate Marriage.* Ann Arbor: University of Michigan Press.

Hochschild, Arlie. 1983. *The Managed Heart: Commercialization of Human Feeling.* Berkeley: University of California Press.

Hodalgo Fernández, Isabel. 2000. *"¡No es facil!"* Barcelona: Icaria/Antrazyt.

Hodge, Derrick. 2001. "Colonization of the Cuban Body: The Growth of Male Sex Work in Havana." *NACLA* 34 (5) (March–April): 20–23.

———. 2005. "Colonization of the Cuban Body: Nationalism, economy, and masculinity of male sex work in Havana." Ph.D. diss., City University of New York.

Hondagneu-Sotelo, Pierrette. 2001. *Doméstica: Immigrant Workers Cleaning and Caring in the Shadows of Affluence.* Berkeley: University of California Press.

Hoy. 2000. "Trabajadoras sexuales piden del Gobierno servicios de salud gratuitos y de calidad." Santo Domingo, Dominican Republic. April 12: 20.

ILO (International Labour Organization). 2001. *Human Resources Development, Employment and Globalization in the Hotel, Catering and Tourism Sector.* Geneva: International Labour Office.

———. 2002. *Women and Men in the Informal Economy: A Statistical Picture.* Geneva: International Labour Office.

International Labour Office. 1972. *Employment, Incomes and Inequality: A Strategy for Increasing Productive Employment in Kenya.* Geneva: International Labour Office.

Ioannides, Dimitri, and Keith G. Debbage, eds. 1998. *The Economic Geography of the Tourism Industry: A Supply-Side Analysis.* London: Routledge

Itzigsohn, José. 2000. *Developing Poverty: The State, Labor Market Deregulation, and the Informal Economy in Costa Rica and the Dominican Republic.* University Park: Pennsylvania State University Press.

Iyer, Pico. 1995. *Cuba and the Night: A Novel.* New York: Knopf.

Jensen, Camilla. 2003. "Socialism, Spillovers and Markets in Cuba." *Post-Communist Economies* 15 (3) (September): 435–59.

Jiménez, Felucho. 1999. *El turismo en la economía Dominicana.* Santo Domingo: Secretaría de Estado de Turismo.

Johnson-Hanks, Jennifer. 2007. "Women on the Market: Marriage, Consumption, and the Internet in Urban Cameroon." *American Ethnologist* 4 (4) (November): 642–659.

Joseph, Miranda. 2005. "The Multivalent Commodity: On the Supplementarity of Value and Values." In *Rethinking Commodification: Cases and Readings in Law and Culture,* edited by Martha M. Ertman and Joan C. Williams, 383–401. New York: New York University Press.

Judson, Fred. 1992. "Cuba and the New World Order." *Monthly Review* (December): 28–39.

Kaplowitz, Donna Rich. 1998. *Anatomy of A Failed Embargo: U.S. Sanctions Against Cuba.* Boulder, Colo.: L. Rienner.

Keller, Peter. 2002. "Introductory Report in WTO Strategic Group: Tourism in a Globalized Society." Madrid, Spain: World Tourism Organization.

Kelsky, Karen. 1994 "Intimate Ideologies: Transnational Theory and Japan's 'Yellow Cabs.'" *Public Culture* 6: 465–78.

Kempadoo, Kamala. 1998. "COIN and MODEMU in the Dominican Republic." In *Global Sex Workers: Rights, Resistance, and Redefinition,* edited by Kamala Kempadoo and Jo Doezema, 260–267. New York: Routledge.

———, ed. 1999. *Sun, Sex, and Gold: Tourism and Sex Work in the Caribbean.* Boulder, Colo.: Rowman and Littlefield.

———. 2004. *Sexing the Caribbean.* New York: Routledge.

Kempadoo, Kamala, and Jo Doezema, eds. 1998. *Global Sex Workers: Rights, Resistance, and Redefinition.* New York: Routledge.

Kendall. 1999. "Women in Lesotho and the (Western) Construction of Homophobia." In *Female Desire: Same-Sex Relations and Transgender Practices across Cultures,* edited by Evelyn Blackwood and Saskia E. Wieringa, 157–178. New York: Columbia University Press.

Kincaid, Jamaica. 1988. *A Small Place.* New York: Farrar, Straus, Giroux.

Kinnaird, Vivian, and Derek Hall, eds. 1994. *Tourism: A Gender Analysis.* London: John Wiley.

Komter, Aafke E., ed. 1996. *The Gift: An Interdisciplinary Perspective.* Amsterdam: University of Amsterdam Press.

———. 2005. *Social Solidarity and The Gift.* Cambridge, UK: Cambridge University Press,

Kumar, Corinne. 2005. "South Wind: Towards a New Political Imaginary." In *Dialogue and Difference: Feminisms Challenge Globalization,* edited by Marguerite Waller and Sylvia Marcos, 165–199. New York: Palgrave MacMillan.

Lacsamana, Anne E. 2004. "Sex Worker or Prostituted Woman? An Examination of the Sex Work Debates in Western Feminist Theory." In *Women and Globalization,* edited by Delia D. Aguilar and Anne E. Lacsamana, 387–403. New York: Humanity Books.

LaForgia, Gerard, Ruth Levine, Arismendi Diaz, and Magadalne Rathe. 2004. "Fend for Yourself: Systemic Failure in the Dominican Health System." *Health Policy* 67: 173–186.

LaFranchi, Howard. 1997. "Havana Rolls out Un-welcome Mat for Its Country Cousins." *Christian Science Monitor,* October 6.

Landau, Saul. 1992. "The Torricelli Bill: Tightening the Chokehold on Cuba." *Nation,* June 15, 818–19.

———. 2002. "The Day the Counterrevolutionaries Had Waited for Arrived, y en eso llegó Fidel." *Latin American Perspectives,* 29 (4) (July): 77–79.

Lea, John. 1988. *Tourism and Development in the Third World.* New York: Routledge.

Leidner, Robin. 1999. "Emotional Labor in Service Work." *Annals of the American Academy of Political and Social Science* 561 (January): 81–95.

López, Juan J. 1998. "Implications of the U.S. Economic Embargo for a Political Transition in Cuba." *Cuban Studies* 28: 40–69.

López Vigil, María. 1999. *Cuba: Neither Heaven nor Hell.* Washington, D.C.: Ecumenical Program on Central America and the Caribbean (EPICA).

Lorde, Audre. 1984. "The Master's Tool Will Never Dismantle the Master's House." In *Sister Outsider.* Freedom, Calif.: Crossing Press.

Löwy, Michael. 2007. *The Marxism of Che Guevara: Philosophy, Economics, Revolutionary Warfare.* 2nd ed. Lanham, Maryland: Rowman and Littlefield.

Lucas, Ann. 2005. "The Currency of Sex: Prostitution, Law, and Commodification." In *Rethinking Commodification: Cases and Readings in Law and Culture*, edited by Martha M. Ertman and Joan C. Williams, 469–514. New York: New York University Press.

Lumsden, Ian. 1996. *Machos, Maricones, and Gays: Cuba and Homosexuality.* Philadelphia: Temple University Press.

Lutjens, Sheryl L. 1995. "Reading between the Lines: Women, the State, and Rectification in Cuba." *Latin American Perspectives* 85 (22): 100–124.

———. 1996. "Fixing Filtraciones: Centralization, the State, and the 1990s in Cuba." *Cuban Studies* 26: 1–33.

Lutz, Catherine. 2004. "Militarization." In *A Companion to the Anthropology of Politics*, edited by David Nugent and Joan Vincent, 317–331. Malden, Mass.: Blackwell Publishing.

Macdonald, Cameron Lynne, and Carmen Sirianni. 1996. "The Service Society and the Changing Experience of Work." In *Working in the Service Economy*, edited by Cameron Lynne Macdonald and Carmen Sirianni, 1–26. Philadelphia: Temple University Press.

Mañon, Melvin. 1986. *Cambio de Mandos.* Santo Domingo: Taller.

Martín de Holán, P., and N. Phillips. 1997. "Sun, Sand, and Hard Currency: The Cuban Tourism Industry." *Annals of Tourism Research* 24 (4) (October): 777–95.

Martínez, Milagros. 1998. "El factor migratorio en las relacciones Cuba–Estados Unidos." In *Cuba: Período especial, perspectivas*, edited by José A. Moreno, Miurka Pérez Rojas, Mark B. Ginsburg, Frank McGlynn, Esteban Morales Domínguez, Jorge Hernández Martínez, Cary Torres Vila, Gilberto Cabrera Trimiño, Gerardo Trueba González, Graciela Chailloux Laffita, María Isabel Domínguez García, and Norma Vasallo, 72–82. Havana: Barrueta, Editorial de Ciencias Sociales.

Mauss, Marcel. 1990. *The Gift: The Form and Reason for Exchange in Archaic Societies.* London: Routledge.

McClintock, Anne. 1995. *Imperial Leather: Race, Gender, and Sexuality in the Colonial Conquest.* New York: Routledge.

McGarrity, Gayle, and Osvaldo Cárdenas. 1995. "Cuba." In *No Longer Invisible*, edited by Minority Rights Group, 77–107. London: Minority Rights Publication.

Meethan, Kevin. 2004. "Transnational Corporations, Globalization, and Tourism." In *A Companion to Tourism*, edited by Alan A. Lew, C. Michael Hall, and Allan M. Williams. London: Blackwell Publishing.

Meillón, Cynthia. 2001. *Holding on to the Promise: Women's Human Rights and the Beijing+5 Review.* New Brunswick, N.J Rutgers: Center for Women's Global Leadership.

Meisch, L. A. 1995. "Gringas and Otaveleños: Changing Tourist Relations." *Annals of Tourism Research* 22: 441–62.

Metz, Allan. 1990. "Why Sosua? Trujillo's Motives for Jewish Refugees Settlement in the Dominican Republic." *Contemporary Jewry* 11 (1): 3–28.

Merry, Sally Engle. 2006. *Human Rights and Gender Violence: Translating International Law into Local Justice.* Chicago: University of Chicago Press.

Mesa-Lago, Carmelo. 2002. "Growing Inequalities and Social Disparities in Cuba: Impact and Recommendations for Change." Institute for Cuban and Cuban-American Studies, University of Miami, Miami, Fla. http://ctp.iccas.miami.edu/research_studies/cmesalago.pdf

Michaloski, Raymond J., and Marjorie S. Zatz. 1990. "The Cuban Second Economy in Perspective." In *The Second Economy in Marxist States,* edited by Maria Los, 101–121. New York: St. Martin's Press.

Miller, Mark M., and Tony L. Henthorne. 1997. *Investment in the New Cuban Tourist Industry: A General Guide to Entrepreneurial Opportunities.* Westport, Conn.: Quorum Books.

Millman, Joel. 1994. "Fidel's New Friends." *Forbes,* February 28, 66–68.

Milne, Simon, and Gordon Ewing. 2004. "Community Participation in Caribbean Tourism: Problems and Prospects." In *Tourism in the Caribbean: Trends, Development, Prospects,* edited by David Timothy Duval, 205–217. London: Routledge.

Minca, Claudio, and Tim Oakes, eds. 2006. *Travels in Paradox: Remapping Tourism.* Lanham, MD: Rowman and Littlefield Publishers.

MODEMU with Laura Murray. 2002. *Laughing on the Outside, Crying on the Inside.* Santo Domingo, Dominican Republic. Editora Gonzalito.

Molyneux, Maxine. 1996. *State, Gender, and Institutional Change in Cuba's "Special Period": The Federación de Mujeres Cubanas.* London: Institute of Latin American Studies.

Morales Domínguez, Esteban. 1998. "Retos de Cuba frente a la política de Estados Unidos en la segunda mitad de la década de los años 90." In *Cuba: Período especial, perspectivas,* edited by José A. Moreno, Miurka Pérez Rojas, Mark B. Ginsburg, Frank McGlynn, Esteban Morales Domínguez, Jorge Hernández Martínez, Cary Torres Vila, Gilberto Cabrera Trimiño, Gerardo Trueba González, Graciela Chailloux Laffita, María Isabel Domínguez García, and Norma Vasallo. Havana: Editorial de Ciencias Sociales.

Moya Pons, Frank. 1995. *The Dominican Republic: A National History.* New Rochelle, N.Y.: Hispaniola Books.

Mullings, Beverly. 1999. "Globalization, Tourism, and the International Sex Trade." In *Sun, Sex, and Gold: Tourism and Sex Work in the Caribbean,* edited by Kamala Kempadoo. Boulder, Colo.: Rowman and Littlefield.

———. 2004. "Globalization and the Territorialization of the New Caribbean Service Economy." *Journal of Economic Geography* 4: 275–98.

Murray, Mary. 1992. *Cruel and Unusual Punishment: The U.S. Blockade against Cuba*. Melbourne: Ocean Press.

Nagle, Jill. 1997. *Whores and Other Feminists*. New York: Routledge.

Nash, Dennison. 1977. "Tourism as a Form of Imperialism." In *The Anthropology of Tourism*, edited by Valene L. Smith, 33–47. Philadelphia: University of Pennsylvania Press.

Navarrete, Julio, and Francisco Calderón. 1997. "Grupos Mantienen Llamado a una Huelga del Nordeste." *Listín Diario*, Julio 1: 1.

Núñez Moreno, Lilia. 1997. "Más allá del cuentrapropismo." *Temas* 11: 41–59.

Núñez Sarmiento, Marta. 2004. "Ideología de género entre profesionales cubanos." *Temas* 37–38 (April–September): 24–36.

Nussbaum, Martha. 2005. "Taking Money for Bodily Services." In *Rethinking Commodification: Cases and Readings in Law and Culture*, edited by Martha M. Ertman and Joan C. Williams, 243–270. New York: New York University Press.

O'Connell Davidson, Julia. 1996. "Sex Tourism in Cuba." *Race and Class* 38: 39–48.

———. 1998. *Prostitution, Power, and Freedom*. Ann Arbor: University of Michigan Press.

OertoOn, Sarah, and Joanna Phoenix. 2001. "Sex/Bodywork: Discourses and Practices." *Sexualities* 4 (4): 387–412.

Oficina Nacional de Estadísticas. 2002. *Censo Nacional de Población y Vivienda*. Santo Domingo, Dominican Republic.

Oppermann, Martin. 1999. "Sex Tourism." *Annals of Tourism Research* 26 (2): 251–66.

Orozco, Manuel. 2002. "Attracting Remittances: Market, Money, and Reduced Costs." Report commissioned by the Multilateral Investment Fund of the Inter-American Development Bank, Washington, D.C., January 28.

Our House in Havana. 2000. Directed and Produced by Stephen Olsson. Co-produced by Carolyn Zaff. Cultural and Educational Media. Sausalito, CA.

Padilla, Mark. 2007. *Caribbean Pleasure Industry: Tourism, Sexuality, and AIDS in the Dominican Republic*. Chicago: University of Chicago Press.

Parreñas, Rhacel. 2001. *Servants of Globalization: Women, Migration and Domestic Work*. Stanford: Stanford University Press.

Pasternostro, Silvana. 2000. "Sexual Revolution." *New Republic* 4 (460–61): 18–22

Pastor, Manuel, Jr., and Andrew Zimbalist. 1995a. "Cuba's Economic Conundrum." *NACLA* 29 (2): 7–12.

———. 1995b. "Waiting for Change: Adjustment and Reform in Cuba." *World Development* 23 (5): 705–20.

———. 1997. "Has Cuba Turned the Corner? Macroeconomic Stabilization and Reform in Contemporary Cuba." *Cuban Studies* 27: 1–20.

Pateman, Carole. 1988. *The Sexual Contract.* Stanford: Stanford University Press.

Pattullo, Polly. 1996. *Last Resorts: The Cost of Tourism in the Caribbean.* London: Cassell.

Pearson, Ruth. 1996. Foreword to *Cuba: Restructuring the Economy—A Contribution to the Debate,* edited by Carranza Valdés, Gutiérrez Urdaneta, and Monreal González, 1–7. London: England. Institute of Latin American Studies.

Pérez, Emma. 1998. "Irigaray's Female Symbolic in the Making of Chicana Lesbian Sitios y Lenguas (Sites and Discourses)." In *Living Chicana Theory,* edited by Carla Trujillo. Berkeley, Calif.: Third Women Press.

Pérez, Louis A., Jr. 1995. *Cuba: Between Reform and Revolution.* 2nd ed. New York: Oxford University Press.

Pérez-López, Jorge F. 1995. *Cuba's Second Economy: From Behind the Scenes to Center Stage.* New Brunswick, NJ: Transaction Publishers.

Pérez Sarduy, Pedro, and Jean Stubbs. 2000. *Afro-Cuban Voices: On Race and Identity in Contemporary Cuba.* Gainesville: University Press of Florida.

Petchesky, Rosalind. 2000. "Sexual Rights: Inventing a Concept, Mapping an International Practice." In *Framing the Sexual Subject: The Politics of Gender, Sexuality, and Power,* edited by Richard Parker Regina Maria Barbosa, and Peter Aggleton, 81–102. Berkeley: University of California Press.

Petchesky, Rosalind, and Sonia Correa. 1994. "Reproductive and Sexual Rights: A Feminist Perspective." In *Population Policies Reconsidered: Health, Empowerment, and Rights,* edited by Gita Sen, Adrienne Germain, and Lincoln C. Chen. Boston: Harvard School of Public Health.

Placencia, Luchy. 1997. "Estima fracasaría plan zonas de tolerancia." *Ultima Hora.* Santo Domingo, Dominican Republic (July 13): 51.

Poon, Auliana. 1990. "Flexible Specialization and Small Size: The Case of Caribbean Tourism." *World Development* 18 (1): 109–23.

Portes, Alejandro, Manuel Castells, and Lauren A. Benton, eds. 1989. *The Informal Economy: Studies in Advanced and Less Developed Countries.* Baltimore: Johns Hopkins University Press.

Portes, Alejandro, and Richard Schauffler. 1993. "Competing Perspectives on the Latin American Informal Sector." *Population and Development Review* 19: 33–60.

Press, Clayton M., Jr. 1978. "Reputation and Respectability Reconsidered: Hustling in a Tourist Setting." *Caribbean Issues* 4: 109–19.

Preston-Whyte, Eleanor, et al. 2000. "Survival Sex and HIV/AIDS in an African City." In *Framing the Sexual Subject: The Politics of Gender, Sexuality, and Power*, edited by Richard Parker Regina Maria Barbosa, and Peter Aggleton, 165–190. Berkeley: University of California Press.

Pruitt, Deborah, and Suzanne LaFont. 1995. "Love and Money: Romance Tourism in Jamaica." *Annals of Tourism Research* 22: 422–40.

PSTT (Private Sector Trade Team). 2004. "Anticompetitive Practices in the Global Tourism Industry: Implications for Barbados." August 1–14. http://tradeteam.bb/cms/pstt/files/issues/Anticompetitive_Practices_Issue_Paper.pdf.

¿Quien diablos es Juliette? (Who the hell is Juliette?): 1998. Directed and produced by Carlos Marcovich. Mexico City: Instituto Mexicano de Cimetografia. United States video and DVD release: Kino Video, New York.

Radu, Michael. 1995. "Cuba's Transition: Institutional Lessons from Eastern Europe." *Journal of Inter-American Studies and World Affairs* 37 (2): 83–111.

Ragano, Frank, and Selwyn Raab. 2002. "In Havana with the Mafia, 1958." In *Travelers' Tales of Old Cuba: From Treasure Island to Mafia Den,* edited by John Jenkins, 158–168. Melbourne: Ocean Press.

Rakowski, Cathy A., ed. 1994. *Contrapunto: The Informal Sector Debate in Latin America.* Albany: State University of New York Press.

Reck, Robert. H., and Virginia P. Reck. 1996. "The role of information systems strategy in making market leaders." *Information Strategy* 12 (4), 6–15.

Reynolds, Maura. 2004a. "Bush Took Quote out of Context, Researcher Says." *Los Angeles Times* July 20, A-15.

———. 2004b. "The Nation; the White House; Castro Promotes Sex Tourism, Bush Says." *Los Angeles Times* July 17, A-14.

Rifkin, Jeremy. 1995. *The End of Work: The Decline of the Global Labor Force and the Dawn of the Post-market Era.* New York: G. P. Putnam.

Ritter, Archibald. 2005. "Survival Strategies and Economic Illegalities in Cuba." http://www.carleton.ca/economics/seminar%20papers/Ritter%20-%204November2005.pdf. Last accessed May 19, 2008.

———. 2004. "The Cuban Economy in the Twenty-first Century: Recuperation or Relapse?" In *The Cuban Economy*, edited by Archibald Ritter, 3–24. Pittsburgh: University of Pittsburgh Press.

———. 1998. "Entrepreneurship, Microenterprise, and Public Policy in Cuba: Promotion, Containment, or Asphyxiation?" *Journal of Inter-American Studies and World Affairs* 40 (2): 63–94.

Ritzker, George, and Allan Liska. 1997. "'McDisneyization' and 'Post-Tourism': Complementary Perspectives on Contemporary Tourism." In *Tourism Cultures: Transformations of Travel and Theory*, edited by Chris Rojek and John Urry, 96–109. London: Routledge.

Robinson, William I. 2004. *A Theory of Global Capitalism: Production, Class, and State in a Transnational World.* Baltimore: Johns Hopkins University Press.

Rodríguez Chávez, Ernesto. 2002. "Notas sobre la identidad Cubana en su relación con la diáspora." *Temas* 28: 44–55.

Roque Cabello, Marta Beatriz, and Manuel Sánchez Herrero. 1998. "Background: Cuba's Current Economic Situation." In *Perspectives on Cuban Economic Reforms*, edited by Jorge F. Pérez-López and Matías F. Travieso-Díaz, 9–17. Tempe: Center for Latin American Studies Press, Arizona State University.

Rubin, Gayle S. 1993. "Thinking Sex: Notes for a Radical Theory of the Politics of Sexuality." In *The Lesbian and Gay Studies Reader*, edited by Henry Abelove, Michèle Aina Barale, and David M. Halperin, 3–44. New York: Routledge.

Ryan, Chris. 2000. "Sex Tourism: Paradigms of Confusion?" In *Tourism and Sex: Culture, Commerce, and Coercion*, edited by Stephen Clift and Simon Carter, 23–40. New York: Pinter.

———. 1991. *Recreational Tourism: A Social Science Perspective*. London; New York: Routledge.

Ryan, Chris, and C. Michael Hall. 2001. *Sex Tourism: Marginal People and Liminalities*. London: Routledge.

Safa, Helen. 1995. *The Myth of the Male Breadwinner: Women and Industrialization in the Caribbean*. Boulder, Colo.: Westview Press.

Sahay, Ratna. 2004. "Stabilization, Debt, and Fiscal Policy in the Caribbean." IMF, Washington, D.C., June 8.

Said, Edward. 1979. *Orientalism*. New York: Vintage Books.

Salas, Sonia. 1996. "Definición de conceptos." In *Memorias primer Congreso Dominicano de trabajadoras sexuales*, 57–59. Dominican Republic: Imprenta La Unión.

Salzinger, Leslie. 2000. "Manufacturing Sexual Subjects: 'Harassment', Desire and Discipline on a Maquiladora Shopfloor." *Ethnography* 1(1): 67–92.

Sánchez Taylor, Jacqueline. 2001. "Dollars Are a Girl's Best Friend? Female Tourists' Sexual Behavior in the Caribbean." *Sociology* 35 (3): 749–64.

———. 2006. "Female Sex Tourism: A Contradiction in Terms?" *Feminist Review* 83 (Summer): 42–59.

Sanky Panky. 2007. Written and directed by José E. Pintor. Santo Domingo, Dominican Republic. Premium Latin Films S.A.

Santos, Boaventura de Sousa. 2002. "Toward a Multicultural Conception of Human Rights." In *Moral Imperialism: A Critical Anthology*, edited by Berta Esperanza Hernández-Truyol, 39–60. New York: New York University Press.

Sassen, Saskia. 1994. "The Informal Economy: Between New Developments and Old Regulations." *Yale Law Journal* 103 (8) (June): 2289–2304.

Satz, Debra. 1995. "Markets in Women's Sexual Labor." *Ethics* 106 (1) (October): 63–85.

Savigliano, Marta E. 1995. *Tango and the Political Economy of Passion*. Boulder, Colo.: Westview Press.

Schoepf, Brook Grundfest. 2004. "AIDS." In *A Companion to the Anthropology of Politics*, edited by David Nugent and Joan Vincent, 37–54. Malden, Mass.: Blackwell Publishing.

Schwartz, Barry. 1967. "The Social Psychology of the Gift." *American Journal of Sociology* 73 (1) (July): 1–11.

Schwartz, Rosalie. 1997. *Pleasure Island: Tourism and Temptation in Cuba.* Lincoln: University of Nebraska Press.

Sen, Amartya. 1999. *Development as Freedom.* New York: Knopf.

Shannon, Thomas Richard. 1989. *An Introduction to the World-System Perspective.* Boulder, Colo.: Westview Press.

Shaw, Gareth, and Allan M. Williams. 1988. *Tourism and Economic Development: European Experiences.* London and New York: Belhaven Press.

———. 2002. *Critical Issues in Tourism: A Geographical Perspective.* Oxford: Blackwell Publishers.

Sheller, Mimi. 2004. "Natural Hedonism: The Invention of Caribbean Islands as Tropical Playgrounds." In *Beyond the Blood, the Beach & the Banana: New Perspectives in Caribbean Studies*, edited by Sandra Courtman, 170–185. Kingston, Jamaica: Ian Randle.

Sierra i Fabra, Jordi. 1997. *Cuba: La noche de la jinetera.* Barcelona: Ediciones del Bronce.

Silié, Rubén, and Manuel Colón. 1994. "Ajuste estructural y modelo neoliberal en República Dominicana." In *Los pequeños países de América Latina en la hora neoliberal*, edited by Gerónimo de Sierra, 89–119. Mexico, D.F: Editorial Nueva Sociedad.

Sinclair, Thea M., ed. 1997. *Gender, Work, and Tourism.* New York: Routledge.

Singer, Linda. 1993. *Erotic Welfare: Sexual Theory and Politics in the Age of Epidemic.* Edited and introduced by Judith Butler and Maureen MacGrogan. New York: Routledge.

Smith, Andrea. 2005. *Conquest: Sexual Violence and American Indian Genocide.* Cambridge, Mass.: South End Press.

Smith, Lois M., and Alfred Padula. 1996. *Sex and Revolution: Women in Socialist Cuba.* London: Oxford University Press.

Smith, Wayne S. 1992. "Washington Should Listen to Cuba's Moderate Dissidents." *Miami Herald*, December 17.

Smith, William C., and Roberto Patricio Korzeniewicz. 1997. "Latin America and the Second Great Transformation." In *Politics, Social Change, and Economic Restructuring in Latin America*, edited by William C. Smith and Roberto Patricio Korzeniewica, 1–20. Boulder, Colo.: Lynne Rienner Publishers.

Spadoni, Paolo. 2008. "Cuba's Current Economic Situation: Macroeconomic Performance, Structural Changes, and Future Challenges." Paper presented at the UC-Cuba Conference, Irvine, CA. May 2.

Stephen, Lynn. 1997. *Women and Social Movements in Latin America: Power from Below.* Austin: University of Texas Press.

Stepick, Alex, and Guillermo Grenier. 1994. "The View from the Back of the House: Restaurant Sand Holes in Miami." In *Newcomers in the Workplace: Immigrants and the Restructuring of the U.S. Economy,* edited by Louise Lamphere, Alex Stepick, and Guillermo Grenier, 181–198. Philadelphia: Temple University Press.

Stoler, Ann Laura. 2002. *Carnal Knowledge and Imperial Power: Race and the Intimate in Colonial Rule.* Berkeley: University of California Press.

Stout, Jan. 1996. "Women, the Politics of Sexuality, and Cuba's Economic Crisis." *Socialist Review* 25: 5–15.

Strathern, Marilyn. 1988. *The Gender of the Gift: Problems with Women and Problems with Society in Melanesia.* Berkeley: University of California Press.

Strongman, Roberto. 2002. "Syncretic Religion and Dissident Sexualities." In *Queer Globalizations: Citizenship and the Afterlife of Colonialism,* edited by Arnaldo Cruz-Malavé and Martin F. Manalansan IV, 176–192. New York: New York University Press.

Suazo, Wilson. 2000. "Si, soy una prostituta y tengo derechos." *Ultima Hora.* Santo Domingo: Dominican Republic. April 5: 36.

Susman, Paul. 1998. "Cuban Socialism in Crisis: A Neoliberal Solution?" In *Globalization and Neoliberalism: The Caribbean Context,* edited by Thomas Klak, 179–208. Lanham, Md.: Rowman and Littlefield.

Symmes, Patrick. 1996. "Taking the Measure of Castro, Ounce by Ounce." *Harper's Magazine* (January): 58–59.

Titley, Gavan. 2004. "All-Sights Reserved: All-Inclusive Resorts and the Imagined Caribbean." In *Beyond the Blood, the Beach & the Banana: New Perspectives in Caribbean Studies,* edited by Sandra Courtman, 205–220. Kingston, Jamaica: Ian Randle.

Thomas, Jim. 2002. *Decent Work in the Informal Sector: Latin America. Working Papers.* Geneva: International Labour Organization.

Thompson, Eric. 2002. "Engineered Corporate Culture on a Cruise Ship." *Sociological Focus* 35: 331–44.

Torres, Rebecca. 2002. "Cancún's Tourism Development from a Fordist Spectrum of Analysis." *Tourist Studies* 2 (1): 87–116.

Torricelli Bill/Cuban Democracy Act, September 18, 1992, *Congressional Record, Senate,* S14135–S14136.

Tracy, Sarah J. 2001. "Becoming a Character for Commerce." *Management Communication Quarterly* 14 (1) (August): 90–128.

Truong, Than Dam. 1990. *Sex, Money, and Morality.* London: Zed Books.

Tucker, Robert C. 1978. *The Marx-Engels Reader.* New York: W. W. Norton and Company.

Tuduri, Carles. 2001a. "El impacto social del turismo en el Caribe: La trastienda del desarrollo turistico." *Editur* (Barcelona, Spain), no. 2134, February 2: 28–34.

———. 2001b. "Todo incluido, un paraporte al paraiso?" *Editur* (Barcelona, Spain), no. 2134, February 2.

Turner, Victor Witter. 1982. *From Ritual to Theatre: The Human Seriousness of Play*. New York, N.Y: Performing Arts Journal Publications.

Tyler, Melissa, and Pamela Abbott. 1998. "Chocs Away: Weight Watching in the Contemporary Airline Industry." *Sociology* 32 (3): 433–50.

UN Committee on the Elimination of Discrimination against Women. "Concluding Observations: Cuba." U.N. Doc. A/51/38, paras. 197–228, 1996. http://www1.umn.edu/humanrts/cedaw/cedaw-cuba.htm.

UNDP (United Nations Development Programme). 2005. *National Human Development Report, Dominican Republic: Towards an Inclusive and Renewed Global Insertion.* http://hdr.undp.org/en/reports/nationalreports/latinamericathecaribbean/dominicanrep/name,3225,en.html.

UN Economic and Social Council. 2000. "Commission on Human Rights, Fifty-sixth Session, Item 12(a) of the Provisional Agenda E/CN.4/2000/68/ Add.2, 8 February." Report, United Nations, New York.

UNWTO. 2003. *Datos esenciales edición*. Madrid, Spain.

———. 2008. *Tourism Highlights: 2008 Edition*. Madrid: World Tourism Organization.

U.S. Government Accountability Office. 2007. "Foreign Assistance: U.S. Democracy Assistance for Cuba Needs Better Management and Oversight." Report. http://www.gao.gov/new.items/d07147.pdf

U.S. Office of the Press Secretary. 2003. "President Discusses Cuba Policy in Rose Garden Speech." October 10. http://www.whitehouse.gov/news/releases/2003/10/20031010-2.html.

Urry, John. 1995. *Consuming Places*. New York: Routledge.

———. 1996. "The Changing Economics of the Tourist Industry." In *The Sociology of Tourism: Theoretical and Empirical Investigations,* edited by Yiorgos Apostolopoulos, Stella Leivadi, and Andrew Yiannakis, 193–218. New York: Routledge.

Valdez, Claudia. 2005. "Genero, discriminación racial and ciudadania: Un studio en la escuela dominicína." In *Miradas desencadenantes: Los estudios de genero en la República Dominicana al inicio del tercer milenio,* edited by Ginetta E. B. Candelario, 231–264. Santo Domingo: Intec.

van der Veen, Marjolein. 2001. "Rethinking Commodification and Prostitution: An Effort at Peacemaking in the Battles over Prostitution." *Rethinking Marxism* 13 (2) (Summer): 30–51.

Vidal-Ortiz, Salvador. 2005. "'Sexuality' and 'Gender' in Santería: Towards a Queer of Color Critique in the Study of Religion." Ph.D. diss., City University of New York.

Villalba Garrido, Evaristo. 1993. *Cuba y el turismo.* Havana: Editorial de Ciencias Sociales.

Waller, Marguerite, and Sylvia Marcos. 2005. Introduction to *Dialogue and Difference: Feminisms Challenge Globalization,* edited by Marguerite Waller and Sylvia Marcos, xix–xxxi. New York: Palgrave Macmillan.

Walkowitz, Judith R. 1980. "The Politics of Prostitution." *Signs* 6 (1): 123–135.

Wardlow, Holly. 2004. "Anger, Economy, and Female Agency: Problematizing 'Prostitution' and 'Sex Work' among the Huli of Papua New Guinea." *Signs: Journal of Women in Culture* 29 (4): 1017–1040.

Wekker, Gloria. 1999. *Female Desires: Same-Sex Relations and Transgender Practices across Cultures,* edited by Evelyn Blackwood and Saskia E. Wieringa. New York: Columbia University Press.

Wiarda, Howard J. and Michael J. Kryzanek. 1992. *The Dominican Republic: A Caribbean Crucible.* Boulder, Colo.: Westview Press.

Williams, Claire. 2003. "Sky Service: The Demands of Emotional Labour in the Airline Industry." *Gender, Work, and Organization* 10 (5) (November): 513–550.

Williams, Randall Jay. 2006. "Appealing Subjects: Reading Across the International Division of Humanity." Ph.D. diss., University of California, San Diego.

Williams, Joan C., and Viviana Zelizer. 2005. "To Commodify or Not to Commodify: That is Not the Question." In *Rethinking Commodification: Cases and Readings in Law and Culture,* edited by Martha M. Ertman and Joan C. Williams, 362–382. New York: New York University Press.

Wilson, Richard Ashby. 2006. "Human Rights." In *A Companion to the Anthropology of Politics,* edited by David Nugent and Joan Vincent, 231–247. Malden, Mass.: Blackwell Publishing.

Wilson, Tamar Diana. 1998. "Approaches to Understanding the Position of Women Workers in the Informal Sector." *Latin American Perspectives* 25 (2): 105–119.

Wolkowitz, Carol. 2002. "The Social Relations of Body Work." *Work, Employment and Society* 16 (3): 497–510.

Wonders, Nancy A., and Raymond Michalowski. 2001. "Bodies, Borders, and Sex Tourism in a Globalized World: A Tale of Two Cities, Amsterdam and Havana." *Social Problems* 48 (4): 545–71.

World Bank. 2004a. "Dominican Republic at a Glance." http://www.worldbank.org/cgi-bin/sendoff.cgi?page=%2Fdata%2Fcountrydata%2Faag%2Fdom_aag.pdf.

———. 2004b. "World Bank Approves $100 Million for the Dominican Republic to Support Key Basic Services for the Poor." Press Release no. 2004/226/LAC. Washington, D.C., February 12. http://web.worldbank.org/WBSITE/EXTERNAL/NEWS/0,,contentMDK:20161499~isCURL:

Y-menuPK:34463-pagePK:64003015-piPK:64003012-theSitePK:4607,00
.html.

———. 2005. "World Bank to Provide up to US$360 Million over Four Years
to Restore Economic Growth and Improve Human Development in the
Dominican Republic." News Release no. 2005/472/LAC. Washington, D.C.,
May 19. http://web.worldbank.org/WBSITE/EXTERNAL/COUNTRIES/
LACEXT/DOMINICANEXTN/0,,contentMDK:20508770-menuPK:
337775-pagePK:141137-piPK:141127-theSitePK:337769,00.html.

World Bank Privatization Database. 2006. "Latin America and the Caribbean."
http://rru.worldbank.org/Privatization/Region.aspx?regionid=435

WTTC (World Tourism and Travel Council). 2005. "Dominican Republic: The
2005 Travel and Tourism Economic Research." http://www.wttc.org/
2005tsa/pdf/1.Dominican%20Republic.pdf.

WTTC (The World Travel & Tourism Council). 2008. "Cuba: The 2008 Travel
and Tourism Economic Research." http://www.wttc.org/bin/pdf/original_
pdf_file/cuba.pdf.

Yan, Yun-xiang. 1996. *The Flow of Gifts: Reciprocity and Social Networks in a
Chinese Village*. Stanford, CA: Stanford University Press.

Yea, Sallie. "Labor of Love: Filipina Entertainer's Narratives of Romance and
Relationships with the GIs in US Military Camp Towns in Korea." *Women's Studies International Forum* 28 (6) (November–December): 456–72.

Zacair, Philippe. 2005. "Haiti on His Mind: Antonio Maceo and Caribbeanness." *Caribbean Studies* 33 (1), (Jan–June): 47–78.

Zelizer, Viviana. 2005. *The Purchase of Intimacy*. Princeton, N.J.: Princeton
University Press.

———. 2006. "Keynote Address: Money, Power, and Sex." *Yale Journal of Law
and Feminism* 8 (1): 303–15.

Index

Amalia L. Cabezas is Assistant Professor in the Department of Women's Studies at the University of California, Riverside, and co-editor of *The Wages of Empire: Neoliberal Policies, Repression and Women's Poverty.*